Socialism, Peace and Democracy

Socialism, Peace and Democracy
Writings, Speeches and Reports
M I K H A I L   S.   G O R B A C H E V

LONDON   ATLANTIC HIGHLANDS

First published 1987 by Zwan Publications
11-21 Northdown Street, London N1 9BN
and Zwan Publications at Humanities Press Inc
Atlantic Highlands, New Jersey 07716, USA

Zwan Publications gratefully acknowledge the
assistance of Novosti Press Agency in the
preparation of this book, with particular
thanks to Mr Alexey Pushkov in Moscow and
Mr Victor Orlik in London

Printed and bound in Great Britain

British Library Cataloguing in Publication Data
Gorbachev, M.S.
    Mikhail Gorbachev: socialism, peace and
    democracy: writings, speeches and reports.
    — (Soviet and East European studies).
    1. Soviet Union — Politics and
    government — 1953 –
    I. Title II. Series
    947.085'4'0924   DK290.3.G6

ISBN 1–85305–011–3

Contents

Abbreviations

ABM	Anti-Ballistic Missile
ASEAN	Association of South East Asian Nations
CMEA	Council for Mutual Economic Assistance
CSCE	Conference of Security and Cooperation in Europe
CPSU	Communist Party of Soviet Union
DPRK	Democratic People's Republic of Korea
DRA	Democratic Republic of Afghanistan
NATO	North Atlantic Treaty Organisation
SDI	Space Defence Initiative
US	United States
USSR	Union of Soviet Socialist Republics

BIOGRAPHICAL NOTE

On 12 March 1985 a plenary meeting of the Soviet Communist Party's Central Committee elected Mikhail Sergeyevich Gorbachev to be its new General Secretary. He thus became leader of a country of nearly 277 million people of more than 100 different nationalities.

In many respects Mikhail Gorbachev's life is typical of a generation of Soviet Communists. He was born on 2 March 1931, in the village of Privolnoye in Stavropol territory. This vast region north of the Caucasian mountains is an important grain and sheep-rearing centre. The people of Stavropol are an industrious and tenacious people who for centuries have grown grain and grazed their flocks under difficult, often harsh, conditions; but they later built canals, developed industries and founded cities and health resorts on the arid steppe.

Mikhail Gorbachev's parents came from peasant stock. His grandfather founded a collective farm and his father, Sergei Andreyevich, a Communist, was an agricultural machine operator who fought at the front of the Great Patriotic War. His mother, Maria Panaleyevna, still lives in the Stavropol region.

Mikhail Gorbachev worked on the land during school vacations and at the age of 18 was awarded the coveted Order of the Red Banner of Labour. After leaving school he enrolled in the Faculty of Law at Moscow State University and graduated in 1955. While still a student he joined the CPSU (he was a Party Congress delegate in 1961). He later undertook postgraduate studies in agricultural economics. In 1955 he returned to the Stavropol territory, and became active in the Young Communist League. From March 1962 he was engaged full-time on party work. He became First Secretary of a City Party Committee, Second Secretary of a Territorial Committee, and from April 1970, First Secretary of one of the Party's most authoritative organisations: that of the Stavropol territory. He was elected to the Central Committee at the 24th Party Congress in March 1971.

Gorbachev's formative experiences in Stavropol included work in many areas of its highly developed and diversified economy. His work involved him in the fields of health and social welfare, science and education, and agriculture and industry. During this period major initiatives were taken in the Stavropol territory to develop mechanical engineering, the chemical industry, resort construction, canal building and irrigation, and in farming and animal husbandry. Gorbachev devoted much attention to the needs and concerns of working people, and for the realities of life at the point of production. From the start Gorbachev was known as someone prepared to spend time in the factories and shops, offices and farms rather than in lecture halls or his private office.

Mikhail Gorbachev is a man with very wide fields of interest. He is interested in literature, the theatre and the arts and has studied political economy, philosophy and law. He has travelled widely in the Soviet Union and abroad.

In 1978 he was elected secretary of the Central Committee and two years later was voted on to the Politburo. He has also for many years been a member of the Soviet parliament – the Supreme Soviet – and has been a member of its Presidium since 1985.

Following his election to the post of General Secretary, Gorbachev began the series of initiatives in the fields of domestic social and economic policy and of international affairs, which have served to reorient and renew Soviet development in the 1980s, after a period of relative stagnation.

Domestically, the reconstruction of social life and the economy have only begun a process which Gorbachev himself has likened to a second revolution. Affecting every area of culture, the arts and the media, and many forms of personal and economic freedom, the broadening of democracy is a facet of contemporary Soviet life which began in 1985 with the April Plenary at which the Central Committee adopted Gorbachev's programme.

The Party has committed itself to the wholesale reconstruction of the national economy on the basis of new technology, raised productivity, and more equitable remuneration at work. In the field of foreign policy a still more radical approach has been adopted, with arms-control initiatives bespeaking a new urgency and seriousness in the search for peace. In asserting that man's 'loss of immortality' is the greatest single issue, transcending all ideological differences, Gorbachev had done no more than begin a far-reaching process whose first consequences were manifest at the Reykjavik summit.

The observation that Gorbachev's political and personal style are reminiscent of Lenin (whose approach was also imbued with informality, personal humility, directness and realism) is not confined to Soviet commentators and to friends. His emphasis on the value of collective leadership, and of direct contact with, and appeals to, the people, are widely acknowledged. They have come to characterise his period in office.

The search for a genuine peace rather than a nuclear armistice is Gorbachev's overriding concern, and it is on the success of this search that his period in office (and much more besides) will eventually be judged.

We do not understand how nuclear weapons can be lauded when there are four tons of explosives for everyone in the world, including children, and when the explosion of even a small part of the existing nuclear arsenals will jeopardise life on earth. We cannot agree to this from the point of view of either politics or morality.

Mikhail Gorbachev's wife, Raise Gorbacheva, is a graduate of the Department of Philosophy of Moscow State University. She is a candidate of philosophy and is a senior lecturer. Their daughter, Irina, is a physician. Her husband Anatoli is a surgeon. The Gorbachevs' granddaughter, Ksenia, is eight years old.

MARK JONES

Part 1
International Relations

1

A World in Crisis

Comrades, the draft new edition of the Programme of the Party contains a thorough analysis of the main trends and features of the current development of the world. It is not the purpose of the Programme to anticipate the diversity of the concrete developments of the future. That would be a futile occupation. But here is another, no less important point: if we want to follow a correct, scientifically grounded policy, we must clearly understand the key tendencies of the current reality. To penetrate deep into the dialectic of the events, into their objective logic, to draw the right conclusions that reflect the motion of the times, is no simple thing, but it is imperatively necessary.

In the days before the October Revolution, referring to the capitalist economy alone, Lenin noted that the sum-total of the changes in all their ramifications could not have been grasped even by seventy Marxes. But, Lenin continued, Marxism has discovered 'the *laws* . . . and the *objective* logic of these changes and of their historical development . . . in its chief and basic features' (*Collected Works*, vol. 14, p. 325).

The modern world is complicated, diverse and dynamic, and shot through with contending tendencies and contradictions. It is a world of the most intricate alternatives, anxieties and hopes. Never before has our home on earth been exposed to such great political and physical stresses. Never before has man exacted so much tribute from nature, and never before has he been so vulnerable to the forces he himself has created.

World developments confirm the fundamental Marxist-Lenninist conclusion that the history of society is not a sum of fortuitous elements, that it is not a disorderly 'Brownian motion' but a law-governed onward process. Not only do its contradictions pass sentence on the old world, on everything that impedes the advance; they are also a source and motive force behind the progress of

Excerpt from the Political Report of the CPSU Central Committee to the 27th Party Congress, 25 February 1986 society in the setting of struggle that is inevitable as long as exploitation and exploiting classes still exist.

The liberation revolutions triggered by the Great October Revolution are determining the image of the twentieth century. However considerable the achievements of science and technology, and however great the influence on the life of society of the rapid scientific and technological progress, nothing but the social and spiritual emancipation of man can make him truly free. And no matter what difficulties, objective and artificial, the old world may create, the course of history is irreversible.

The social changes of the century are altering the conditions for the further development of society. New economic, political, scientific, technical, internal and international factors are beginning to operate. The interconnection between states and between peoples is increasing. And all this is setting new, especially rigid, demands upon every state, whether in foreign policy, in economic and social activity, or the spiritual image of society.

The progress of our time is rightly identified with socialism. World socialism is a powerful international entity with a highly developed economy, substantial scientific resources, and a dependable politico-military potential. It accounts for more than one-third of humanity, for dozens of countries and peoples opening up in every way the intellectual and moral wealth of man and society. A new way of life has taken shape, based on the principles of socialist justice, with neither oppressors nor oppressed, neither exploiters nor exploited, where power belongs to the people. Its distinctive features are collectivism and comradely mutual assistance, triumph of the ideas of freedom, unbreakable unity between the rights and duties of every member of society, the dignity of the individual, and true humanism. Socialism is a realistic option open to all humanity, an example projected into the future.

Socialism sprang up and was built in countries that were far from economically and socially advanced at that time, differing greatly from one another in mode of life and their historical and national traditions. Each one of them advanced to the new social system along its own way, confirming Marx's prediction about the 'infinite variations and gradations' of the same economic basis in its concrete manifestations (*Capital*, vol. III, p. 779).

The way was neither smooth nor simple. It was exceedingly difficult to raise the backward or ruined economy, to teach millions of people to read and write, to provide them with a roof over their heads, with food and free medical aid. The very novelty of the social tasks, the ceaseless military, economic, political – and psychological pressure of imperialism, the need for tremendous efforts to ensure defence – all this could not fail to influence the course of events, their character, and the rate at which the socioeconomic programmes and transformations were carried into effect. Nor were mistakes in politics, and various subjectivist deviations, avoided.

But such is life; it always takes the shape of diverse contradictions, sometimes quite unexpected ones. The other point is much more important: socialism has demonstrated its ability to resolve social problems on a fundamentally different basis than before, namely a collectivist one, has brought the countries to higher levels of development, and has given the working people a decent and secure life.

Socialism is continuously improving social relations, multiplying its achievements purposefully, building up the impact and credibility of its example, and demonstrating the tangible humanism of the socialist way of life. By so doing, it is erecting an increasingly dependable barrier to the ideology and policy of war and militarism, reaction and force, to all forms of man-hating, and is actively furthering social progress. It has grown into a powerful moral and material power, and has shown what opportunities are arising for modern-day civilisation.

The course of social progress is tied in closely with anti-colonial revolutions, national liberation movements , the renascence of quite a few countries, and the emergence of dozens of new ones. Having won political independence, they are working hard to overcome backwardness, poverty and sometimes desperate misery – the entire painful legacy of their history of enslavement. They, who were once rightless objects of imperialist policy, are now making history by themselves.

Social progress is expressed in the development of the international communist and working-class movement and in the growth of the new massive democratic movement of our time, including the anti-war and anti-nuclear movement. It is apparent, too, in the stratification of the political forces of the capitalist world, notably in the US,the metropolitan centre of imperialism. Here, progressive tendencies are forcing their way forward through a system of monopolistic totalitarianism, and are exposed to the continuous pressure of organised reactionary forces, including their enormous propaganda machine which floods the world with stupefying misinformation.

Marx compared progress in exploiting society to 'that hideous pagan idol, who would not drink the nectar but from the skulls of the slain' (*Selected Works*, vol I, p.499). He amplified:

> In our days everything seems pregnant with its contrary. Machinery, gifted with the wonderful power of shortening and fructifying human labour, we behold starving and overworking it. The new-fangled sources of wealth, by some strange weird spell, are turned into sources of want. The victories of art seem bought by the loss of character. At the same pace that mankind masters nature, man seems to become enslaved to other men or to his own infamy. Even the pure light of science seems unable to shine but on the dark background of ignorance. All our inventions and progress seem to result in endowing material forces with intellectual life, and in stultifying human life into a material force. (*Selected Works*, vol. I, p. 500)

Marx's analysis is staggering for its historical sweep, accuracy, and depth. It has, indeed, become still more relevant with reference to the bourgeois reality of the twentieth century that it was in the nineteenth. On the one hand, the swift advance of science and technology has opened up unprecedented possibilities for mastering the forces of nature and improving the conditions of the life of man. On the other, the 'enlightened' twentieth century is going down in history as a time marked by such imperialist outgrowths as the most devastating wars, an orgy of militarism and fascism, genocide and the destitution of millions of people. Ignorance and obscurantism go hand in hand in the capitalist world with lofty achievements of science and culture. That is the society we are compelled to be neighbours of, looking for ways of cooperation and mutual understanding. Such is the command of history.

The progress of humanity is also directly connected with the scientific and technological revolution. It matured slowly and gradually, and then, in the final quarter of the century, gave the start to a gigantic accretion of man's material and spiritual resources. They were of two kinds. A qualitative leap has been registered in humanity's productive forces. But there is also a qualitative leap in means of destruction, in the military matters, 'endowing' man for the first time in history with the physical capacity for destroying all life on earth.

The facets and consequences of the scientific and technological revolution vary in the different sociopolitical systems. The capitalism of the 1980s, the capitalism of the age of electronics and information science, computers and robots, is leaving more millions of people, including young and educated people, without jobs. Wealth and power are being increasingly concentrated in the hands of a few. Militarism is gorging itself on the arms race beyond reason, and also wants to gain control little by little over the political levers of power. It is becoming the ugliest and the most dangerous monster of the twentieth century. By its efforts, the most advanced scientific and technical ideas are being converted into weapons of mass destruction.

To the developing countries the scientific and technological revolution is setting this most acute question: are they fated to enjoy the achievements of science and technology in full measure in order to gain strength for combating neocolonialism and imperialist exploitation or will they remain on the periphery of world development? The scientific and technological revolution shows in bold relief that many socioeconomic problems impeding progress in that part of the world are unresolved.

Socialism has everything it needs to place modern-day science and technology at the service of the people. But it would be wrong to think that the scientific and technological revolution is creating no problems for socialist society. Experience shows that its advance involves improvement of social relations, a change of mentality, the forging of a new psychology, and the acceptance of dynamism as a way and a rule of life. It calls insistently for continuous reassessment and renewal of the prevailing patterns of management. In other words the scientific and technological revolution not only opens up prospects, but also sets higher demands on the entire organisation of home and international affairs. Certainly, scientific and technological progress cannot abolish the laws of social development or the social purpose and content of such development. But it exercises a tremendous influence on all the processes that are going on in the world, on its contradictions.

It is quite obvious that the two socioeconomic systems differ substantially in their readiness and also in their capacity to conceptualise and resolve the arising problems.

Such is the world we are living in on the threshold of the third millennium. It is a world full of hope, because people have never before been as amply equipped for the further development of civilisation. But it is also a world overloaded with dangers and contradictions, prompting the thought that this is perhaps the most alarming period in history.

The first and most important group of contradictions in terms of humanity's future is connected with the relations between countries of the two systems, the two formations. These contradictions have a long history. Since the Great October Revolution in Russia and the split of the world on the social-class principle, fundamental distinctions have come to light in the assessment of current affairs and in the views concerning the world's social perspective.

Capitalism regarded the birth of socialism as an 'error' of history which must be 'rectified'. It was to be rectified at any cost, by any means, irrespective of law and morality: by armed intervention, economic blockade, subversive activity, sanctions and 'punishments', or refusal of any and all cooperation. But nothing could interfere with the consolidation of the new system and its historical right to live.

The difficulty that the ruling classes of the capitalist world have in understanding the realities, the periodical recurrence of attempts at resolving by force the whole group of contradictions dividing the two worlds are of course anything but accidental. Imperialism is prompted by its intrinsic mainsprings and socioeconomic essence to translate the competition of the two systems into the language of military confrontation. By dint of its social nature, imperialism ceaselessly generates aggressive, adventurist policy.

Here we can speak of a whole complex of compelling motives: the predatory appetites of the arms manufacturers and the influential military-bureaucratic groups, the selfish interest of the monopolies in sources of raw materials and sales markets, the bourgeoisie's fear of the ongoing changes, and, lastly, the attempts to resolve its own, snowballing problems at socialism's expense.

The latter are especially typical of US imperialism. It was nothing but imperial ideology and policy, the wish to create the most unfavourable external conditions for socialism and for the USSR that prompted the start of the race of nuclear and other arms after 1945, just when the crushing defeat of fascism and militarism was, it would seem, offering a realistic opportunity for building a world without wars, and a mechanism of international cooperation – the United Nations – had been created for this purpose. But imperialism's nature asserted itself that time again.

Today, too, the right wing of the US monopoly bourgeoisie regards the stoking up of international tensions as something that justifies military allocations, claims to global supremacy, interference in the affairs of other states, and an offensive against the interests and rights of the US working people. No small role seems to be played by the idea of using tensions to exercise pressure on the allies, to make them implicitly obedient, to subordinate them to Washington's dictates.

The policy of total contention, of military confrontation, has no future. Flight into the past is no response to the challenges of the future. It is rather an act of despair which, however, does not make this posture any less dangerous. Washington's deeds will show when and to what extent it will understand this. We, for our part, are ready to do everything we can in order to radically improve the international situation. To achieve this socialism need not renounce any of its principles or ideals. It has always stood for and continues to stand for the peaceful coexistence of states belonging to different social systems.

As distinct from imperialism, which is trying to halt the course of history by force, to regain what it had in the past, socialism has never, of its own free will, related its future to any military solution of international problems. This was borne out at the very first big discussion that took place in our country after the victory of the Great October Revolution. During that discussion, as we may recall, the views of the 'Left Communists' and the Trotskyites, who championed the theory of 'revolutionary war' which they claimed would carry socialism to other countries, were firmly rejected. This position, as Lenin emphasised in 1918, 'would be completely at variance with Marxism, for Marxism has always been opposed to "pushing" revolutions, which develop with the growing acuteness of the class antagonisms that engender revolutions' (*Collected Works*, vol. 27, pp. 71–2). Today, too, we are firmly convinced that pushing revolutions from outside, and doubly so by military means, is futile and inadmissible.

The problems and crises experienced by the capitalist world arise within its own system and are a natural result of the internal antagonistic contradictions of the old society. In this sense capitalism negates itself as it develops. Unable to cope with the acute problems of the declining phase of capitalism's development, the ruling circles of the imperialist countries resort to means and methods that are obviously incapable of saving the society which history has doomed.

The myth of a Soviet or Communist 'threat' that is being circulated today, is meant to justify the arms race and the imperialist countries' own aggressiveness. But it is becoming increasingly clear that the path of war can yield no sensible solutions, either international or domestic. The clash and struggle of the opposite approaches to the perspectives of world development have become especially complex in nature. Now that the world has huge nuclear stockpiles and the only thing experts argue about is how many times or dozens of times humanity can be destroyed, it is high time to begin an effective withdrawal from the brink of war, from the equilibrium of fear, to normal, civilised forms of relations between the states of the two systems.

In the years to come the struggle will evidently centre on the actual content of the policy that can safeguard peace. It will be a hard and many-sided struggle, because we are dealing with a society whose ruling circles refuse to assess the realities of the world and its perspectives in sober terms, or to draw serious conclusions from their own experience and that of others. All this is an indication of the wear and tear suffered by its internal 'systems of immunity', of its social senility, which reduces the probability of far-reaching changes in the policy of the dominant forces and augments its degree of recklessness.

That is why it is not easy at all, in the current circumstances, to predict the future of the relations between the socialist and the capitalist countries, the USSR and the US. The decisive factors here will be the correlation of forces on the world scene, the growth and activity of the peace potential, and its capability of effectively repulsing the threat of nuclear war. Much will depend, too, on the degree of realism that Western ruling circles will show in assessing the situation. But is is unfortunate when not only the eyesight but also the souls of politicians are blind. With nuclear war being totally unacceptable, peaceful coexistence rather than confrontation of the systems should be the rule in inter-state relations.

The second group of contradictions consists of the intrinsic contradictions of the capitalist world itself. The past period has amply confirmed that the general crisis of capitalism is growing keener. The capitalism of today, whose exploitative nature has not changed, is in many ways different from what it was in the early and even the middle twentieth century. Under the influence and in the setting of the scientific and technological revolution, the conflict between the productive forces, which have grown to gigantic proportions, and the private-owner social relations, has become still more acute. Here there is growth of unemployment and deterioration of the entire set of social problems. Militarism, which has spread to all areas, is applied as the most promising means of enlivening the economy. The crisis of political institutions, of the entire spiritual sphere, is growing. Reaction is exercising fierce pressure all along the line – in home and foreign policy, economy and culture, and the use of the achievements of human genius. The traditional forms of conservatism are giving place to authoritarian tendencies.

Special mention should be made of anti-Communism and anti-Sovietism, a most dangerous aspect of the crisis of capitalism. This concerns not only external policy. In the modern-day system of imperialism it is also a most important area of internal policy, a means of pressure on all the advanced and progressive elements that live and fight in the capitalist countries, in the non-socialist part of the world.

True, the present stage of the general crisis does not lead to any absolute stagnation of capitalism and does not rule out the possible growth of its economy and the emergence of new scientific and technical trends. It 'allows for' sustaining concrete economic, military, political and other positions, and in some cases even for possible social revenge, the regaining of what had been lost before. But lacking positive aims and guidelines that would express the interests of the working masses, capitalism now has to cope with an unprecedented interlacement and mutual exacerbation of all groups of its contradictions. It faces so many social and other impasses as it has never known before in all the centuries of its development.

Among the first to grow more acute are the contradictions between labour and capital. In the 1960s and 1970s, with the onset of a favourable economic situation, the working class, and the working people generally, managed to secure a certain improvement of their condition. But from the mid-1970s on, the proliferating economic crises and another technological modernisation of production changed the situation, and enabled capital to go on the counter-offensive, depriving the working people of a considerable part of their social gains. For a number of standard of living indicators, the working people were flung many years back. Unemployment has reached a postwar high. The condition of peasants and farmers is deteriorating visibly: some farms are going bankrupt, with their former owners joining the ranks of wage workers, while others become abjectly dependent on large argicultural monopolies and banks. The social stratification is growing deeper and increasingly striking. In the US, for example, 1 per cent of the wealthiest families own riches that exceed by nearly 50 per cent the total wealth of 80 per cent of all US families, who make up the lower part of the property pyramid.

Imperialism's ruling circles are doubtlessly aware that such a situation is fraught with social explosions and political destabilisation. But this is not making their policies more considered. On the contrary, the most irreconcilable reactionary groups of the ruling class have, by and large, taken the upper hand in recent years. The period is marked by an especially massive and brutal offensive of the monopolies on the rights of the working people.

The whole arsenal of means at capitalism's disposal is being put to use. The trade unions are persecuted and economically blackmailed. Anti-labour laws are being enacted. The left and all other progressives are being persecuted. Continuous control or, to be more precise, surveillance of people's state of mind and behaviour has become standard. Deliberate cultivation of individualism, of the principle that might is right in the fight for survival, immorality, and hatred of all that is democratic – this is practised on an unprecedented scale.

The future, the working people's fight for their rights, for social progress, will show how that basic contradiction between labour and capital will develop and what conclusions will be drawn from the prevailing situation. But mention must be made of the serious danger to international relations of any further substantial shift of policy, of the entire internal situation in some capitalist countries, to the right. The consequences of such a development are hard to predict, and we mut not underrate their danger.

The last decades of the century are marked by new outbreaks of inter-imperialist contradictions and the appearance of their new forms and tendencies. This group of capitalist contradictions has not been eliminated either by class affinity, the interest in uniting forces, by military, economic and political integration, or by the scientific and technological revolution. The latter has incontestably accelerated the internationalisation of capitalist production, has given added impetus to the evening up of levels as well as to the leap-like development of capitalist countries. The competition that has grown more acute under the impact of scientific and technological progress is hitting those who have dropped behind still more mercilessly. The considerable complication of the conditions of capitalist reproduction, the diversity of crisis processes, and the intensification of international competition have made imperialist rivalry especially acute and bitter. The commercial and economic struggle in the world market is witnessing ever greater reliance on the power of national state-monopoly capitalisms, with the role of the bourgeois state becoming increasingly aggressive and egoistic.

The transnational monopoly capital has gained strength rapidly. It is seizing control of, and monopolising, whole branches or spheres of production both on the scale of individual countries and in the world economy as a whole. By the early 1980s, the transnational corporations accounted for more than one-third of the industrial production, more than one half of the foreign trade, and nearly 80 per cent of the patents for new machinery and technology in the capitalist world.

The core of the transnational corporations consists of US firms. Their enterprises abroad use an additional army of wage and salary workers equalling half the number employed in manufacturing in the US. At present they produce something like 1.5 trillion dollars worth of goods and services a year, or nearly 40 per cent of gross US output.

The size of the 'second economy' of the US is double or triple that of the economies of such leading West European powers as the Federal Republic of Germany, France, and Britain, and second only to that of Japan. Today the biggest US transnational monopolies are empires whose economic activity is comparable to the gross national product of entire countries.

The new knot of contradictions has appeared and is being swiftly tightened between the transnational corporations and the nation-state form of society's political organisation. The transnational corporations are undermining the sovereignty both of developing and of developed capitalist countries. They make active use of state-monopoly regulation when it suits their interests, and come into sharp conflict with it when they see the slightest threat to their profits from the actions of bourgeois governments. But for all that, the US transnational supermonopolies are, as a rule, active conductors of state hegemonism and the imperial ambitions of the country's ruling circles.

The relations between the three main centres of present-day imperialism – US, Western Europe and Japan – abound in visible and concealed contradictions. The economic, financial, and technological superiority which the US enjoyed over its closest competitors until the end of the 1960s has been put to serious trial. Western Europe and Japan managed to outdo their US patron in some things, and are also challenging the US in such a traditional sphere of US hegemony as that of the latest technology.

Washington is continuously calling on its allies not to waste their gunpowder on internecine strife. But how are the three centres of modern-day imperialism to share one roof if the US itself, manipulating the dollar and the interest rates, is not loath to fatten its economy at the expense of Western Europe and Japan? Wherever the three imperialist centres manages to coordinate their positions, this is more often than not the effect of US pressure or outright dictation, and works in the interests and aims above all of the US. This in turn sharpens, rather than blunts, the contradictions.

It appears that people are beginning to wonder about this cause-and-effect relationship. For the first time governments of some West European countries, the social democratic and liberal parties, and the public at large, have begun to openly discuss whether present US policy coincides with Western Europe's notions about its own security and whether the US is going too far in its claims to 'leadership'. The partners of the US have had more than one occasion to see that someone else's spectacles cannot substitute for one's own eyes.

The clash of centrifugal and centripetal tendencies will no doubt continue as a result of changes in the correlation of forces within the imperialist system. Still, the existing complex of economic, politico-military and other common interests of the three 'centres of power' can hardly be expected to break up in the prevailing conditions of the present-day world. But within the framework of this complex Washington should not expect unquestioning obedience to US dictates on the part of its allies and competitors, and especially when this is to the detriment of their own interests.

The specificity of the inter-imperialist contradictions of the current period also encompasses a possible change of their configuration in the coming decades, with new capitalist centres of power coming on the scene. This will doubtless lead to a further growth of the bulk of contradictions, to their closer interlacement and aggravation.

The new, complex and changing set of contradictions has taken shape between imperialism and the developing countries and peoples. The liberation of former colonies and semi-colonies was a strong political and ideological blow to the capitalist system. It has ceased to exist in the shape that it assumed in the nineteenth century and in which it extended into the first half of the twentieth. A slow, arduous, but irreversible process of socio-economic transformations is under way in the life of nations comprising the majority of mankind. This process, which has brought about no few fundamental changes, has also encountered considerable difficulties.

By political manoeuvring, blandishments and blackmail, military threats and intimidation, and all too often by direct interference in the internal affairs of the newly free countries, capitalism has in many ways managed to sustain the earlier relationships of economic dependence. On this basis imperialism managed to create and adjust the most refined system of neocolonialist exploitation, and to tighten its hold on a considerable number of newly free states.

The consequences of this are tragic. The developing countries with a total population of more than two billion, have in effect become a region of wholesale poverty. In the early 1980s the per capita income in the newly free countries was on the whole less than 10 per cent that of the developed capitalist states. And in the past thirty years, far from shrinking, the gap has grown wider. Nor is it a question of just comparative poverty. There is illiteracy and misery, chronic undernourishment and hunger, appalling child mortality, and epidemics that afflict hundreds and millions of people.

This is a disgrace for civilised humanity! And its culprit is imperialism. Not only from the point of view of history, that is, of colonial plunder on entire continents which left behind a heritage of unbelievable backwardness, but equally in terms of present-day practices. In just the past ten years, the profits squeezed out of the developing countries by US corporations exceeded their inputs fourfold. And in Latin America and the Caribbean, in the same period, the profits of US monopolies were over eight times greater than their inputs.

It is no exaggeration to say that to a large extent the imperialist system is still living off the plunder of the developing countries, off their totally merciless exploitation. The forms and methods are changing, but the essence remains. In the US, for example, a tangible portion of the national income comes from these very sources. The developing countries are being exploited by all the imperialist states, but, unquestionably, US imperialism is doing it with the least consideration for them. Non-equivalent exchange, unequal trade, juggling and abuse of interest rates, the pumps of the transnational corporations are being used to one and the same end. They are adding still more to the poverty and misery of some, and to the wealth of others, and increasing the polarisation in the capitalist world economy.

The distressing condition of the developing countries is a major worldwide problem. This and nothing else is the true source of many of the conflicts in Asia, Africa, and Latin America. Such is the truth, however hard the ruling circles of the imperialist powers may invoke the 'hand of Moscow' in order to vindicate their neocolonialist policy and global ambitions.

Take the problem of debts. Together with the profits shipped out yearly from the developing countries, the accumulated debt means just one thing: the prospects of their development have shrunk, and a further deterioration of the already terrible social, economic and other problems is inevitable.

In the existing circumstances these countries will not of course be able to repay their debts. And if no fair solution is devised, the situation is fraught with grave socioeconomic and political consequences on the international scene. It would be wrong to say that the imperialist ruling circles are blind to the underlying danger here. But all their concerns boil down to one thing – how to save the present system of enrichment through the exploitation and super-exploitation of the peoples of the developing countries.

This other thing is certain as well: there is an irrefutable causal connection between the trillion-sized debt of these countries and the more than trillion-sized growth of US military expenditures in the past ten years. The 200-odd billion dollars that are being annually pumped out of the developing countries and the practically equal size of the US military budget in recent years, are no coincidence. That is why militarism has a direct stake in maintaining and tightening the system of neocolonial super-exploitation.

It is also obvious that with capitalism's contradictions growing sharper and its sphere of predominance shrinking, neocolonialism is becoming an increasingly important source of means that provide monopoly capital with the possibility for social manoeuvring, reducing social tension in the leading bourgeois states, and for bribing some sections of the working people. It is a truly extraordinary source, for a worker's hourly rate in the advanced capitalist states is higher, sometimes several times higher, than a day's earnings in the countries of Asia, Africa and Latin America.

All this cannot go on forever. But of course no miracle can be expected: the situation is not going to straighten itself out on its own. The military force that the US is counting on to maintain the status quo, to safeguard the interests of the monopolies and the military-industrial complex, and to prevent any further progressive change in the newly free countries, can only complicate the situation and precipitate new conflicts. The bags of money are liable to become kegs of gunpowder. Sooner or later, in this area too, capitalism will have to choose between the policy of force and shameless plunder, on the one hand, and the opportunity for cooperation on an equitable basis, on the other. The solutions must be radical – in the interests of the peoples of the developing states.

Analysis of yet another group of contradictions – those on a global scale, affecting the very foundations of the existence of civilisation, leads to serious conclusions. This refers first of all to pollution of the environment, the air and oceans, and to the exhaustion of natural resources. The problems are aggravated not only by excessive loads on the natural systems as a consequence of the scientific and technological revolution and the increasing extent of man's activity. Engels, in his time, foresaw the ill effects of exposing nature to the blind play of market forces. The need for effective international procedures and mechanisms that would make for the rational use of the world's resources as an asset belonging to all humanity, is becoming increasingly apparent.

The global problems, affecting all humanity, cannot be resolved by one state or a group of states. This calls for cooperation on a worldwide scale, for close and constructive joint action by the majority of countries. This cooperation must be based on completely equal rights and respect for the sovereignty of each. It must be based on conscientious compliance with accepted commitments and with the standards of international law. Such is the categorical call of the times in which we live.

Capitalism also causes an impoverishment of culture, an erosion of the spiritual values created over the centuries. Nothing elevates man more than knowledge. But in probably no other period of history has mankind experienced any stronger pressure of falsehood and deceit than it does now. Bourgeois propaganda shovels ingeniously doctored information on people all over the world, imposing thoughts and feelings, and programming a civic and social attitude advantageous to the ruling forces. What knowledge, what values and moral standards are implicit in the information dispensed to the people and in the system of education is first and foremost a political problem.

Life itself brings up the question of safeguarding culture, of protecting it from bourgeois corruption and vandalisation. That is one of the most important worldwide tasks. We cannot afford to neglect the long-term psychological and moral consequences of imperialism's current practices in the cultural sphere. Its impoverishment under the onslaught of unbridled commercialisation and the cult of force, the propagation of racism, the propaganda of lowly instincts, of the ways of the criminal world and the 'lower depths' of society, must be, and certainly will be, rejected by mankind.

The problems, as you see, comrades, are many, and they are large-scale and intricate. But it is clear that their conceptualisation is on the whole lagging behind the scope and depth of the current tasks. The imperative condition for success in resolving the topical issues of international life is to reduce the time of search for political understandings and to secure the swiftest possible constructive action.

We are pefectly well aware that not everything by far is within our power and that much will depend on the West, on its leaders' ability to see things in sober perspective at important crossroads of history. The US President said once that if our planet were threatened by a landing from another planet, the USSR and the US would quickly find a common language. But isn't a nuclear disaster a more tangible danger than a landing of extraterrestrials? Isn't the ecological threat big enough? Don't all countries have a common stake in finding a sensible and fair approach to the problems of the developing states and peoples?

Lastly, isn't all the experience accumulated by mankind enough to draw perfectly justified practical conclusions today rather than wait until some other crisis breaks out? What does the US hope to win in the long term by producing doctrines that can no longer ensure US security within the modest dimensions of our planet?

To keep in the saddle of history, imperialism is resorting to all possible means. But such a policy is costing the world dearly. The nations are compelled to pay an even higher price for it. To pay both directly and indirectly. To pay with millions of human lives, with a depletion of national resources, with the waste of gigantic sums on the arms race. With the failure to solve numerous, increasingly difficult problems. And in the long run, perhaps, with the highest possible price that can be imagined.

The US ruling circles are clearly losing their realistic bearings in this far from simple period of history. Aggressive international behaviour, increasing militarisation of politics and thinking, contempt for the interests of others – all this is leading to an inevitable moral and political isolation of US imperialism, widening the abyss between it and the rest of humanity. It is as though the opponents of peace in that country are unaware that when nuclear weapons are at the ready, the time and space for civilisation lose their habitual outlines, and mankind becomes the captive of an accident.

Will the ruling centres of the capitalist world manage to embark on the path of sober, constructive assessments of what is going on? The easiest thing is to say: maybe yes and maybe no. But history denies us the right to make such predictions. We cannot take 'no' for an answer to the question: will mankind survive or not? We say: the progress of society, the life of civilisation, must and will continue.

We say this not only by dint of the optimism that is usual for Communists, by dint of our faith in people's intelligence and common sense. We are realists and are perfectly well aware that the two worlds are divided by very many things, and deeply divided, too. But we also see clearly that the need to resolve most vital problems affecting all humanity must prompt them to interaction, awakening humanity's heretofore unseen powers of self-preservation. And here is the stimulus for solutions commensurate with the realities of our time.

The course of history, of social progress, requires ever more insistently that there should be constructive and creative interaction between states and peoples on the scale of the entire world. Not only does it so require, but it also creates the requisite political, social and material premisses for it.

Such interaction is essential in order to prevent nuclear catastrophe, in order that civilisation could survive. It is essential in order that other world-wide problems that are growing more acute should also be resolved jointly in the interests of all concerned. The prevailing dialectics of present-day development consist in a combination of competition and confrontation between the two systems and in a growing tendency towards interdependence of the countries of the world community. This is precisely the way, through the struggle of opposites, through arduous effort, groping in the dark to some extent, as it were, that the controversial but interdependent and in many ways integral world is taking shape.

The Communists have always been aware of the intrinsic complexity and contradictoriness of the paths of social progress. But at the centre of these processes – and this is the chief distinction of the Communist world outlook – there unfailingly stands man, his interests and cares. Human life, the possibilities for its comprehensive development, as Lenin stressed, is of the greatest value; the interests of social development rank above all else. That is what the CPSU takes its bearing from in its practical policy.

As we see it, the main trend of struggle in contemporary conditions is to create worthy, truly human material and spiritual conditions of life for all nations, to see to it that our planet should be habitable, and to deal with its riches rationally. Above all, to deal rationally with the chief value of all – with people and all their potentialities. That is exactly where we offer the capitalist system to compete with us in a setting of lasting peace.

2

The Significance of the Victory over Fascism

Dear Comrades,
Friends,
Dear guests,

The four years of war were long and harsh for our people. The road to victory was hard. And then came that bright day in May when Soviet soldiers, Soviet people could say: The right cause has triumphed! The enemy has been smashed! Victory is ours!

The Soviet people and their valiant armed forces inflicted a crushing defeat on Nazi Germany, defended their homeland's freedom and independence, and brought liberation to the peoples of Europe. The defeat of fascism and the victorious end of the war were an event of fundamental, history-making importance, which opened up before mankind, that had been saved, new paths of social progress and the prospect of a just and lasting peace on this planet. Our victory is not a thing of the past. It is a living victory relevant to the present and the future.

The Central Committee of the CPSU, the Presidium of the Supreme Soviet of the USSR and the Soviet government wholeheartedly congratulate the heroic Soviet people upon the fortieth anniversary of the great victory. A happy holiday to you, my dear fellow-countrymen!

Today the country is paying tribute to the courage, valour and heroism of its sons and daughters, of everyone who, weapons in hand, did their patriotic duty to the full, and did everything for the coming of the spring of victory.

Report at a Meeting in the Kremlin Palace of Congress on the Fortieth Anniversary of the Soviet People's Victory in the Great Patriotic War, 8 May 1985.

A happy holiday to you, dear heroes – frontline soldiers, partisans and underground fighters! Glory to your combat achievement in the name of your native land, for the sake of life on earth!

Carry on with dignity and honour the high title of veteran of the Great Patriotic War, which is so dear to the entire Soviet people!

Today the country is paying tribute to the dedicated work and unmatched staunchness of those who remained in the rear, of each and every one of those who made the weapons, smelted metal, and grew grain, who were bringing nearer the hour of victory at factory shops and coal mines, on railways, in the fields and on livestock farms, at research laboratories and in design offices.

A happy holiday to you, dear comrades! Honour and glory to all those whose life and work in the war years were devoted to one sacred duty: 'Everything for the front, everything for victory!'

The Soviet people have infinite respect for, and are infinitely grateful to the war and labour veterans. It is to you, comrades, that the country owes its victory, and it will never forget what you accomplished then, from 1941 to 1945, both by fighting on the battlefields and by working with unprecedented intensity.

More and more generations of Soviet people are being brought up with your glorious accomplishments as a model to emulate, learning to be brave, courageous and staunch, boundlessly loyal to Communist ideals, and ready to surmount all obstacles and to overcome all difficulties when the country calls on them to do so.

The sacrifices made by our people for the sake of victory are great indeed. The war claimed over 20 million Soviet lives. Almost every family lost some of its loved ones, and was scarred by the war. Never will the pain of bereavement and sorrow for the fallen fade away. But if they had not heroically given their lives to the country, there would have been no victory.

The memory of the immortal exploits of those who were the first to go into battle, blocked embrasures with their bodies, rammed enemy planes, threw themselves under enemy tanks with handgrenades, who, as sailors, engaged in hand-to-hand fighting with the enemy, who sank enemy ships, derailed enemy trains, courageously fought on the intelligence front, who braved death on the battlefields, who remained staunch under torture and in facist dungeons and camps will for ever remain in the Eternal Flame, in majestic memorials and modest obelisks, in literary works and works of art, in the hearts of our contemporaries and our posterity.

Everlasting glory to the heroes who fell in action for the freedom and independence of the Soviet homeland!

Let us now observe a minute of silence in tribute to their memory.

Comrades, a united front consisting of many countries and peoples was formed in order to repel the aggression of German fascism and Japanese militarism. Soviet people remember and highly value the contribution made by all who fought in the Second World War to the defeat of the common enemy and appreciate their combat valour in the struggle for freedom, peace and justice.

Allow me to convey my heartfelt greetings to the foreign guests who have come to Moscow to celebrate with the Soviet people the fortieth anniversary of the great historic event which is held dear by all honest people on our planet.

Comrades, the last war went down in the history of our country as the Great Patriotic War. Soviet people fully realised that in that life-and-death struggle the future of their socialist homeland would be decided – whether our peoples would be free or become slaves, whether they would have their own statehood, language and culture or lose everything and sink into historical oblivion. The mortal danger that hung over the country and the tremendous force of patriotism roused the whole country so that the war became a people's war, a sacred war. Soviet people drew strength from the great Leninist ideas. They were inspired by the heroic chapters of our history and our people's struggle against foreign invaders. They rose to the defence of their homeland.

In terms of its class essence, our war against Nazi Germany was the biggest armed conflict between socialism and the striking forces of imperialism. The young Soviet state, formed less than a quarter of a century before, was carrying out large-scale social reforms. The new social system was revealing more and more fully its creative potentialities. We needed peace and only peace. The Party and the Soviet government did everything to prevent the war. Our foreign policy and diplomatic efforts were directed towards attaining that objective.

As the danger of war grew, our country made preparations so as to be able to give effective rebuff tot he eventual aggressor. The Party educated Soviet people in the spirit of vigilance, hatred for fascism and readiness to defend their socialist state. It did everything to provide the army with reliable weaponry and modern equipment. The powerful industry built in the first five-year-plan periods formed the basis for strengthening the country's defence capacity.

A great deal was done in the prewar period. However, for various reasons, we failed to do everything we needed to do and on time. We had too little time.

The beginning of the war was harsh for us. We were attacked by a cruel and treacherous enemy, which had already tested its war machine and made the economies of the European countries it had occupied work for it. Its aggregate military and economic potential was twice that of the Soviet Union. Besides, it had the advantage of launching a surprise attack. And the effects of our own miscalculations were also felt.

Fighting pitched battles, the Red Army retreated deep into the country. That retreat to Moscow, Leningrad, the Volga and the Caucasus was our bitterest experience. The Nazi invasion brought on people unheard-of suffering, pain and hardships. We also faced critical situations during the war.

But from the very start it revealed the great moral force inherent in socialist society and a profound realisation that the future of the country depended on the effort of everyone. Even in the most difficult hours the people did not lose their belief in victory, their trust in the Party and the conviction that our just cause would triumph. The whole world admired the endurance of the Soviet soldiers and the courage of a great people.

The blitzkrieg plan, worked out by the German generals, was frustrated even in 1941 owing to the heroic rebuff given to the enemy on Soviet soil. The world remembers the unflinching staunchness of the defenders of the Brest Fortress, of Moscow, Leningrad and Stalingrad, Kiev and Minsk, Odessa and Sevastopol, Novorossiisk and Kerch, Tula, Smolensk and Murmansk. Cities become heroes because their defenders are heroes. The war convincingly proved this. On the defence lines of Sevastopol alone as many enemy soldiers and officers were killed as Hitler's army had lost in all the theatres of operations before its attack on the USSR. In fierce battles our army bled the enemy white, amassed experience and strength and learned to win.

Our country held out and turned the tide. The Soviet forces routed the Nazi hordes near Moscow, Stalingrad and Leningrad, and in the Caucasus and dealt crushing blows at the enemy on the Kursk Bulge, in the Ukraine west of the Dnieper, Byelorussia and in the Jassy-Kishinev, Vistula-Oder and Berlin operations.

What determined the victorious outcome of these battles, each of which had no equal in history? What enabled us to win the war which had begun so inauspiciously for us?

The sources of victory were the nature of socialism, of the Soviet way of life, and the popular, national character of the Great Patriotic War. The war, as a most severe test has strikingly and fully confirmed that it is the popular masses that are the decisive force of history. Soviet citizens of different nationalities stood by their socialist homeland, showing mass heroism in battles and labour. They were united and inspired by the example of the great Russian people, whose courage, fortitude and indomitable spirit instilled in them an unconquerable will to attain victory.

The millions participating in the war were not a faceless mass in that battle of unprecedented scale. Their heroism vividly reflected the high personal qualities of the soldiers of the Great Patriotic War – from Private Alexander Matrosov to Marshal Georgi Zhukov.

The combat banners of our armed forces are covered with everlasting glory. The Red Army, born of the October Revolution, was a people's army. The Soviet soldiers were distinguished by total devotion to their country and by courage and high combat skill. In fierce battles they displayed their great moral qualities. Neither the immense sacrifices we made during the war nor the atrocities perpetrated by the enemy darkened their minds with a blind thirst for vengeance. Having entered the territory of Germany as victors, the Soviet people did not spread their hatred of Nazism to the German people. The fighting was still going on when they helped the German people to start building a peaceful life.

The talent of our generals and military commanders vividly manifested itself in unprecedentedly great battles. Born in the midst of the masses and reared and educated by the Party, they proved to be worthy heirs and successors to the country's best traditions of the art of warfare. The superiority of Soviet military science and generalship – their strategic foresight, the creative character of the decisions they took, their persistence and dedication in attaining the set goals, and their ability to fuse the high morale of the offices and men with the all-crushing might of the newest military technology – was clearly seen in battles against a strong and experienced enemy. The whole country knows the glorious names of the prominent generals and military commanders of the Great Patriotic War. All war veterans, our armed forces and all Soviet people are proud of them.

The involvement of all Soviet people in the war found vivid expression in the formation of the two-million-strong volunteer force, in the struggle of the underground fighters on territory temporarily occupied by the enemy, and in the large-scale partisan movement. Behind the frontline, in the enemy rear, there was one more front, that of the partisans. Over one million partisans took part in the fighting. The ground burned under the aggressors' feet, and quite a number of the invaders' divisions perished in the flames of the just cause of the partisans.

'War tests all the economic and organisational forces of a nation,' Vladimir Lenin used to say.[1] And the Soviet economy withstood this greatest test with honour. The socialist organisation of industry and agriculture had convincingly proved its advantages.

In the most difficult situation, within time limits which seem fantastic even today, we moved more than 1,500 large factories and plants and a considerable amount of material resources and assets deep into the country. Just one year after the enemy attack the eastern regions of the Soviet Union accounted for more than three-quarters of the country's military output. The advantage of the socialist economy was demonstrated most convincingly in its high efficiency. Though our output of steel and coal was only one-third and one-fifth respectively of that of Germany and the countries occupied by it, we produced nearly twice as much military hardware.

What made the Soviet wartime economy effective was the firm authority of the state plan, the discipline, strict responsibility, initiative, resourcefulness, and bold ideas and selfless efforts of the workers, collective farmers, engineers, designers and scientists, and the organising abilities of production managers.

Faced with a moral danger, the whole country contributed to the war effort. The Soviet working class dispalyed unprecedented heroism and staunchness. At most critical moments workers' battalions joined the army in the field while plants continued to operate even when the enemy was near and shells and bombs exploded close by. With its political consciousness and organisation the working class reaffirmed its role as Soviet society's leading force, having done everything for victory.

The worker-peasant alliance, the socialist system of agriculture and collective farming stood the test of the war. Despite the fact that the country's main grain-growing areas had been captured by the enemy and despite the shortage of manpower and machinery, the countryside provided troops at the front and workers in the rear with food, and industry with raw materials. Collective farmers, state-farm workers and the personnel of machine-and-tractor stations spared no effect to smash the enemy and discharged with honour their patriotic duty.

Like the rest of the country, professional people did all they could for victory. Our talented and hardworking scientists, designers and engineers produced aircraft, tanks, guns, mortars, and other weaponry which surpassed the military equipment of the enemy. That was truly invincible weaponry designed for victory.

Impassioned journalism and prose writings, and patriotic songs, films, plays, poems and posters inspired people to a determined struggle against the enemy.

The exploits of Komsomol members and of all young people of those fiery years of the 1940s, whose adolescence and early manhood coincided with the war, will forever remain in the people's memory. The young people who fought the enemy in battles belonged to the generation that was born after the October Revolution and moulded by the socialist system. From childhood they had absorbed its revolutionary and collectivist morals and psychology. And they did not flinch, boldly moving forward to the firing lines. Having gone through all the trials of the hard war years, they demonstrated that a country capable of bringing up and educating such young people could not be conquered.

It was the same in the rear. Young men and women, teenagers, worked hard at factories and plants, in the fields of collective and state farms. It is often said that they worked without knowing fatigue. Of course they knew what fatigue was, but they also knew that their efforts were badly needed by the embattled country. And today millions of our contemporaries are particularly moved when they recall their wartime childhood and youth.

It is with a feeling of deep gratitude that we speak of the heroism of Soviet women. Indeed, war is not for women. But defying danger, they went into attack with the men, fought courageously against the hated enemy, removed wounded soldiers from the battlefield, and nursed them back to health at medical stations and hospitals. Millions of soldiers owe their lives to the valour and kindheartedness of women. Nor will the Soviet people ever forget the women's glorious feats on the labour front. Soviet women bore all the hardships of wartime life and the grief of loses, displaying tremendous will-power and retaining the warmth of never-fading love. Our admiration for Soviet women patriots is immense and our gratitude for what they did for the sake of victory is deep.

The fascists, planning aggression against our country, had hoped to bring the peoples of the Soviet Union into conflict with one another and to incite national strife. These hopes were dashed by what actually happened. Mankind knows no other instance where war brought all nations and nationalities of a country so close together in order to fight an aggressor. The fraternal unity of the peoples demonstrated with full force the wisdom and foresight of the Leninist nationalities policy. The great socialist union remained firm and unshaken.

The gigantic efforts at the front and in the rear were guided by the Party, its Central Committee, by the State Defence Committee headed by Joseph Stalin, General Secretary of the Central Committee of the All-Union Communist Party (Bolsheviks).

Party committees became real military headquarters and political organisers of the masses. Everywhere, in soldiers' trenches, in partisan detachments and underground, Party organisations were active, and political instructors inspired soldiers with impassioned words and personal example. 'The history of the Great Patriotic War', *Pravda* wrote in 1942, 'will include as one of the glorious and honourable figures that of the political instructor who, submachine gun in hand and wearing a camouflage cape and helmet, was always in the forefront and leading the soldiers to the achievement of a lofty and noble goal – the defeat of the German fascists and the liberation of the homeland.'[2]

Communists went to the most dangerous and crucial areas of the struggle. Four in five of them either fought in the army or worked at munitions plants. Members of the Central Committee and the best Party cadres were sent there. Three million Communists died in battles against the fascist invaders. Over five million people joined the Party in those heroic years.

Lenin's Party was a fighting party which had become one with the people at war. During the most difficult period – the war period – of our history it lived up to its great responsibility for the fate of the country and led it to victory. The political and moral prestige of our Party grew in the war years; the name of Communist rose further in the people's esteem. And we members of Lenin's Party will always cherish and be proud of this.

It was not only our weapons, economy and political system that won in the war. It was a victory of the ideas for which the revolution had been made and Soviet citizens had fought and died. It was a victory of our ideology and morality, which embody the high principles of humanism and justice, over the man-hating fascist ideology.

The Soviet army carried out with honour its great liberating mission. It came to enslaved Europe as the liberator, and fought in order to end war and fascism and to ensure that the peoples of Europe would enjoy a durable peace.

In observing Victory Day, we pay due respect to the valour of the soldiers of the Allied US, British and French armies. We shall never forget the steadfastness and courage of the Yugoslav people and their People's Liberation Army.

We highly respect the selfless struggle of occupied but unsubdued Poland. The Polish and Czechoslovak armies fought shoulder to shoulder with our forces on Soviet territory, and then in freeing their own countries.

Partisans, underground fighters and, in the last phase of the war, the armies of Bulgaria and Romania along with Hungarian units contributed to the defeat of Hitlerism. The Albanian and Greek peoples fought with determination against the occupation troops. We remember the courageous, though unequal combat of the German Communists and all anti-fascists against the Hitler regime.

The Soviet people highly appreciate the bravery of Resistance Movement fighters. In the forefront of the movement were the Communist Parties of France, Italy, Norway, Denmark, Belgium, Holland and other West European countries. They inspired and rallied their peoples to fight against Nazi tyranny and for their freedom and national independence. Many Communists gave their lives for victory over the enemy. The French Communist Party went down in history as a party of men shot and killed.

True to its Allied commitment in the Second World War to the end, our country played a tremendous role in defeating militarist Japan. We acted in close military cooperation with the great Chinese people. The soldiers of the Mongolian People's Republic fought the common enemy together with us. The patriots of Vietnam, Korea and other Asian countries resolutely fought the Japanese invaders.

Recalling the events of that time and the joint struggle waged by peoples against their common enemy, we can proudly say that the outcome of the Second World War was decided on the Soviet-German front. There the fascist aggressor sustained more than 70 per cent of all its losses.

The Soviet people's feat in the Great Patriotic War is a great and unforgettable one. The years of the war are a record of an infinite number of experiences – the bitterness of loss, the joy of victory, the valour displayed in fierce battles and the unostentatious greatness of day-to-day work.

Our victory greatly enhanced the Soviet Union's international prestige. It brought about a surge of patriotism in Soviet people. For us that victory has been and will continue to be a source of inspiration, from which we shall always draw strength in carrying out our great development plans and in increasing the might and prosperity of our land, the Union of Soviet Socialist Republics.

Our victory in the Great Patriotic War is a holiday we shall always celebrate.

Comrades, the main, the most valuable thing the victory gave us is the possibility to live and work in peace. The war was a test that showed that our social system is invincible and that its vitality is inexhaustible.

Peacetime puts forth its own great demands and is a serious test of society's ability to ensure steady economic growth and constantly perfect social relations, and improve people's working conditions and living standards.

Summing up the results of the past 40 years, one has every reason to say that in peaceful development as well socialism has convincingly demonstrated its vast potentialities and great advantages.

People of the older generation remember the horrible picture of destruction in regions liberated from the invaders. They remember bomb-scarred earth, houses burned to cinders, and blast furnaces and coal mines in disuse or destroyed. Almost 1,700 cities and towns and 70,000 villages lay in ruins. Nearly 25 million people were homeless. Tens of thousands of industrial and agricultural enterprises were destroyed. The fire of war devoured nearly one third of the national wealth created by the people. But no one can ever measure the most horrible and irreparable loss, the loss of millions of lives of Soviet people.

The enemies of socialism hoped that the destruction and damage inflicted upon this country would make it backward and dependent on the West. They miscalculated once again. The hard and dedicated work of the workers, collective farmers and members of the intelligentsia raised from the ashes the cities, villages, factories and plants destroyed by the enemy. It took the Soviet Union just three years to restore industrial production to the prewar level and five years to restore agricultural.output.

That was another feat, a feat in constructive work, which the Soviet people accomplished in the difficult postwar years. It showed most forcefully what a people inspired by the great goals of socialist construction can accomplish. Since then this country has made great progress in all fields of economic, social, political and cultural development.

Soviet society today is a society with a highly developed economy. The country's national income is more than 16 times what it was before the war, and its industrial output has grown 24 times. Our industry has been increasing its output twice as fast as that of advanced capitalist countries. Today the USSR produces more pig-iron, steel, oil, natural gas, cement, mineral fertilisers, machine tools, tractors, grain combine-harvesters and many other goods than any other country in the world.

There have been deep-going changes in the structure of scientific and technological standards of production. New industries, such as the atomic, aerospace, electronics and microbiological industries, have been set up. Powerful production complexes have been or are being built in the country's central regions and in the Urals, Siberia, the Soviet Far East, Soviet Central Asia and Transcaucasia, in fact, in all regions. The country has a ramified network of power transmission lines and oil and gas pipelines. Canals stretch for thousands of kilometres. The once arid steppes are no longer what they used to be, and marshlands have become fertile. The country's economic map has changed beyond recognition over these decades.

The major productive force of this society, its creative potential, has essentially changed. The USSR has well-trained and highly-educated manpower today. The professional skill, general culture and specialist knowledge of factory workers and collective farmers have increased substantially. We have the biggest contingent of engineers and scientists in the world. In the postwar period, Soviet science and technology have more than once achieved outstanding successes in major areas of world scientific and technological progress. The Soviet Union built the first-ever nuclear power station and nuclear-powered ice-breaker, and launched the first sputnik. Soviet citizen Yuri Gagarin was the first man to see the Earth from space.

Soviet society today is a society of continually rising living standards. Rapid economic development has made it possible, without paying less attention to further building up the national economic potential, to start moving towards satisfying more fully the working people's needs and to score impressive results in this respect. Real per capita incomes are more than six times as high as the prewar level. Housing construction has assumed vast proportions. The network of hospitals and out-patient clinics, kindergartens and day nurseries, and public service facilities has appreciably expanded.

Soviet society today is a society of high standards in education and culture, a society where the people enjoy a rich intellectual life. While before the war only 5 in every 100 workers primarily engaged in physical labour had a higher or secondary education, the figure now has reached 82. Our contemporary is a person of a broad cultural and political vision and high intellectual requirements.

Soviet society today is a society which has resolved major social problems. The entire system of social relations has reached a higher stage of maturity. The alliance between the working class, the peasantry and the intelligentsia has been strengthened. We have made progress in eliminating the essential distinctions between town and countryside, between physical and mental labour. The progress made by nations and nationalities is integral to their all-round drawing together. A sense of belonging to a single family – the Soviet people, is a new social and international community without precedent in history – is deeply ingrained in everybody's mind and heart.

Soviet society today is a society of authentic, real democracy, respect for the dignity and rights of citizens, and their great responsibility. The working people's involvement in the affairs of the nation and of their individual production group is becoming increasingly active and extensive. The system of the people's socialist self-government is being perfected.

Forty years after the great victory, the Soviet Union is a mighty and flourishing power, confidently blazing the trail into the Communist future.

Our achievements are clear to see. But the dialectics of development are such that the targets reached extend the historical horizons and place more complex and more challenging tasks before people. We also have such tasks before us today. They mean, essentially, that we have to achieve a new qualitative state of society with regard to its economy, its system of social and political relations and institutions, and the totality of the working and living conditions for millions of Soviet people.

The April 1985 Plenary Meeting of the CPSU Central Committee centred on urgent issues. The Party sees its main task in greatly accelerating the social and economic progress of the nation, which is required by life itself – both by domestic factors and the international situation. We must first of all ensure intensive and dynamic economic growth on the basis of the latest achievements in science and technology. This will enable us to further raise living standards, enhance the economic and defence might of our country, and improve our society of developed socialism in every respect.

Good end results with the most effective utilisation of resources are now the main yardstick of economic performance. It is from this angle that we must view today's economic situation. We must within a short period of time reach the highest possible levels of productivity, quality and efficiency. This is one of today's vital demands.

The way to achieve this is through scientific and technological progress. Our growth rates and the course of our economic competition with capitalism are going to depend largely on how we accelerate this progress and the introduction of the achievements of science and technology into the economy.

In short, at this new historic stage Soviet society is confronted with formidable tasks. We have all we need to cope with them and will undoubtedly reach our targets.

We are confident that the advantages of the socialist system will serve us well in the new historical conditions too. But it is important that we take urgent and often new measures without delay to bring the forms and methods of socialist economic management and social and economic administration into correspondence with the current demands and future requirements.

Our strategy of managerial streamlining is based on Lenin's idea that 'socialism must achieve this advance *in its own way*, by its own method – or, to put it more concretely, by *Soviet* methods'.[3] We must develop forms and structures in the economic machinery to maximise efficiency, improve quality and further scientific and technological progress.

Constructive initiative by the people ensures our advancement. The working people's profound interest in the life of their socialist homeland, and their labour and political activity have always promoted social progress, helping us overcome all difficulties and obstacles. Today it is very important to give ample scope to public initiative and direct it towards bringing about faster social and economic growth.

Nothing promotes a working man's activity so much as confidence that the principle of social justice will be applied without fail. The Party shall do all in its power to ensure this. By erecting a firm barrier to all departures from socialist principles and to all sorts of negative phenomena, by blocking all sources of unearned income and at the same time enhancing the role of material and moral incentives for conscientious and effective work, we shall carry out major socioeconomic, political, ideological and educational tasks, arouse the profound interest of millions of working people in the attainment of the targets set and raise even further their social consciousness and level of organisation.

In looking forward to the next (27th) CPSU Congress, the Party Central Committee is taking steps to ensure that the Party's political line fully meets the requirements of social development, the interests and aspirations of the broadest sections of the working people. It is for this very reason that the Party is constantly improving its work, the forms of Party and state guidance.

Today it is exceptionally important for us to know how to act, as Lenin taught us, by virtue of authority, energy, greater experience, greater versatility, and greater talent. There must be less talk, assurances and promises and more real work, practical results, responsibility, integrity, coordination of efforts, attention to people, and personal modesty. This is the main yardstick for assessing all personnel, their ideological integrity and competence; this is the substance of Party requirements as to style and methods of work.

The efforts to intensify social and economic development, to have firm order everywhere, to tighten organisation and discipline are meeting with the warm approval and complete support of the Soviet people. The CPSU Central Committee, its Political Bureau and the Soviet government appreciate and value the people's trust in the Party's policy and will exert every effort to justify it.

The Party's entire policy is based on its profound faith in the creative powers and abilities of the Soviet people. A people who conquered the enemy in open battle, held out in the difficult years of postwar recovery and scored outstanding achievements in developing their socialist homeland will likewise prevail in the new historical conditions and meet in a fitting manner any challenge posed by the times.

The Party clearly sees the tasks facing the country and the ways in which they can be successfully accomplished, and it is mobilising the Soviet people to bring about a new and powerful upsurge in the economy in order to raise further their living standards. In this we see a worthy continuation of the cause for which the Soviet people fought with dedication during the harsh years of the war and in the years of peaceful socialist construction.

Comrades, returning now in our minds and hearts to the victorious spring of 1945, we naturally ask whether the hopes of the millions of people who fought so that we, our children and grandchildren could live in peace and happiness have materialised.

· Yes, they have! But a great deal remains to be done to preserve our planet, the common home of mankind, both for us, who are living now, and for future generations, and to eliminate wars from people's lives once and for all.

Forty years is not a short period of time by any standards. Time passes. Those who were born after the victory have become mature people, and their children are grown up, too. For most people today the Second World War is an event outside their personal experience. But the war left such a legacy that its results and lessons continue to influence the whole course and nature of the world's development and the people's consciousness.

The Second World War emerged long before the first battles took place on the fields of Europe and on the ocean expanses. Its sinister shadow was looming over mankind when some politician failed and others did not want to prevent Nazism coming to power. Today we have better knowledge than we did at that time about who helped and how they helped the Nazi ruling clique to arm itself, build up a potential for aggression and prepare for military adventures.

The attempts by leading groups of monopoly capital to manipulate German fascism's expansion, directing it eastwards, were the height of political irresponsibility. The Munich deal will go down forever in the book of shame covering the names of those who so persistently instigated Hitler to attack the Soviet Union. And one has to suffer from a profound political amnesia not to remember this.

There is no need now to recall the names of the bourgeois politicians and statesmen of the 1930s who sincerely erred and those who were motivated by their selfish class interests. History will not change its verdict: the 'Munich policy' of the Western powers and their connivance at Nazi aggression resulted in a great tragedy for all the peoples of Europe. Criminal was the policy pursued by those who, ignoring persistent calls from the Soviet Union, refused to act in a united front to stop the Nazi adventurists. Time will never lift from them the responsibility for a holocaust which could have been prevented if hostility towards socialism had not blinded the leaders of the West at that time.

Unfortunately, history is repeating itself. And today, more than ever before, it is imperative to display vigilance against the intrigues of those who are pushing the world to an abyss, only this time a nuclear abyss. One should have a clear idea as to where the threat to mankind today is emanating from. The Soviet Union makes this statement just as forcefully as before the war, warning against the menacing danger. Another reason for mentioning this is that the ill-intentioned myth of a 'Soviet military threat', so noisily exploited by Nazism, is still in circulation.

Despite all the efforts of the falsifiers of history to rewrite it, the people of the world know that the Soviet Union was the first country to sound the alarm and warn against the growing danger of fascism. It was the Communists who proposed a clear-cut programme of struggle against the brown plague when it was still in embryo. Last but not least, it was the Soviet Union that put forward a series of proposals aimed at curbing the aggressor who was casting off all restraint. But at that time, too, it was all dismissed as 'Communist propaganda'.

The occupation of almost the whole of Western Europe, the seizure of Paris, the bombardment of London and the attack on Pearl Harbour dashed those cynical calculations and illusory hopes. It was only after the Red Army had won a number of brilliant victories that agreements on cooperation with the Soviet Union in the struggle against fascism began to materialise.

The expansion of the fascist threat made Western politicians look at the world in a more realistic fashion. The history of the anti-Hitler coalition indisputably shows that states with different social systems can join forces in the fight against a common enemy, find mutually acceptable solutions and work effectively for a common cause.

Soviet people remember the material help which the Allies gave this country. True, it was not as great as the West is wont to claim, but we are grateful for that help and regard it as a symbol of cooperation. The opening of the second front in Europe, though belated, was a substantial contribution to the common struggle.

The favourable atmosphere of cooperation between the countries of the anti-Hitler coalition and a realistic assessment of the new situation in the world after the defeat of fascism were reflected in the postwar settlement and in the decisions made by the Allied conferences in Teheran, Yalta and Potsdam. Those decisions along with the United Nations Charter and other international agreements of that time are imbued with a spirit of cooperation. They ensured that a solution would be found to the complex problems of the postwar settlement, including territorial questions, a settlement meeting the objective of attaining the long-awaited peace.

It is particularly appropriate to recall all these things today when all peoples have one common enemy, the threat of nuclear war, and one supreme goal – that of removing this threat.

Twice this century the imperialist forces unleashed bloody world wars in a bid to achieve their class aims, strengthen their positions and further their selfish interests. But history decreed otherwise. No wonder that both wars, which started out as ventures of imperialism, which was arrogant, confident of its impunity and convinced that international law was written with the invader's fist, ended in the defeat of those who unleashed them and provoked each time a series of crises which shook the very system that breeds wars.

In defending their country's freedom and independence, the Soviet people also carried out the great international mission of saving world civilisation from fascism. The defeat of fascism consolidated the positions of progressive democratic forces, which resulted in the triumph of a new social system in a number of European and Asian countries. A first workers' and peasants' state was also born on German soil. During the popular struggle against Nazism and Japanese imperialism, a struggle which closely merged with the aspirations of the masses for deep social change, the appeal of socialist ideas visibly grew, while the Communist parties in many countries gained in strength and development into a powerful force.

The postwar years have seen the formation of a world socialist system and its considerable progress; a community of socialist states has emerged. The new social system that has established itself in the world has proved its vitality. It has awakened the creative power of millions and enabled history-making accomplishments to be achieved within a short period of time. Today socialism is a mighty world system, one which is exerting enormous influence on the development of mankind and its future, and is an invincible factor for peace and a guarantor of the security of the peoples.

The states of this great community possess invaluable experience and an efficient mechanism of coordinating their policy. They act as one on international matters and steadfastly uphold the cause of peace and disarmament, the principles of peaceful coexistence. The Warsaw Treaty Organisation, its Political Consultative Committee and the Joint Armed Forces of the allied countries have a special role to play in this respect. So long as there is a threat to peace and security, the Warsaw Treaty member countries will do everything necessary as they have always done to safeguard themselves against any encroachments. Proof of this has been provided by the extension, unanimously approved by all its signatories, of the Treaty for another team.

Profound changes in the postwar world have also taken place following the collapse of colonialism, with dozens of independent states springing up where colonies and semi-colonies used to be. True, their development has been uneven, there have been ups and downs, achievements and tragedies. True, the developing countries are faced with very difficult problems – some inherited from the past and some due to the policy of neocolonialism.

But it is also true that the system of colonialism has now been eradicated almost completely and that many young national states are playing an increasingly prominent and progressive role in world politics. With the active support of the socialist countries they are making persistent efforts to establish a new and fairer world economic order. The non-aligned movement has become an important factor in present-day international relations.

As we see, comrades, the political map of the world has undergone radical changes in the forty years that have passed since the victory.

The sphere in which imperialism is able to dominate has perceptibly narrowed. Its opportunities for manoeuvre and for imposing its will on sovereign states and peoples with impunity have been substantially reduced. The alignment of forces inside the capitlist world has also changed. The defeat in the Second World War of such a predator as German imperialism, the defeat of militarist Japan, and the weakening of the once-powerful British and French rivals of US imperialism have enabled it to lead the capitalist world in all the major indicators – economic, financial and military. The fact that the US is actually the only major country to have fabulously enriched itself on the war has also boosted the claims of the US ruling class to world hegemony.

In the very first years of the postwar period imperialist reaction, displeased with the social and international-political results of the war, tried to take a kind of historic revenge, to roll back socialism and other democratic forces. This strategy was spearheaded against the Soviet Union while the economic might of the US and its temporary monopoly of atomic weapons served as levers.

This monopoly was looked upon by the ruling circles in the US as a means of pressuring us and other socialist countries militarily and politically, and for intimidating all peoples.

That is why, when we speak about the results of the decades since the war, it would be wrong to see only those which we sincerely welcome and support. Unfortunately we see many things which cause growing anxiety. Of course the world today does not in the least resemble the world of the 1930s, but by no means has everyone in the West given up attempts to use threats when talking to the Soviet Union.

The cold war launched by militaristic circles in the West was nothing less than an attempt to revise the results of the Second World War, to deprive the Soviet people, the world forces of progress and democracy, of the fruits of their victory. Actually, these goals were never concealed. They found their expression in the ideology and policy of 'rolling back socialism', 'massive retaliation', 'brinkmanship', etc. This undermined trust between nations and greatly reduced the opportunities for the constructive international cooperation which had been launched within the framework of the anti-Hitler coalition.

US militarism is in the forefront of the forces which threaten mankind with war. The increasingly bellicose US policies have become a constant negative factor in international relations, which we cannot afford to overlook. The aggressive designs of the US ruling elite have revealed themselves in its attempts to upset the military-strategic balance, the bulwark of international security, in its instigation of the arms race, especially the nuclear arms race, and in its dangerous plans for the militarisation of space. Some barbarous doctrines and concepts concerning the use of nuclear weapons are being devised, and hundreds of military bases and facilities have been set up around the world. A policy of state-backed terrorism is being pursued with respect to Nicaragua, and an undeclared war is being waged against Afghanistan.

The US has been trying to impose on the world community of nations its claims for an exclusive and special mission in history. Nothing else can explain its imperial demands for 'zones of vital interests', for the 'right' to interfere in the internal affairs of other states, to 'encourage' or 'punish' sovereign nations in any way which suits Washington. Even the US's political and legal commitments are being violated.

It should be said in quite definite terms that the danger of West German revanchism, in whose revival the current US leadership is so deeply involved, has been growing. The leaders of the seven leading caitalist states, who gathered in Bonn the other day to 'mark' the fortieth anniversary of the end of the Second World War in their own way, even dared to question the territorial and political realities in Europe that had emerged as a result of Nazi Germany's defeat and postwar developments. Some politicians are prepared to forget and even justify SS cutthroats, moreover to render homage to them, which is an insult to the very memory of the millions shot, burned and gassed.

Realising the scope of the military danger and being aware of our responsibility for the future of the world, we will not let the military and strategic balance between the USSR and the US, between the Warsaw Treaty Organisation and NATO, be upset. We will continue to pursue this policy, as we have learnt well, once and for all, what history has taught us.

To put it briefly, the situation remains complicated and even dangerous, but we believe there are genuine opportunities for curbing the forces of militarism. The conviction that a world without wars and weapons can really be reached, that such a world can be built in our time, that now, today, we should actively strive for it, struggle for it, is becoming strongly implanted in the minds of people the world over.

This conviction is being proven by the experience of the policy of peaceful coexistence and the practical results of cooperation between the states of the two systems. There are quite a number of such examples. They are encouraging more and more people to oppose aggression and violence in international relations. There is a growing realisation that peace will only be durable if peaceful constructive coexistence, equal and mutually beneficial cooperation between states with different social systems become supreme universal laws governing international relations. There can be no doubt that the anti-war movement will continue to grow, more and more effectively obstructing adventurist moves by the forces of aggression.

The only sensible way out today is to promote vigorous cooperation between all states in the interests of a universal peaceful future, and also establish, utilise and develop such international mechanisms and institutions which would enable us effectively to balance the interests of individual peoples and countries with the interests of mankind as a whole.

We urge the most diverse social and political forces to promote sincere cooperation based on goodwill for the sake of peace. It is a far from easy task which cannot be solved on a short-term basis and requires a sufficiently high degree of trust in relations between nations. The course of events could be altered radically if tangible progress were attained at the Soviet-US talks on nuclear and space weapons in Geneva. This is our conviction.

The experience of the 1970s, in our view, is truly invaluable in this respect. It was at that time that good political, legal, moral and psychological foundations were laid for the cooperation between the states belonging to the two systems in new historical circumstnaces, covering, for example, such sensitive areas as the security of sides. But the results could have been even more substantial had the West shown a responsible attitude towards the gains of détente.

We are solidly in favour of the process of détente being restarted. But that does not mean simply going back to what was achieved in the 1970s. We must set our sights much higher. Détente is not the ultimate objective of politics in our estimation. It is an indispensable, yet no more than transitional, stage from a world crammed with weapons to a reliable and comprehensive system of international security.

The Soviet Union is prepared to proceed along these lines. Looking for every opportunity to remove the danger of nuclear war must become the highest duty of governments and responsible statesmen. I would like to repeat once more today, on this anniversary which is memorable for all of us, that the Soviet Union is resolutely in favour of a world without wars, a world without arms. We declare again and again that the outcome of historical competiton between the two systems cannot be decided by military means.

Our allegiance to the policy of peaceful coexistence is evidence of the strength of the new social system and of our faith in its historic potential. This allegiance meets the interests of all nations. It is permeated with a spirit of true humanism, with the ideals of peace and freedom which also inspired the Soviet people in the years of the last war.

To uphold man's sacred right to live, to ensure a lasting peace is the duty of the living to the millions of those who fell for freedom and social progress, our common duty to present and future generations.

Dear Comrades,

The great Soviet people, whether in a soldier's greatcoat or a workman's overalls, led by the Bolshevik Party were the main hero of the war and the architect of the victory.

As we celebrate Victory Day, we bow to the memory of the fine, courageous sons and daughters of our country who gave their lives for the sacred cause of defending the homeland.

As we celebrate Victory Day, we honour war veterans and labour veterans, the Soviet people, whether as soldiers or working people, our heroic working class, collective farmers, and people's intelligentsia.

As we celebrate Victory Day, we honour all this country's nations and nationalities, united in the unbreakable fraternal family – the Union of Soviet Socialist Republics.

As we celebrate Victory Day, we honour the Soviet soldier and our valiant armed forces.

As we celebrate Victory Day, we honour the Leninist Communist Party, the Party of the victorious people.

Let the Soviet people's exploit in the Great Patriotic War live through the ages!

Notes

1 V.I. Lenin, 'Address to the Second All-Russia Congress of Communist Organisations of the Peoples of the East, 22 November 1919', *Collected Works*, vol. 30, 1977, p. 154.

2 *Pravda*, 22 March 1942.

3 V.I. Lenin, 'The Immediate Tasks of the Soviet Government', *Collected Works*, vol. 27, 1977, p. 248.

3

General Disarmament: a Soviet Proposal

A new year, 1986, has begun. It will be an important year, one might say a turning point in the history of the Soviet state, the year of the 27th Congress of the CPSU. The Congress will chart the guidelines for the political, social, economic and intellectual development of Soviet society in the period up to the next millennium. It will adopt a programme for accelerating our peaceful construction.

All efforts of the CPSU are directed towards ensuring a further improvement of the life of the Soviet people.

A turn for the better is also needed on the international scene. This is the expectation and the demand of the peoples of the Soviet Union and of the peoples throughout the world.

Being aware of this, at the very start of the new year the Political Bureau of the CPSU Central Committee and the Soviet government have adopted a decision on a number of major foreign policy measures that are of a fundamental nature. They are designed to promote to a maximum degree an improvement of the international situation. They are prompted by the need to overcome the negative confrontational tendencies that have been growing in recent years and to clear the ways towards curbing the nuclear arms race on earth and preventing it in outer space, towards an overall reduction of the war danger and towards confidence-building as an integral part of relations among states.

The most important of these measures is a concrete programme aimed at the complete elimination of nuclear weapons throughout the world within a precisely defined period of time.

The Soviet Union proposes that a step-by-step, consistent process of ridding the earth of nuclear weapons be implemented and completed within

Statement by Mikhail Gorbachev, 15 January 1986.

the next fifteen years, before the end of this century.

The twentieth century has given mankind the gift of the energy of the atom. However, this great achievement of the human intellect can turn into an instrument of mankind's self-annihilation.

Is it possible to resolve this contradiction? We are convinced that it is possible. Finding effective ways of eliminating nuclear weapons is a feasible task, provided it is tackled without delay.

The Soviet Union proposes that a programme of ridding mankind of the fear of a nuclear catastrophe be carried out beginning in 1986. The fact that this year has been proclaimed by the UN the International Year of Peace provides an additional political and moral stimulus for this. What is required here is that we should rise above national selfishness, tactical considerations, differences and disputes, whose significance is nothing compared to the preservation of what is most cherished – peace and a secure future. The energy of the atom should be placed solely at the service of peace, a goal that our socialist state has consistently pursued and continues to pursue.

Our country was the first to raise, back in 1946, the question of prohibiting the production and use of atomic weapons and to make nuclear energy serve peaceful purposes, for the benefit of mankind.

How does the Soviet Union envisage today in practical terms the process of reducing nuclear weapons, both delivery vehicles and warheads, up to their complete elimination? Our proposals on this subject can be summarised as follows.

Stage One. Within the next five to eight years the USSR and the US will reduce by one half of the nuclear weapons that can reach each other's territory. As for the remaining delivery vehicles of this kind, each side will retain no more than 6,000 warheads.

It stands to reason that such a reduction is possible only if both the USSR and the US renounce the development, testing and deployment of space-strike weapons. As the Soviet Union has repeatedly warned the development of space-strike weapons will dash the hopes of a reduction of nuclear armaments on earth.

The first stage will include the adoption and implementation of a decision on the complete elimination of medium-range missiles of the USSR and the US in the European zone – both ballistic and cruise missiles – as a first step towards ridding the European continent of nuclear weapons.

At the same time the US should undertake not to transfer its strategic and medium-range missiles to other countries, while Britain and France should pledge not to build up their respective nuclear arsenals.

The USSR and the US should from the very beginning agree to stop all nuclear explosions and call upon other states to join in such a moratorium as soon as possible.

The reason why the first stage of nuclear disarmament should concern the Soviet Union and the US is that it is they who should set an example for the other nuclear powers. We said that very frankly to President Reagan of the US during our meeting in Geneva.

Stage Two. At this stage, which should start no later than 1990 and last for five to seven years, the other nuclear powers will begin to join the process of nuclear disarmament. To start with, they would pledge to freeze all their nuclear arms and not to have them on the territories of other countries.

In this period the USSR and the US will continue to carry out the reductions agreed upon during the first stage and also implement further measures aimed at eliminating their medium-range nuclear weapons and freezing their tactical nuclear systems.

Following the completion by the USSR and the US of a 50 per cent reduction of their respective armaments at the second stage, another radical step will be taken: all nuclear powers will eliminate their tactical nuclear weapons, that is, weapons having a range (or radius of action) of up to 1,000 kilometres.

At this stage the Soviet-US accord on the prohibition of space-strike weapons would become multilateral, with the mandatory participation in it of the major industrial powers.

All nuclear powers would stop nuclear weapon tests.

There would be a ban on the development of non-nuclear weapons based on new physical principles, whose destructive power is close to that of nuclear arms or other weapons of mass destruction.

Stage Three will begin no later than 1995. At this stage the elimination of all remaining nuclear weapons will be completed. By the end of 1999 there will be no nuclear weapons on earth. A universal accord will be drawn up that such weapons should never again come into being.

We envisage that special procedures will be worked out for the destruction of nuclear weapons as well as for the dismantling, conversion or scrapping of delivery vehicles. In the process, agreement will be reached on the number of weapons to be scrapped at each stage, the sites of their destruction and so on.

Verification of the destruction or limitation of arms could be carried out both by national technical means and through on-site inspections. The USSR is ready to reach agreement on any other additional verification measures.

Adoption of the nuclear disarmament programme that we are proposing would unquestionably have a favourable impact on the negotiations conducted at bilateral and multilateral forums. The programme would envisage clearly-defined routes and reference points, establish a specific timetable for achieving agreements and implementing them and would make the negotiations pur-poseful and task-oriented. This would stop the dangerous trend whereby the momentum of the arms race is greater than the progress of negotiations.

Thus we propose that we should enter the third millennium without nuclear weapons, on the basis of mutually acceptable and strictly verifiable agreements. If the US administration is indeed committed to the goal of the complete elimination of nuclear weapons everywhere, as it has repeatedly stated, it now has a real opportunity to carry it out in practice. Instead of spending the next 10 to 15 years in developing new space weapons, which are extremely dangerous for mankind, weapons allegedly designed to make nuclear arms useless, would it not be more sensible to start eliminating those weapons and finally doing away with them altogether? The Soviet Union, I repeat, proposes precisely that.

The Soviet Union calls upon all peoples and states, and naturally, above all, nuclear states, to support the programme of eliminating nuclear weapons before the year 2000. It is absolutely clear to any unbiased person that if such a programme is implemented, nobody would lose and all stand to gain. This is a problem common to all mankind and it can and must be solved only through joint efforts. And the sooner this programme is translated into practical deeds, the safer life on our planet will be.

Guided by the same approach and a desire to take another practical step within the context of the nuclear disarmament programme, the Soviet Union has adopted an important decision.

We are extending by three months our unilaterial moratorium on all nuclear explosions, which expired on 31 December 1985. Such a moratorium will remain in force even longer if the US for its part also stops nuclear tests. We propose once again to the US that it join this initiative whose significance is evident to practically everyone in the world.

Obviously the adoption of such a decision has by no means been simple for us. The Soviet Union cannot indefinitely display unilaterial restraint with regard to nuclear tests. But the stakes are too high and the responsibility too great for us not to try every possibility of influencing the position of others by force of example.

All experts, scientists, politicians and military men agree that the cessation of tests would indeed reliably block the channels of perfecting nuclear weapons. And this is a top-priority task. A reduction of nuclear arsenals alone, without a prohibition of nuclear weapon tests, does not provide a way out of the dilemma of nuclear threat, since the remaining weapons would be modernised and there would still be the possibility of developing increasingly sophisticated and lethal nuclear weapons and appraising their new types at test ranges.

Therefore the cessation of tests is a practical step towards eliminating nuclear weapons.

I wish to say the following at the outset. Any references to verification as an obstacle to the establishment of a moratorium on nuclear explosions are totally groundless. We declare unequivocally that for us verification is not a problem. Should the US agree to stop all nuclear explosions on a reciprocal basis, appropriate verification of compliance with the moratorium would be fully ensured by national technical means as well as with the help of international procedures, including on-site inspections when necessary. We invite the US to reach agreement with us to this effect.

The USSR resolutely stands for making the moratorium a bilateral, and later, a multilateral measure. We are also in favour of resuming the tripartite negotiations, involving the USSR, the US and Great Britain, on the complete and general prohibition of nuclear weapon tests. This could be done immediately, even this month. We are also prepared to begin without delay multilateral test-ban negotiations withiin the framework of the Geneva Conference on Disarmament, with all nuclear powers taking part.

Non-aligned countries have proposed that consultations be held with the aim of extending the 1963 Moscow Treaty Banning Nuclear Weapon Tests in the Atmosphere, in Outer Space and Under Water to cover also underground tests, whose ban is not envisaged in the Treaty. The Soviet Union agrees to this, too.

Since last summer we have been calling upon the US to follow our example and stop nuclear explosions. Washington has not yet done that despite protests and demands on the part of the public, and contrary to the will of most states in the world. By carrying out more and more nuclear explosions the US side continues to pursue its elusive dream of achieving military superiority. This policy is futile and dangerous, a policy which is not worthy of the level of civilisation that modern society has attained.

In the absence of a positive response from the US, the Soviet side had every right to resume nuclear tests starting 1 January 1986. If one were to follow the usual 'logic' of the arms race, that, presumably, would have been the thing to do.

But the whole point is that it is precisely such logic, if one can call it that, that has to be resolutely rejected. We are making yet another attempt in this direction. Otherwise the process of military rivalry will assume gigantic proportions and any control over the course of events would be impossible. To yield to the anarchic force of the nuclear arms race is impermissible. This would be acting against reason and the human instinct of self-preservation. What are required are new and bold approaches, fresh political thinking and a heightened sense of responsibility for the destinies of the peoples.

The US administration is once again given more time to consider our proposals on stopping nuclear explosions and to give a positive answer to them. It is this kind of response that people everywhere in the world will expect from Washington.

The Soviet Union appeals to the US President and Congress, to the US people: there is an opportunity to halt the process of perfecting nuclear arms and developing new weapons of that kind. The opportunity must not be missed. The Soviet proposals put the USSR and the US in an equal position. These proposals are not an attempt to outwit or outsmart the other side. We propose embarking on a road of sensible and responsible decisions.

In order to implement the programme of reducing and eliminating nuclear arsenals it is necessary to activate the entire existing system of negotiations and to ensure the highest possible efficiency of the disarmament mechanism.

In a few days the Soviet-American talks on nuclear and space arms will be resumed in Geneva. When we met with President Reagan last November in Geneva we had a frank discussion on the whole range of problems which are the subject of those negotiations, namely on space, strategic offensive armaments and medium-range nuclear systems. It was agred that the negotiations should be accelerated and this agreement must not remain a mere declaration.

The Soviet delegation in Geneva will be instructed to act in strict compliance with that agreement. We expect the same constructive approach from the US side, above all on the question of space. Space must remain peaceful, strike weapons must not be deployed there. Neither must they be developed. And there must also be introduced very strict control, including the opening of relevant laboratories for inspection.

Mankind is at a crucial stage of the new space age. And it is time to abandon the thinking of the stone age, when the chief concern was to have a bigger stick or a heavier stone. We are against weapons in space. Our material and intellectual capabilities make it possible for the Soviet Union to develop any weapon if we are compelled to do so. But we are fully aware of our responsibility to the present and future generations. It is our profound conviction that we should approach the third millennium not with the Star Wars programme, but with large-scale projects of peaceful space exploration by all mankind. We propose to start practical work in developing and implementing such projects. This is one of the most important ways of ensuring progress on our entire planet and establishing a reliable system of security for all.

To prevent the arms race from spreading to outer space means to remove the obstacle barring the way to drastic reductions in nuclear weapons. On the negotiating table in Geneva is a Soviet proposal to reduce by one half the corresponding nuclear arms of the Soviet Union and the US, which would be an important step towards the complete elimination of nuclear weapons. To block all possibility of resolving the problem of space indicates a lack of desire to stop the arms race on earth. This should be stated in clear and straightforward terms. It is not by chance that the proponents of the nuclear arms race are also ardent supporters of the Star Wars programme. These are two sides of the same policy, hostile to the interests of people.

Let me turn to the European aspect of the nuclear problem. It is a matter of extreme concern that in defiance of reason and contrary to the national interests of the European peoples, US first-strike missiles continue to be deployed in certain West European countries. This problem has been under discussion for many years now. Meanwhile the security situation in Europe continues to deteriorate.

It is time to put an end to this course of events and cut this Gordian knot.

The Soviet Union has long been proposing that Europe should be freed of both medium-range and tactical nuclear weapons. This proposal remains valid. As a first radical step in this direction we now propose, as I have said, that even at the first stage of our programme all medium-range ballistic and cruise missiles of the USSR and the US in the European zone should be eliminated.

The achievement of tangible practical results at the Geneva talks would give meaningful material substance to our programme to eliminate nuclear arms completely by the year 2000.

The Soviet Union considers fully feasible the task of completely eliminating still in this century such barbaric weapons of mass destruction as chemical weapons.

At the talks on chemical weapons within the framework of the Geneva Conference on Disarmament certain signs of progress have recently become evident. However, these talks have been inadmissibly drawn out. We are in favour of intensifying the talks on the conclusion of an effective and verifiable international convention prohibiting chemical weapons and destroying the existing stockpiles of those weapons, as was agreed upon with US President Reagan at Geneva.

In the matter of banning chemical weapons, as in other disarmament matters, all participants in the talks should take a fresh look at things. I would like to make it perfectly clear that the Soviet Union is in favour of prompt and complete elimination of those weapons and of the industrial base for their production. We are prepared to make a timely announcement of the location of enterprises producing chemical weapons and ensure the cessation of their production; we are ready to start developing procedures for destroying the corresponding industrial base and to proceed, soon after the convention enters into force, to eliminate the stockpiles of chemical weapons. All these measures would be carried out under strict control, including international on-site inspections.

A radical solution to this problem would also be facilitated by certain interim steps. For example, agreement could be reached on a multilateral basis not to transfer chemical weapons to anyone and not to deploy them in the territories of other states. As for the Soviet Union it has always strictly abided by these principles in its practical policies. We call upon other states to follow this example and exercise equal restraint.

In addition to eliminating weapons of mass destruction from the arsenals of states, the Soviet Union proposes that conventional weapons and armed forces become subject to agreed-upon reductions.

Reaching an agreement at the Vienna negotiations could signal the beginning of progress in this direction. It now appears that an outline is discernible of a possible decision to reduce Soviet and US troops and subsequently freeze the level of armed forces of the opposing sides in Central Europe. The Soviet Union and our Warsaw Treaty allies are determined to achieve success at the Vienna talks. If the other side also truly wants this 1986 could become a landmark for the Vienna talks too. We proceed from the understanding that a possible agreement on troop reductions would naturally require reasonable verification. We are prepared for this. As for observing the commitment to freeze the number of troops, in addition to national technical means permanent verification posts could be established to monitor any military contingents entering the reduction zone.

Let me now mention such an important forum as the Stockholm Conference on Confidence- and Security-Building Measures and Disarmament in Europe. It is called upon to create barriers against the use of force or covert preparations for war, whether on land, at sea or in the air. The possibilities for this have now become evident.

In our view, especially in the current situation, it is essential to reduce the number of troops participating in major military manoeuvres which are notifiable under the Helsinki Final Act.

It is time to begin dealing effectively with the problems still outstanding at the Conference. The bottleneck there, as we know, is the issue of notifications regarding major ground force, naval and air force exercises. Of course these are serious problems and they must be addressed in a serious manner in the interests of building confidence in Europe. However, if their comprehensive solution cannot be achieved at this time, why not explore ways for partial solution, for instance, reach an agreement now about notifications of major ground force and air force exercises, postponing the question of naval activities until the next stage of the Conference.

It is not by chance that a significant part of the new Soviet initiatives is addressed directly to Europe. Europe could play a special role in bringing about a radical turn towards the policy of peace. That role is to erect a new edifice of détente.

For this Europe has a necessary, often unique historical experience. Suffice it to recall that the joint efforts of the Europeans, the US and Canada produced the Helsinki Final Act. If there is a need for a specific and vivid example of new thinking and political psychology in approaching the problems of peace, cooperation and international trust, that historic document could in many ways serve as such an example.

Ensuring security in Asia is of vital importance to the Soviet Union, a major Asian power. The Soviet programme for eliminating nuclear and chemical weapons by the end of the current century is harmonious with the sentiments of the peoples of the Asian continent, for whom the problems of peace and security are no less urgent than for the peoples of Europe. In this context one cannot fail to recall that Japan and its cities of Hiroshima and Nagasaki became the victims of the nuclear bomb, and Vietnam a target for chemical weapons.

We highly appreciate the constructive initiatives put forward by the socialist countries of Asia, by India and other members of the non-aligned movement. We view as very important the fact that the two Asian nuclear powers, the USSR and the People's Republic of China, have undertaken a pledge not to be the first to use nuclear weapons.

The implementation of our programme would fundamentally change the situation in Asia, rid the nations in that part of the globe as well of the fear of nuclear and chemical warfare, bring security in that region to a qualitatively new level.

We see our programme as a contribution to a search, together with all the Asian countries, for an overall comprehensive approach to establishing a system of secure and lasting peace on this continent.

Our new proposals are addressed to the entire world. Initiating active steps to halt the arms race and reduce weapons is a necessary prerequisite for coping with increasingly acute global problems – those of the deteriorating state of man's environment and of the need to find new energy sources and combat economic backwardness, hunger and disease. The pattern imposed by militarism – arms in place of development – must be replaced by the reverse order of things – disarmament for development. The noose of the trillion-dollar foreign debt, currently strangling dozens of countries and entire continents, is a direct consequence of the arms race. The more than 250,000 million dollars annually siphoned out of the developing countries is practically equal to the size of the mammoth US military budget. Indeed this is no chance coincidence.

The Soviet Union wants each measure limiting and reducing arms and each step towards eliminating nuclear weapons not only to bring nations greater security but also to make it possible to allocate more funds for improving people's lives. It is natural that the peoples seeking to put an end to backwardness and rise to the level of industrially developed countries associate the prospects of freeing themselves from the burden of foreign debt to imperialism, which is draining their economies, with limiting and eliminating weapons, reducing military expenditures and transferring resources to the goals of social and economic development. This subject will undoubtedly figure most prominently at the international conference on disarmament and development to be held in Paris next summer.

The Soviet Union is opposed to making the implementation of disarmament measures dependent on so-called regional conflicts. Behind this lie both an unwillingness to follow the path of disarmament and a desire to impose upon sovereign nations what is alien to them and a system that would make it possible to maintain profoundly unfair conditions whereby some countries live at the expense of others, exploiting their natural, human and intellectual resources for the selfish imperial purposes of individual states or aggressive alliances. The Soviet Union will continue as before to oppose this. It will continue consistently to advocate freedom for the peoples, peace, security, and a stronger international legal order. The Soviet Union's goal is not to whip up regional conflicts but to eliminate them through collective efforts on a just basis, and the sooner the better.

There is no shortage today of statements professing commitment to peace. What is in short supply are concrete actions to strengthen the foundations of peace. All too often peaceful words conceal war preparations and power politics. Moreover, some statements made from high rostrums are in fact intended to eliminate any trace of that new 'spirit of Geneva' which is having a salutary effect on international relations today. It is not only a matter of statements. There are also actions clearly designed to incite animosity and mistrust, to revive confrontation, the antithesis of détente.

We reject such a way of acting and thinking. We want 1986 to be not just a peaceful year but one that will enable us to reach the end of the twentieth century under the sign of peace and nuclear disarmament. The set of new foreign policy initiatives we are proposing is intended to make it possible for mankind to approach the year 2000 under peaceful skies and with a peaceful outer space, without fear of nuclear, chemical or any other threat of annihilation and fully confident of its own survival and of the continuation of the human race.

The new resolute measures being taken by the Soviet Union to defend peace and improve the overall international situation give expression to the substance and the spirit of our internal and foreign policies and their organic unity. They reflect the fundamental historic law which was emphasised by Vladimir Lenin. The whole world sees that our country is holding high the banner of peace, freedom and humanism which was raised over our planet by the Great October Revolution.

In questions of preserving peace and saving mankind from the threat of nuclear war, let no one remain indifferent or stand aloof. This concerns all and everyone. Each state, large or small, socialist or capitalist, has an important contribution to make. Every responsible political party, every public organisation and every person can also make an important contribution.

No task is more urgent, more noble or humane, than that of uniting all efforts to achieve this lofty goal. This task must be accomplished by our generation, not shifted on to the shoulders of those who will succeed us. This is the imperative of our time. This, I would say, is the burden of historic responsibility for our decisions and actions in the time remaining until the beginning of the third millennium.

The course of peace and disarmament will continue to be pivotal in the foreign policy of the CPSU and the Soviet state. In actively pursuing this course, the Soviet Union is prepared to engage in wide-ranging cooperation with all those who proceed from positions of reason, goodwill and an awareness of the responsibility to ensure mankind's future – a future without wars or weapons.

4

Soviet Policy towards Asia

These are our common plans and concerns, comrades. They show the Soviet Union's true intentions better than any verbal subterfuges. However much the ruling forces of imperialism may try to distort them, we have said openly and honestly and will continue saying to all peoples and governments: yes, we need peace; we again and again issue the call to end the arms race, stop nuclear madness and eliminate nuclear weapons, and to search persistently for a political settlement to regional conflicts.

We are witnessing phenomena of paramount importance. The realisation that there should be peace for all is forcefully grasping the minds of the peoples even where the governments continue to think that weapons and war are tools of politics. It is precisely for all, since a nuclear war would not be a clash of only two blocs, two confronting forces. It would lead to a global disaster, in which human civilisation would be threatened with destruction.

Our initiatives on nuclear disarmament, a considerable reduction of conventional weapons and armed forces, verification, and creation of a healthier international atmosphere have been met in different ways.

The friendly countries have expressed support for them. The countries of the socialist community regard them with good reason as a component part of the general policy of socialism in the world arena. And not only because these initiatives have been coordinated with them, not only for principled inter-nationalist considerations, but also because we are all engaged in a purely peaceful undertaking – the perfection of our societies. The salutary process of our drawing closer together is intensified on that basis, economic integration is filled with new contents, concrete steps are made to create joint plants and amalgamations, human contacts are broadened. In a word, a progressive, mutually beneficial process of deepening cooperation and fraternity among the peoples of the community is under way.

Speech at the Meeting in Vladivostok to Award the City the Order of Lenin, 28 July 1986 (abridged).

The developing world shows much interest in our plans and intentions – both internal and international ones. We note that many developing countries wish to expand and deepen economic, scientific and cultural cooperation with the Soviet Union. We are prepared for that.

It would be fair to say that the Western public at large and representatives of the business community who have a realistic view of things, who do not suffer from anti-Communist paranoia and do not associate themselves with profits from the arms race, regard our plans seriously and with interest. They also stand for peace and cooperation, for the development of healthy economic, scientific and cultural ties with the Soviet Union. We welcome such an approach.

Yet in many capitalist countries the tone is set, as before, by forces that have been in the past and will in the future be blinded by animosity towards socialism, by imperial ambitions, or that have close links with the war business. And this business, as is known, is extremely voracious and ruthless. Yesterday it needed millions, today it needs billions, and tomorrow it will need trillions. It will never start manufacturing, of its own free will, toys for children instead of missiles. Such is its nature.

The ruling circles of the US and some countries allied to it are trying either to picture our peace initiatives as sheer propaganda or to make it appear that only the Soviet Union stands to gain from them. Yes, we stand to gain from disarmament, if we are to use that expression, just as all peoples whose governments now spend billions on the arms race stand to gain from disarmament. Yet this is only a part of the truth. I will even say, a small part of the truth. The most important truth is that our initiatives stem from a profound concern for the future of mankind.

In the face of nuclear threat it is absurd and criminal to act according to an old, already dead scheme: what is good for the socialist countries must be rejected. Here one can clearly see class narrow-mindedness, a primitive ideological mechanical approach, and the growing political influence of militarism. Yet I am not inclined to believe that the military-industrial complex is omnipotent. We see that the world public realises ever more clearly the danger of militarism. We see that in the US, too, despite the constant whipping up of chauvinistic sentiments, a sense of realism is growing, and the realisation is deepening that the source of military threat to the US is not the Soviet people, not the socialist countries, not the peasants of Nicaragua, not the faraway Vietnamese or Libyans, but its own arms manufacturers, the irresponsible politicians serving them, and the adventuristic military.

Of course we are aware that the arms race, which is gaining momentum, serves not only the aims of making superprofit and of war preparations, but also – and this is not of the least importance – other immoral aims, which are essentially to exhaust the Soviet Union economically, frustrate the Party's course for achieving a further rise in the living standards of the people, and hamper the implementation of our social programme. We also know who are those that continue to cherish the hope of bringing about a planned, systematic destruction of the USSR and of other socialist countries, using to that end economic, moral-psychological, propaganda, political and military methods.

But it can be said that this is a futile attempt; it always has been and still is today. The time has come to reckon with the realities rather than to make policy on the basis of illusions and misconceptions. If no accords are reached, this will not bring relief to the world, no tranquillity will set in. Fear will not disappear until certain rulers in the West give up the attempts, which are perhaps consoling for them, but fruitless, and above all dangerous, to bring the Soviet Union to its knees, split socialist society and hamper our advance.

The time urgently demands a new understanding of the present stage in the development of civilisation, of international relations, of the world. The world is full of contradictions, it is complex, but it is objectively united by bonds of interdependence. International relations are such that, with all the differences and clashes of interest, one can no longer live according to the millennia-old traditions of 'fist law'. And civilisation has demonstrated an unprecedented strength of the human mind and human labour and at the same time its own fragility, its vulnerability to the forces released by the human genius but placed at the service of destruction.

All that dictates the need for and makes urgent a radical break with many customary attitudes to foreign policy, a break with traditional political thinking, traditional views on problems of war and peace, on defence, on the security of individual states and international security. In this connection it is clear that our radical, global, in the full sense of the word, proposals such as the programme for the elimination already in this century of nuclear and other mass destruction weapons, a total ban on nuclear weapons tests, a ban on chemical weapons, proposals on cooperation in the peaceful uses of outer space, and a whole set of other proposals, concern the whole world, all countries.

The main problem confronting mankind today – that of survival – is equally acute and urgent for Europe, Africa, America and Asia. Yet in each part of the world it looks different. Therefore, while being here, in Vladivostok, it is natural to look at international policy issues from the Asian-Pacific standpoint.

We are in favour of building together new, fair relations in Asia and the Pacific.

Recently I have had many meetings with leaders of European states, with various political figures of European countries. I cannot help comparing the situation in Asia with that of Europe.

On the whole the Pacific region has not as yet been militarised to the extent Europe has. But the potentialities of its militarisation are truly immense, and the consequences are extremely dangerous. One only needs to look at a map to be convinced of this. Major nuclear powers are situated here. Large land armies, navies and air forces have been established. The scientific, technological and industrial potential of many countries – from the western to the eastern fringes of the ocean – makes it possible to step up any arms race. The situation is being exacerbated by the preservation of conflict situations. Let us not forget: it is in Asia that US imperialism waged the two biggest wars since 1945 – the war in Korea and the war in Indochina. In the last four decades there is hardly a period of even just a few years when the flames of war did not blaze in one or another part of the Asian or Pacific region.

In Europe, whether it is working well or not, the Helsinki process of dialogue, negotiations and agreements is under way. This creates a certain stability and reduces the probability of armed conflicts. In the region under consideration this is absent, or nearly absent. If something has changed lately, it has not been for the better. Since the second half of the 1970s the US has undertaken large-scale measures to build up armed forces in the Pacific Ocean. The militarised triangle of Washington, Tokyo and Seoul is being set up under its pressure. And although two out of the three nuclear powers in the region – the People's Republic of China and the USSR – pledged not to be the first to use nuclear weapons, the US has deployed nuclear weapon delivery vehicles and nuclear warheads in one of the zones of crisis – in the Korean peninsula, and nuclear weapon delivery vehicles on Japanese territory.

One has to state that militarisation and the escalation of the war threat in this part of the world are taking place at a dangerously fast pace. The Pacific Ocean is turning into an arena of military and political confrontation. This is what gives rise to growing concern among the peoples living here. This is alarming also for us from all points of view, including for considerations of security in the Asian part of our country.

The Soviet Union's policy towards Asia and the Pacific region is an integral part of the general platform of the CPSU's international activity worked out by the April Plenary Meeting and the 27th Congress. But a platform is not a chart that can be applied to any situation. Rather it is a set of principles and a method based on experience.

How, then, should one envisage the process of establishing international security and peaceful cooperation in this vast region?

First of all, in keeping with its principled policy as approved by the 27th Congress, the Soviet Union will try to invigorate its bilateral relations with all countries in the region without exception. We shall strengthen in every way friendship and promote many-sided relations with the Mongolian People's Republic, the Democratic People's Republic of Korea (DPRK), the Socialist Republic of Vietnam, the Lao People's Democratic Republic and the People's Republic of Kampuchea. We regard relations with our friends, built on the principles of equality and solidarity, as an integral part of overall Asian and Pacific security.

At present, for instance, a question of withdrawing a substantial part of Soviet troops from Mongolia is being considered jointly by the Soviet and Mongolian leadership.

We are prepared to expand ties with Indonesia, Australia, New Zealand, the

Philippines, Thailand, Malaysia, Singapore, Burma, Sri Lanka, Nepal, Brunei, the Republic of Maldives, and the youngest independent participants in the region's political life. With some of these – Papua New Guinea, Western Samoa, the Kingdom of Tonga, Fiji, the Republic of Kiribati, the Republic of Nauru, Tuvalu and the Republic of Vanuatu – we already maintain diplomatic relations.

Speaking in a city which is but a step from the People's Republic of China, I would like to dwell on the most important issues in our relations. These relations are extremely important for several reasons, starting with the fact that we are neighbours, that we share the world's longest land border and that for this reason alone we, our children and grandchildren are destined to live near each other 'for ever and ever'.

Of course there is more to the question than that. History has entrusted the Soviet and the Chinese peoples with an extremely responsible mission. Much in international development depends upon these two major socialist nations.

Relations between our two countries have improved noticeably in recent years. I would like to reaffirm that the Soviet Union is prepared – at any time and at any level – to enter into discussion with China on additional measures for establishing an atmosphere of good-neighbourliness. We hope that the border dividing us (I would prefer to say linking) will become in the near future a line of peace and friendship.

The Soviet people respond with understanding and respect to the objective advanced by the Communist Party of China – to modernise the country and build in the future a socialist society worthy of a great people.

As far as it is possible to judge, the Soviet Union and China have similar priorities – to accelerate social and economic development. Why not support each other, why not cooperate in implementing our plans wherever this is clearly to the benefit of both sides? The better our relations, the more we shall be able to share our experience.

We note with satisfaction that a positive shift has become visible in economic ties. We are convinced that the historically established complementarity between the Soviet and the Chinese economies offers great opportunities for expanding these ties, including in the border regions. Some of the major problems of cooperation are literally knocking at the door. For instance, we do not want the Amur, which runs along the Chinese-Soviet border, to be viewed as a 'water barrier'. Let the basin of this mighty river unite the efforts of the Chinese and the Soviet peoples in using the river's rich resources for mutual benefit and in building water-management projects. A relevant intergovernmental agreement is already being jointly worked out. And the official border could pass along the main ship channel.

The Soviet government is preparing a positive reply concerning the question of assistance in building a railway connecting the Xinjiang-Uygur Autonomous Region with Kazakhstan.

We have suggested cooperation with China in space exploration, which could include the training of Chinese cosmonauts. The opportunities for mutually beneficial exchanges in the sphere of culture and education are great. We are prepared for and sincerely desire all this.

On relations with Japan signs are emerging indicating a turn for the better here as well. It would indeed be a positive development if the turn did take place. The objective position of our two countries in the world demands profound cooperation on a sound and realistic basis, and in a calm atmosphere free from problems of the past. A beginning was made this year. Foreign ministers exchanged visits and an exchange of top-level visits is on the agenda.

Economic cooperation is of mutual interest. The main issue here is our coastal regions which already have business contacts with Japanese firms. It is possible to discuss the question of establishing joint enterprises in adjacent and nearby regions of the USSR and Japan. Why not establish long-term cooperation in the investigation and comprehensive use of the ocean resources; why not correlate programmes of the peaceful study and use of outer space? The Japanese, it seems, have a method of making relations more dynamic which is called 'economic diplomacy'. This time let it serve Soviet-Japanese cooperation.

The Soviet Union also shares the border with the US in the Pacific region. It is our next-door neighbour in the literal meaning of the word, with only seven kilometres dividing us – the exact distance between the Soviet island of Big Diomede and the US island of Little Diomede.

We recognise clearly that the US is a great Pacific power. Primarily because a considerable part of the country's population lives on the shores of this ocean, the western part of the US, gravitating towards this area, is playing a growing part in the country's development and is a dynamic force. Furthermore the US, undoubtedly, has important and legitimate economic and political interests in the region.

No doubt, without the US and its participation, it is not possible to resolve the problem of security and cooperation in the Pacific Ocean to the satisfaction of all nations in the region. Regrettably Washington has thus far shown no interest in this issue. It is not even contemplating a serious talk on the Pacific issue. If the issue is taken up, it inevitably leads to the trodden path of the 'Soviet threat' and to sabre-rattling corroborating this myth.

Our approach to relations with the US is well known. We are for peaceful, good-neighbourly, equitable relations, and mutually beneficial cooperation which offers, incidentally, considerable opportunities in the Far East as well as in the Pacific.

A few words concerning the most important aspect of our relations with the US at present – on the termination of the arms race. Since the Geneva meeting the Soviet Union has put forward many large-scale proposals on the entire range of problems involved in reducing and eliminating arms and verifying this process. We have not noticed any movement to meet us even half-way. In fact, our proposals met the same response as before the Geneva summit.

In an attempt to overcome the standstill we went a step further: new large-scale proposals of compromise were put forward in my June letter to the US president. When visiting here, in the Far East, I received a reply from President Reagan. The reply sets one thinking and we have begun to study it. We shall treat it with responsibility and attention. The most important thing from our point of view is the extent to which the proposals contained in the letter meet the principle of equal security and whether they make it possible to reach effective joint solutions in ending the arms race and preventing its spread into outer space. We shall determine our further steps accordingly.

As far as a new Soviet-US summit meeting is concerned I can repeat: we favour such a meeting. But we are resolutely against interpreting the accords reached at the previous meeting in Geneva as a promise to have more meetings. No. The main thing on which we agreed last time with President Reagan and what we signed is the consent to strive for the normalisation of relations between the USSR and the US and for the improvement of the international situation, and to speed up the course of talks on the reduction of armaments. This should also be the purpose of a new summit meeting.

We frequently hear from abroad all kinds of stories to the effect that the Soviet Union is building up its military power in the east of the country. Let me state with full responsibility: we are not doing anything and shall not do anything over and above the level that corresponds to the minimal requirements of our own defence, and the defence of our friends and allies, especially in the light of the US, military activity not far from our and their frontiers.

This applies in full measure to the medium-range missiles. Those who do not want to see the lessening of world tensions continue to allege that we will be able to move our SS-20 missiles from the west to the east and from the east to the west. This is why I emphasise one more time – we suggest that both US and Soviet medium-range missiles in Europe *be eliminated*. Eliminated – not moved somewhere else. This quite clearly promotes the interests of the Asian countries as well.

I would also like to state that the Soviet Union is a dedicated advocate of disbanding the military groupings, renouncing the possession of military bases in Asia and the Pacific Ocean and withdrawing troops from the territories of other countries. The USSR is a member of the Warsaw Treaty; but this is a European defensive alliance and it operates strictly within the stipulated geographical limits. In our turn we are strongly opposed to the US attempts to extend NATO's 'competence' to the entire world, including Asia and the Pacific Ocean.

Our views about security in the Asian-Pacific region did not come out of thin air. They take into account the experience of the past and of today. The principles of 'Pancha Shila' and of Bandung have not sunk into oblivion. The positive examples of the truce in Korea, the 1954 Geneva meeting on Indochina, the Indo-Pakistani agreement in Tashkent live on in diplomatic experience. Nowadays, too, we have witnessed the efforts of a number of states to solve in practice common economic problems and the attempts somehow to regulate conflicts. In the activities of the ASEAN and in bilateral ties many positive steps have been taken. After the plan for a 'Pacific community' had been rejected, the discussions began on the idea of 'Pacific economic cooperation'. We approached this idea without bias and we are ready to join in the deliberations on the possible foundations of such cooperation; this is, of course, if it is not conceived in a forced, bloc-oriented, and anti-socialist pattern, but is rather the result of free discussion without any discrimination. The sufficiently vast arsenal of scientific and political ideas on the issue of establishing a new world economic order and the experience of integration in the West and the East could become a solid foundation for such discussions.

For an objective, however remote, we would like to propose a conference in the mould of the Helsinki conference, to be attended by all countries gravitating towards the Ocean. When an agreement is reached on its convocation (if an agreement is reached at all, of course) it will be possible to establish the place for this conference. Hiroshima is a possible option. Why should that city, the first victim of nuclear evil, not become a 'Helsinki' for Asia and the Pacific Ocean?

In summary I would like to emphasise that we stand for integrating the Asian-Pacific region into the general process of establishing a comprehensive system of international security proposed at the 27th Congress of the CPSU.

What are our concrete views on this issue?

First, the issues of regional settlement inevitably arise. I'll speak of Afghanistan separately. Now let me speak of South-East Asia and Kampuchea.

The Khmer people sustained terrible losses. That country, its cities and villages were victims of US bombing raids more than once. Through its suffering that country has earned itself the right to choose its friends and allies. It is impermissible to try and draw it back into its tragic past, to decide the future of that state in distant capitals or even in the UN.

Here, as with other problems of South-East Asia, much depends on the normalisation of Sino-Vietnamese relations. It is a sovereign matter of the governments and the leadership of both countries. We can only express our interest in seeing the border between these socialist states become again a border of peace and good-neighbourly relations, in seeing friendly dialogue resumed and the unnecessary suspicion and mistrust removed. It seems that the moment is right, and all of Asia needs this change.

In our opinion there are no insurmountable obstacles in the way of establishing mutually acceptable relations between the countries of Indochina and ASEAN. Given goodwill and the absence of foreign interference they could solve their problems which would simultaneously benefit the cause of security in Asia.

There is a possibility for not only relieving the dangerous tensions in the Korean peninsula, but also for beginning the solving of the national problem of the entire Korean people. As far as the truly Korean interests are concerned, there are no sensible reasons for evading a serious dialogue which has been proposed by the DPRK.

Second, we are for blocking the proliferation and buildup of nuclear weapons in Asia and the Pacific Ocean.

As is known the USSR has pledged not to increase the number of medium-range nuclear missiles in the Asian part of the country.

The USSR supports proclaiming the southern part of the Pacific a nuclear-free zone and urges all nuclear powers to guarantee its status in a unilateral or multilateral way.

The implementation of the proposal of the DPRK for the creation of a nuclear-free zone in the Korean peninsula would be a significant contribution. The idea of creating such a zone in South-East Asia has aroused well-deserved attention.

Third, we propose to start talks on the reduction of the activity of naval forces in the Pacific, in particular, nuclear-armed ships. Restriction of the rivalry in the sphere of anti-submarine weapons, specifically, the arrangement to refrain from anti-submarine activity in certain zones of the Pacific, would help strengthen stability. This could become a substantial confidence-building measure.

In general I would like to say that if the US gave up its military presence, say, in the Philippines, we would not leave this step unanswered.

We remain strongly in favour of resuming the talks on establishing the Indian Ocean as a peace zone.

Fourth, the Soviet Union attaches great importance to the radical reduction of armed forces and conventional armaments in Asia to limits of reasonable sufficiency. We realise that this problem should be tackled gradually, stage by stage, by starting with one certain region, say, the Far East. In this context the USSR is prepared to discuss with China concrete steps aimed at the commensurate lowering of the level of land forces.

Fifth, the Soviet Union believes that it is high time to switch to practical discussions on confidence-building measures and on the non-use of force in this region. Simpler measures could serve as the beginning: for instance, measures for the security of sea lanes in the Pacific, and for the prevention of international terrorism.

A conference to discuss and work out such measures could be held in one of the Soviet maritime cities. By the way, with time the question of opening Vladivostok to visits by foreigners could be solved. If the situation in the Pacific actually changes for the better, Vladivostok could become a major international centre, a commercial and cultural centre, a city for festivals, sports events, congresses, and scientific symposia. We would like it to be our window opened widely on the East. And then the words of our great Pushkin: 'the ships of every flag and nation will hail our shores' will apply to Vladivostok as well.

And in conclusion, about Afghanistan. It was declared from the rostrum of the 27th CPSU Congress that we are ready to recall Soviet troops stationed in

Afghanistan at the request of its government. As is known the Party now firmly adheres to the principle that words should be confirmed by deeds.

Having thoroughly assessed the current situation and having held consultations with the government of the Democratic Republic of Afghanistan (DRA), the Soviet leadership has adopted the decision which I officially announce today: six regiments will be returned home from Afghanistan before the end of 1986 – one armoured regiment, two motorised infantry regiments, and three anti-aircraft artillery regiments – with their regular equipment and armaments. These units will be returned to the areas of their permanent deployment in the Soviet Union, and in a manner that these moves will be obvious to all those who take an interest in this.

Taking this serious step, of which we informed the states concerned in advance, including Pakistan, the Soviet Union is striving to speed up and give further impetus to a political settlement. The Soviet Union expects that those who organise and implement the armed intervention against the Democratic Republic of Afghanistan, will correctly understand and duly appreciate this unilateral step we have taken. It must be answered by the curtailment of outside interference in the affairs of the Democratic Republic of Afghanistan.

Certain progress has been achieved recently at the Afghan-Pakistani talks held through the mediation of a representative of the UN Secretary General. As soon as a political settlement is finally worked out the recall of all Soviet troops from Afghanistan can be accelerated. Schedules for their stage-by-stage recall have been agreed upon with the Afghan leadership.

But all who encourage and finance the undeclared war against Afghanistan and from whose territory it is waged, should know that if the intervention against the DRA continues, the Soviet Union will come to the defence of its neighbour. This position stems from our internationalist solidarity with the Afghan people and from the interests of the Soviet Union's security.

We support the policy of the present Afghan leadership aimed at national reconciliation and at widening the social base of the April National-Democratic Revolution. This includes the creation of a government in which would participate those political forces that have found themselves beyond the country's borders but who are prepared to participate sincerely in the nation-wide process of building new Afghanistan.

Comrades,

The present generations have inherited many difficult and painful problems. In order to reach a solution to these problems it is necessary to get rid of the burden of the past, to seek new approaches, guiding oneself by one's responsibility for the present and the future.

The Soviet state calls upon all Asian and Pacific nations to cooperate for the sake of peace and security. Everyone who strives towards these goals and who hopes for a better future for their people, will find that we are willing to talk and are honest partners.

Mankind is living through a difficult and dramatic time. But it has a reserve of strength, which allows it not simply to survive, but also to learn to live in a new, civilised world, in other words, to live without the threat of war, and to live in freedom, when the highest criterion will be mankind's benefit and the maximum development of the individual's abilities. But this requires a persistent struggle against the common enemy – the threat of universal annihilation.

Mobilisation of the existing potential of common sense and the partnership of reason are now more important than ever before to stop the slide towards catastrophe. Everyone can rest assured, all peoples in all countries, that our resolve to do our utmost for this cause remains unchanged. This, in brief, is the state of our domestic affairs at present and the state of the general international situation, in the development of which the Asian and Pacific part of the world is to play an ever increasing role. We should draw practical conclusions from all this in order to act ever more vigorously to rebuild and improve our life.

5

What Happened at Reykjavik

Good evening, dear comrades.

As you know, my meeting in Iceland with the President of the United States, Ronald Reagan, concluded the day before yesterday, on Sunday. A press conference on its results has been televised. The text of my statement and my replies to journalists have been published.

Having returned home, I consider it my duty to tell you how the meeting went and how we assess what took place in Reykjavik.

The results of the meeting in the capital of Iceland have just been discussed at a meeting of the Politburo of the CPSU Central Committee. A report wil be published tomorrow outlining the opinion our Party's leadership has formed about this major political event, the consequences of which, we are convinced, will be felt in international relations for a long time to come.

Before Reykjavik much was said and written about the forthcoming meeting. As is usually the case in such situations, there was a myriad of conjectures and views. This is normal. And in this case there was speculation as well.

Now the meeting is over its results are in the centre of attention of the world public. Everybody wants to know: What happened? What results did it produce? What will the world be like after it?

We strove to give the main questions of world politics – ending the arms race and nuclear disarmament – top priority at the meeting in Reykjavik. And that is how it was.

What are the motives for our persistence in this matter? One often hears conjectures abroad that the reason lies in our domestic difficulties. There is a thesis in Western calculations that the Soviet Union will ultimately be unable to endure the arms race economically, that it will break down and bow to the West. One need only squeeze the Soviet Union harder and step up the position of strength. Incidentally, the US President made a remark to this

Speeches on Soviet television, 14 and 22 October 1986.

effect in an address after our meeting.

I have said repeatedly that such plans are not only built on air; they are dangerous as they may result in fatal political decisions. We know our own problems better than anyone else. We do have problems which we openly discuss and resolve. We have our own plans and approaches on this score, and there is a common will of the Party and the people. In general, I would have to say that the Soviet Union's strength today lies in its unity, dynamism, and the political activity of its people. I think that these trends and, consequently, the strength of our society will be growing. The Soviet Union has the capacity to respond to any challenge, should the need arise. The Soviet people know this; the whole world should know this, too. But we are opposed to playing power games, for this is an extremely dangerous thing in the nuclear-missile age.

We are firmly convinced that the protracted feverish state of international relations harbours the threat of a sudden and fatal crisis. We must take joint Soviet-US efforts, efforts on the part of the entire international community, in order to radically improve international relations.

For the sake of these goals, we, the Soviet leadership, carried out extensive preparatory work on the eve of the meeting, even before we received President Reagan's consent to attend it. Taking part in this work, in addition to the Politburo and the Secretariat of the CPSU Central Committee, were the Ministry of Foreign Affairs and the Defence Ministry, plus some other departments, representatives of science, military experts, and specialists from various branches of industry. The positions we worked out for the Reykjavik meeting were the result of wide-scale, repeated discussion with our friends, with the leaderships of the socialist community countries. We sought to make the content of the meeting as meaningful as possible, putting forth far-reaching proposals.

Now the meeting itself, how events developed there. This should be discussed not only in order to affirm the truth, which is already being distorted by our partners in the Reykjavik talks, but more importantly, to inform you of what we plan to do next.

The first conversation with President Reagan started on Saturday, at 10.30 a.m. After the greetings necessary on such occasions and a brief conference with journalists, the two of us remained alone; only our interpreters were present. We exchanged views on the general situation, on the way the dialogue betweeen our two countries was developing, and outlined the problems to be discussed.

Then I asked the President to listen to our concrete proposals on the main questions which prompted our meeting. I already spoke at length about them during the press conference. Still, I will recall them here in brief.

A whole set of major measures was submitted to the talks. These measures, if accepted, would usher in a new era in the life of mankind – a nuclear-free era. Herein lies the essence of the radical change in the world situation, the possibility of which was obvious and realistic. The talk was no longer about limiting nuclear arms, as was the case with the SALT-1, SALT-2 and other treaties, but about the elimination of nuclear weapons within a comparatively short period of time.

The first proposal concerned strategic offensive weapons. I expressed our readiness to reduce them by 50 per cent within the next five years. The strategic weapons on land, water and in the air would be halved. In order to make it easier to reach accord, we agreed to a major concession by revoking our previous demand that the strategic equation include US medium-range missiles reaching our territory and American forward-based systems. We were also ready to take into account the US concern over our heavy missiles. We regarded the proposal on strategic arms in the context of their total elimination, as we had suggested on 15 January this year.

Our second proposal concerned medium-range missiles. I suggested to the President that both Soviet and US missiles of this class in Europe be completely eliminated. Here, too, we were willing to make a substantial concession: we stated that, contrary to our previous stand, the nuclear-missile weapons of Britain and France need not be taken into account. We proceeded from the necessity to pave the way to détente in Europe, to free the European nations of the fear of a nuclear catastrophe, and then to move further – towards the elimination of all the nuclear weapons. You will agree that this was another bold step on our part.

Anticipating the possible objections, we said we would agree to freeze missiles with a range of under 1,000 kilometres and immediately begin talks on what is to be done with them in the future. As for the medium-range missiles in the Asian part of our country – this issue was invariably present in President Reagan's 'global version' – we suggested that talks be started immediately on this subject as well. As you see, here, too, our proposals were serious and far-reaching, facilitating a radical solution of this problem as well.

The third question I raised during my first talk with the President, one that formed an integral part of our proposal package, was the existing Anti-Ballistic Missile (ABM) Treaty and the Nuclear Test Ban Treaty. Our approach is as follows: since we are entering a totally new situation which will witness the beginning of substantial reductions in nuclear weapons and their complete elimination in the foreseeable future, it is necessary to protect oneself from any unexpected developments. We are speaking of weapons which to this day make up the core of this country's defences. Therefore it is necessary to exclude everything that could undermine equality in the process of disarmament, to preclude any chance of developing weapons of a new type which would ensure military superiority. We regard this stance as perfectly legitimate and logical.

This being the case, we have firmly stated the need for strict observance of the 1972 ABM Treaty of unlimited duration. Moreover, in order to consolidate its regime, we proposed to the President that a mutual pledge be taken by the US and the Soviet Union to refrain from pulling out of the treaty for at least ten years, during which time strategic weapons would be abolished.

Taking into account the particular difficulties the US administration created for itself on this problem when the President personally committed himself to space weapons, to the so-called SDI, we did not demand termination of work in this field. The implication was, however, that all provisions of the ABM Treaty would be fully honoured – that is, research and testing in this sphere would not go beyond laboratories. This restriction applies equally to the US and to the USSR.

Listening to us, the President made remarks, asked for clarification on certain points. During the conversation we presented the question of verification firmly and with resolve, linking it with the post-nuclear situation. This situation demands special responsibility. I told the President that if both countries embark on nuclear disarmament, the Soviet Union will make its position on verification stricter. Verification must be plausible, comprehensive and indisputable. It must create full confidence in reliable compliance with the agreement and include the right to on-site inspection.

I must tell you, comrades, that the President's initial reaction was not entirely negative. He even said: 'What you have just stated is reassuring.' But it did not escape our attention that our US interlocutors (George Shultz as well as Comrade Shevardnadze had joined the conversation on these issues by then) appeared to be somewhat confused. At the same time immediate doubts and objections cropped up in their separate remarks. Straight away, the President and the Secretary of State started talking about divergencies and disagreement. In their words we clearly discerned the familiar old tones we had heard at the Geneva negotiations for many months: we were reminded of all sorts of sub-levels on strategic nuclear armaments, the 'interim proposal' on missiles in Europe, and that we, the Soviet Union, should join the SDI and should replace the existing ABM Treaty with some new agreement, and many other things in the same vein.

I expressed my surprise. How can this be? We propose to accept the US 'zero option' in Europe and take up negiotiations on medium-range missiles in Asia while you, Mr President, are abandoning your previous stand. This is incomprehensible.

As for the ABM Treaty, we propose to preserve and strengthen this fundamentally important agreement, and you want to give it up and even propose to replace it with some new treaty, and thereby – following renunciation of SALT-2 – to wreck this mechanism standing guard over strategic stability. This, too, is incomprehensible.

We grasped the essence of the SDI plans as well, I said. If the US creates a three-tiered ABM system in outer space, we shall respond to it. However, we are concerned about another problem: the SDI would mean the transfer of weapons to a new medium, which would destabilise the strategic situation, make it even worse than it is today. If this is the US's purpose, this should be stated plainly. But if you really want reliable security for your people and for the world in general, then the US stand is totally ungrounded.

I told the President directly: we have put forward major new proposals. However, what we are hearing from you is precisely what everybody is fed up with and what can lead us nowhere. Mr President, please, re-examine our proposals carefully and give us an answer point by point. I gave him an English translation of a draft of possible instructions that had been drawn up in Moscow and which, in the event that agreement is reached in principle, could be given to the foreign ministers and other departments to draw up three draft agreements. They could be signed later during my visit to the US.

In the afternoon, we met again. The President announced the stand that had been drawn up during the break. As soon as he uttered the first phrases it became clear that they were offering us the same old moth-eaten trash, as I put it at the press conference, from which the Geneva talks are already choking: all sorts of intermediate versions, figures, levels, sub-levels and so on. There was not a single new thought, fresh approach or idea which would contain even a hint of a solution, of advance.

It was becoming clear, comrades, that the US representatives had come to Reykjavik with nothing at all to offer. The impression was that they had come there empty-handed to gather fruits in their basket.

The situation was taking a dramatic turn.

The US President was not ready to take any radical decisions on questions of principle, to meet the Soviet side half-way, so as to give a real impetus to productive and encouraging negotiations. This is precisely what I impressed upon the President in my letter, in which I put forward the idea that an urgent meeting be held in order to give a powerful impetus at the level of the top leaders of the two countries – an impetus to negotiations on nuclear disarmament.

Confident that our proposals were well-balanced and took the partner's interests into account we decided not to abandon our efforts to bring about a breakthrough at the meeting. A ray of hope on strategic armaments appeared, following many clarifying questions. Clinging to this we took one more great step in search of a compromise. I told the President: we both recognise that there is a triad of strategic offensive armaments: ground-based missiles, strategic submarines and strategic bombers. So let us make a 50-per cent reduction in each part of the triad. And then there will be no need for all sorts of levels and sub-levels, for all sorts of calculations.

After lengthy debate, we managed to reach mutual understanding on that issue.

Then the discussion turned to the problem of medium-range missiles. The US delegation stubbornly stuck to the so-called interim proposal which provides for the preservation of a part of their missiles, including Pershing-2 missiles in Europe, and, naturally, of our corresponding SS-20 missiles. We categorically opposed this, for reasons I have already described. Europe deserves to be free of nuclear weapons, to stop being held nuclear hostage. As for the President, it was difficult for him to fight his own 'zero option' which he had promoted for so long. And still, we sensed their intention to thwart agreement under the guise of special concern for their allies in Asia.

The US side said much that was ungrounded. It is embarrassing to repeat it here. The talks began to move forward only when on this issue, too, we took one more step to meet the US side and agreed to the following formula: zero missiles in Europe, 100 warheads on medium-range missiles in the eastern part of our country and, accordingly, 100 warheads on medium-range missiles on US territory. Most importantly, we managed to agree on eliminating nuclear weapons on the European continent.

Thus accord was reached on the problem of medium-range missiles, too, and a major breakthrough was made in this direction of nuclear disarmament. The US administration failed to hold out against our insistent striving to achieve positive results.

However, there still remained the ABM issue and the ban on nuclear explosions.

Two groups of experts, one from each side, worked through the night before we met on Sunday for our third talk, which was scheduled to be the concluding one. They thoroughly analysed what had been discussed at the two previous meetings with the President and reported the results of their night-time debates respectively to the President and myself.

The result? A possibility arose of undertaking to work out agreements on strategic offensive armaments and on medium-range missiles.

The ABM Treaty in this situation acquired key significance; its role was becoming even more important. Could one destroy, I asked, what has made it possible so far to somehow restrain the arms race? If we now begin reducing strategic and medium-range nuclear weapons, both sides should be confident that during that time nobody will develop new systems which would undermine stability and parity. Therefore, in my view, it would be perfectly logical to fix the timeframe – the US representatives mentioned seven years, and we proposed ten years – within which nuclear weapons must be eliminated. We proposed ten years during which neither the Soviet nor the US side may avail itself of the right – and they have such a right – to withdraw from the ABM Treaty, and during which research and tests may be conducted in laboratories only.

Thus, I think, you understand why we chose exactly ten years. This was no random choice. The logic is plain and fair. 50 per cent of strategic armaments are to be reduced in the first five years, the other half in the next five years. This makes ten years.

In connection with this I proposed that our high-ranking representatives be instructed to start full-scale talks on the discontinuation of nuclear explosions and thus in the end an agreement could at last be worked out completely banning explosions. In the course of working out the agreement – and here again we displayed flexibility and assumed a constructive stand – specific issues connected with nuclear explosions could be resolved.

The reasoning President Reagan used in his response is a familiar one to us in that we have come across it earlier both in Geneva and in his public statements: SDI is a defence system. If we begin eliminating weapons, how will we protect ourselves from some madman who might get hold of them? And Reagan is ready to share with us the results obtained within the research done on SDI. In answering this last remark I said: Mr President, I do not take this idea seriously, your idea about sharing with us the results of research on SDI. You do not even want to share with us oil equipment or equipment for the dairy industry, and still you expect us to believe your promise to share the research developments in the SDI project. That would be something like a 'Second American Revolution', and revolutions do not occur that often. I told President Reagan that we should be realists and pragmatists. This is a more reliable approach, for the issues at hand are very serious.

By the way, when trying to justify his position on SDI yesterday, the President said that he needed this programme to ensure that the US and its allies remain invulnerable to a Soviet missile attack. As you see, he did not even make any mention of madmen. And the 'Soviet threat' was again brought to light.

But this is nothing but a trick. We proposed that not only strategic armaments, but also all the nuclear armaments in the possession of the US and the USSR, be eliminated under strict control.

How can there be a need to protect the 'freedom of America' and its friends from Soviet nuclear missiles if these missiles no longer exist?

If there are no nuclear weapons, why should we need to protect ourselves from them? Thus the entire Star Wars undertaking is purely militaristic in nature and is directed at obtaining military superiority over the Soviet Union.

Let us return, however, to the talks. Although an agreement on strategic arms and medium-range missiles had been reached, it was premature to believe that everything had been completely settled as a result of the first two sessions. An entire day was ahead, nearly eight hours of non-stop and intense discussions in which these issues, which seemed to have been agreed upon already, were to be raised again and again.

The President sought to touch upon ideological issues as well in these discussions and in this way demonstrated, to put it mildly, total ignorance and the inability to understand the socialist world and what is happening there. I rejected the attempts to link ideological differences to issues of ending the arms race. I persistently drew the President and the Secretary of State back to the subject that had brought us to Reykjavik. It was necessary to remind our interlocutors repeatedly about the third element of our package of proposals, without which it would be impossible to reach accord on the whole. I have in mind the need to comply strictly with the ABM Treaty, to consolidate the regime of this major treaty and to ban nuclear tests.

We had to draw attention again and again to things that seemed to be perfectly clear: having agreed to major reductions in nuclear arms, attempts –

both in deed and in thought – to shake strategic stability and to circumvent the agreements should be made to be impossible. That is why we should have confidence in the preservation of the ABM Treaty which has no time-limit. You, Mr President, I said, ought to agree that if we are begining to reduce nuclear weapons, there should be the full assurance that the US will do nothing behind the back of the USSR, while the Soviet Union will also do nothing to jeopardise US security, to devalue the agreement or to create difficulties.

Hence the key task to strengthen the ABM regime: to keep the results of the research under this programme in the laboratory and prevent them from being applied in outer space. It is necessary that the right to pull out of the ABM Treaty is not used for ten years in order to create the confidence that in settling the issue of arms reduction at the same time we are ensuring security for both sides and for the world as a whole.

But the US delegation obviously had other intentions. We saw that the US actually wants to defeat the ABM Treaty, to revise it so as to develop a large-scale space-based ABM system for its own conceited ends. It would simply be irresonsible of me to agree to this.

As far as nuclear testing is concerned, it was perfectly clear here as well why the US side does not want to conduct serious talks on this issue. It would have preferred to carry these talks on endlessly and thus postpone the settlement of the issue of banning nuclear tests for decades. And once again we had to reject attempts to use the talks as a cover and to get a free hand in the field of nuclear explosions. I said bluntly that I was having doubts about the honesty of the US position and questioned whether there wasn't something in it damaging for the Soviet Union. How can an agreement on the elimination of nuclear arms be reached if the US continues to perfect these weapons? Still we were under the impression that the SDI was the main snag. If it could have been removed it would have been possible to reach an accord on banning nuclear explosions as well.

At a certain point in the talks, when it became absolutely clear that to continue the discussion would be a waste of time, I reminded the other side that we had proposed a definite package of measures and asked them to consider it as such. If we have worked out a common position on the possibility of making major reductions in nuclear arms and at the same time have failed to reach agreement on the issue of the ABM Treaty and nuclear testing, then everything we have tried to create here falls apart, I said.

The President and the Secretary of State reacted poorly to our firm position, but I could not pose the question in any other way. This is a matter concerning the security of our country, the security of the entire world, all peoples and all continents.

Our proposals were major, truly large-scale and clearly in the nature of compromise. We made concessions. But we did not see even the slightest desire on the US side to respond in kind or to meet us half-way. We were deadlocked. We began thinking about how to conclude the meeting. And nevertheless we continued our efforts to engage our partners in constructive dialogue.

During the conversation that was supposed to be the concluding one we ran out of time. Instead of going our separate ways – we to Moscow and they to Washington – yet another break was announced to allow the sides to think everything over and meet one more time after dinner. On returning to the house of the city's mayor after the break, we made yet another attempt to end the meeting successfully. We proposed the following text as the basis for summing up the positive results.

Here is the text:

> The Soviet Union and the US will oblige themselves not to use their right to withdraw from the ABM Treaty, which has no time-limit, for a period of ten years and during this period to ensure strict observance of all of its provisions. All testing on the space elements of the ABM defence in outer space will be prohibited excluding research and testing conducted in laboratories.
>
> In the first five years of this decade (until 1991 inclusive) the strategic offensive arms of both sides wil be reduced by 50 per cent.
>
> In the next five years of this period the remaining 50 per cent of the strategic offensive arms of both sides will be eliminated.
>
> Thus, the strategic offensive arms of the USSR and the US will be completely eliminated by the end of the year 1996.

Commenting on this text I made an important addition in reference to the document which had been given to the President at the end of our first conversation. This document is basically a proposal to hold special negotiations after the ten years are up and nuclear weapons no longer exist in order to work out mutually acceptable decisions as to what should be done next.

But this time, too, our attempts to reach an agreement were to no avail. For four hours we again tried to make our interlocutors understand that our approach was well founded, that it was not at all threatening, and did not affect the interests of the genuine security of the US. But with every hour it became more obvious that the US representatives would not agree to keep SDI research and testing in the laboratories. They are bent on going into outer space with weapons.

I said firmly that we would never agree to help undermine th ABM Treaty with our own hands. We consider this an issue of principle, as well as a national security issue.

We were thus literally two or three steps from making possibly historic decisions for the entire nuclear-space era, but we were unable to make those last steps. A turning point in the world's history did not take place, even though, I will say again with full confidence, it could have.

Our conscience is clear, however, and we cannot be reproached. We did everything we could.

The scope of our partners' approach was not broad enough. They did not grasp the uniqueness of the moment, and ultimately, they did not have enough courage, sense of responsibility or political resolve which are all so needed to settle key and pressing issues in world politics. They stuck to old positions which had already eroded with time and did not correspond to the realities of today.

Foreigners in Iceland and my comrades here have asked me what in my opinion were the main reasons for the attitude of the US delegation at the Reykjavik meeting. There are a number of reasons, both subjective and objective, but the main one is that the leadership of that great country relies too heavily on the military-industrial complex, on the monopolistic groups which have turned the nuclear and other arms races into a business, into a way of making money, into the object of their existence and the meaning of their activities.

In my opinion, the US representatives are making two serious mistakes in their assessment of the situation.

The first is a tactical mistake. They believe that sooner or later the Soviet Union will reconcile itself to the fact that the US is attempting to revive its strategic diktat, that it will agree to the limitation and reduction of only Soviet weapons. It will do so because, so they think, the USSR is more interested in disarmament agreements than the US. But this is a grave delusion. The sooner the US administration overcomes it – I repeat perhaps for the hundredth time – the better it will be for them, for our relations and for the world situation in general.

The other mistake is a strategic one. The US seeks to exhaust the Soviet Union economically with a buildup of sophisticated and costly space arms. It wants to impose hardships of all kinds on the Soviet leadership, to foil its plans, including those in the social sphere and those for improving our people's living standards, and thus spread discontent. Another aim is to restrict the Soviet Union's potential in its economic ties with developing countries which, in such a situation, would all be compelled to bow down before the US. These are far-reaching designs. The strategic course of the current US administration also rests on delusions. Washington, it seems, does not wish to burden itself with a thorough analysis of the changes taking place in our country, does not wish to draw the appropriate practical conclusions for itself and for its course, but is rather busy with wishful thinking. It is building its policy toward the USSR on the basis of this delusion. It is of course difficult to predict all the long-term consequences of such a policy. One thing is clear to us already now: it will not and cannot benefit anyone, including the US.

Before addressing you I read through the US President's statement on Reykjavik. I noticed that the President gives himself all the credit for all the proposals discussed. Well it seems as though these proposals are so attractive to the US people and the peoples throughout the world that it's possible to resort to such a ruse. We are not consumed by vanity but it is important that people get the true picture of what happened in Reykjavik.

So what is next? I already said at the press conference that the work done before the meeting and that done in Reykjavik was not in vain. We ourselves did a lot of thinking in connection with the meeting and re-examined a great deal. We have now better cleared the way to continue the fight for peace and disarmament. We freed ourselves from obstructions that had developed, from insignificant issues, and from stereotypes which hindered new approaches in the important area of our policies.

We know where we stand and see the possibilities available to us more clearly. The preparations for the Reykjavik meeting helped us to formulate a platform – a new, bold platform which promises greater chances for ultimate success. It meets the interests of our people and society at this new stage of socialist development. This platform also meets the interest of other countries and nations and thereby merits trust. We are confident that it will be received with understanding in many countries of the world and in the most differing political and public circles.

I think that many people around the world, including leaders vested with power, can and must draw weighty conclusions from the Reykjavik meeting. Everyone will have to think again and again about the essence of the matter, and about why such persistent efforts to achieve a breakthrough and start advancing towards a non-nuclear world and towards a universal security have thus far failed to produce the needed result.

I would like to hope that the President also has a better insight now into our analysis, the intentions of the Soviet Union, and into the possibilities and limits for adjusting the Soviet stand. And I hope Mr Reagan understands our analysis more fully and more precisely since receiving first-hand explanations of our constructive measures for stabilising and improving the international situation.

The US leadership will obviously need some time.

We are realists and we clearly understand that the issues that have remained unsettled for many years and even decades can hardly be settled at a single sitting. We have a great deal of experience in doing business with the US. And we are aware that the domestic political climate can change there quickly and that the opponents of peace across the ocean are strong and influential. There is nothing new here for us.

If we do not despair, if we do not slam the door and give vent to our emotions – although there is more than enough reason for this – it is because we are sincerely convinced that new efforts are needed aimed at building normal inter-state relations in the nuclear epoch. There is no other alternative.

And another thing: after Reykjavik, the infamous SDI became even more conspicuous as an epitome of obstructing peace, as a strong expression of militaristic designs and an unwillingness to get rid of the nuclear threat looming over mankind. It is impossible to perceive this programme in any other way. This is the most important lesson of the Reykjavik meeting.

In summing up these eventful days I would like to say the following. The meeting was a major event. A reappraisal was made. A qualitatively new situation developed in that no one can continue to act as he acted before. The meeting was useful. It paved the way for a possible step forward, for a real positive shift, should the US finally adopt realistic positions and abandon delusion in its appraisals.

The meeting has convinced us that the path we have chosen is correct and that a new and constructive mode of political thinking in the nuclear age is necessary.

We are energetic and determined. Having embarked on a programme of reorganisation the country has already traversed a certain path. We have just started this process, but changes have already been made. Growth in industrial production over the past nine months reached 5.2 per cent, labour productivity grew by 4.8 per cent. National income produced rose 4.3 per cent as compared to the previous year.

All this is the strongest support for the Party's policies on the part of the people, for this is the support by deed.

This shows that under new conditions the people's efforts are helping to accelerate the growth of the country's economic potential and are thus consolidating its defence capabilities.

The Soviet people and the Soviet leadership have unanimously agreed that the policy of socialism can and must be a policy of peace and disarmament. We shall not swerve from the course of the 27th CPSU Congress.

*   *   *

Good evening, dear comrades.

I speak with you agin, and the subject is again the same – Reykjavik. This is a very serious issue. The outcome of the meeting with the US President has stirred the entire world. A great deal of new data have come out over the past days demanding assessments which I would like to share with you today.

You will remember that I said at the press conference in Reykjavik that we shall return again and again to this meeting between the leaders of the USSR and the US.

I am convinced that we have not yet realised the full significance of what happened. But we will reach this realisation. If not today, then tomorrow. We will grasp the full significance of Reykjavik and will do justice to the accomplishments and gains, as well as to the missed opportunities and losses.

Dramatic as the course of the talks and their results were, the Reykjavik meeting greatly facilitated, perhaps for the first time in many decades, our search for a way to achieve nuclear disarmament.

I believe that as a result of the meeting we have now reached a higher level, not only in analysing the situation, but also in determining the objectives and the framework of possible accords on nuclear disarmament.

Having found ourselves a few steps from an actual agreement on such a difficult and vitally important issue, we all grew to understand more fully the danger facing the world and the need for immediate solutions. And what is most important, we now know that it is both realistic and possible to avert the nuclear threat.

I would like to point out here that the Soviet programme for eliminating nuclear arms by the year 2000 was until recently described by many 'experts' in world politics as illusory, as an unrealisable dream.

This is indeed the case when past experience is neither wealth nor counsel, but a burden that makes the search for solutions all the more difficult.

Reykjavik generated more than just hopes. Reykjavik also highlighted the difficulties encountered on the way to a nuclear-free world.

If this fact is not understood it is impossible to assess correctly the results of the Icelandic meeting.

The forces opposed to disarmament are great. We felt that during the meeting and we feel this today. Reykjavik is being talked about a great deal.

Those who look realistically at the facts assess the meeting in Iceland as a major political event.

They welcome the fact that as a result of this meeting progress was made toward new qualitative levels in the fight against nuclear weapons. The results of Reykjavik, as they are viewed by the Soviet leadership, are encouraging to all who seek a change for the better.

Interesting assessments are being made in many countries at the state level, in public circles and in the scientific community. The opportunities that have been opened up are being characterised as corresponding to the aspirations of all mankind.

It is a common view that the meeting has raised both the Soviet-US dialogue and the East-West dialogue as a whole to a new level.

For the dialogue has been taken out of the plane of technical estimates and numerical comparisons and has been placed on to one with new parameters and dimensions.

From this height new prospects can be seen for the settlement of today's urgent issues. I am referring to security, nuclear disarmament, the prevention of new spirals in the arms race, and a new understanding of the opportunities that have opened up before mankind.

One could say that the debate over the results of the meeting has only just begun. I believe, I am even confident, that this debate will grow. And we believe the joint efforts of the people, of political figures and of public organisations will grow as well in an endeavour to take advantage of the opportunities that opened up in Reykjavik.

A course was outlined there for settling vitally important issues on which the very fate of mankind depends.

In the time that has passed since Reykjavik, however, something else has become clear.

Those groups linked with militarism and making profits from the arms race are obviously scared. They are doing their utmost to cope with the new situation and, coordinating their actions, are trying in every way possible to mislead the people, to control the sentiment of broad sections of the world public, to suppress the people's quest for peace, and to impede governments from taking a clear-cut position at this decisive moment in history.

These groups have at their disposal political power, economic leverage, and the powerful mass media. Of course one should not overestimate their strength, but one should not underestimate it either. All indications are that the battle will be a difficult one.

Forces are being regrouped in the camp of the enemies of détente and disarmament. Feverish efforts are being made to create obstacles in order to stem the process started in Reykjavik.

Under these circumstances I consider it necessary to return to the urgent issues which arose in connection with our meeting in Iceland.

Our point of view, which I made public one hour after the meeting, has not changed. I consider it necessary to state this not only in order to reiterate the appraisals made earlier.

I am doing this to draw your attention to the juggling with words and dissonance which we are observing. This might be the result of confusion or perplexity, but this also might be a preplanned campaign to fool the people.

The aims which were set before the meeting are explained differently. The initial negative reports of the Reykjavik meeting have quickly and concertedly become words of praise.

A hectic campaign has been started to misappropriate the other side's proposals.

The greatest efforts are being made to defend SDI, a project that was shown to be worthy of shame in Reykjavik. Generally speaking Washington is now experiencing some hectic times.

But what is this? A pre-election game which needs to depict Reykjavik as a success? Or are we dealing with a policy that will be unpredictable for years to come?

This needs to be studied carefully.

It certainly did catch our attention as to how and where certain political groupings are trying to steer the discussion of the results of the meeting.

The key elements of this campaign are worth mentioning. Efforts are being made in a bid to whitewash the destructive position of the US administration which came to the meeting unprepared. They came, I would say one more time, with the same old baggage. But when the situation demanded definite answers the US side wrecked the chances for concluding the meeting with an accord.

A new situation has developed since Reykjavik, and meanwhile efforts are being made to force the USSR to return to the old approaches, to the unproductive debates about numbers, and to walking in circles in a deadlock situation.

Evidently there is a great number of politicians in the West for whom the Geneva talks serve as a screen, and not as a forum for seeking accords.

What was once disguised thoroughly is now being disclosed: there are powerful forces in the ruling circles of the US and Western Europe which are seeking to frustrate the process of nuclear disarmament. Certain people are once again beginning to claim that nuclear weapons are even a good thing.

A half-truth is the most dangerous lie, as a saying goes. It is extremely disquieting that not only have the mass media, leaning towards the right taken such a stand, but so have leading figures in the US administration. And at times this stand is even one of downright deception.

I have already had the opportunity to report how things went in Reykjavik. We arrived at the meeting with constructive and the most radical arms reduction proposals in the entire history of Soviet-US negotiations. These proposals take into account the interests of both sides.

Upon arrival in Iceland I spoke about this on the eve of the meeting in a conversation with the leaders of that country. The proposals had already been handed over to the President of the US by the middle of my first conversation with him.

Far-reaching and interconnected, these proposals form an integrated package and are based on the programme made public on 15 January for the elimination of nuclear weapons by the year 2000.

The first proposal is to reduce by half all strategic arms with no exceptions.

The second proposal is to eliminate completely Soviet and US medium-range missiles in Europe and to start talks immediately on missiles of this type in Asia, as well as on missiles with a range of less than one thousand kilometres. We suggested that the number of such missiles be frozen immediately.

The third proposal is to consolidate the regime of the ABM Treaty and to start full-scale talks on a total nuclear test ban.

The discussions in Reykjavik, which I described in detail in my previous speeches, opened with the Soviet proposals.

Tremendous efforts and intense arguments resulted in the positions of the two sides drawing reassuringly closer together in two of the three areas.

The talks enabled the two sides to establish specific periods for the elimination of strategic offensive arms. We came to the agreement with President Ronald Reagan that the arms of this type belonging to the USSR and the US can and must be completely eliminated by the year 1996.

An accord was also reached on the complete elimination of US and Soviet medium-range missiles in Europe and on a radical cut in missiles of this type in Asia.

We attach great importance to these accords between the USSR and the

US: they prove that nuclear disarmament is possible.

This is the first half of the truth about the Reykjavik meeting. But there is still the other half and this is, as I have already said, that the US side frustrated an agreement which, it seemed, was quite near at hand.

The US administration is now trying in every way possible to convince the people that the possibility of a major success in reaching definite agreements was not realised on account of the Soviet Union's unyielding position on the issue of the so-called Strategic Defence Iniative (SDI).

It is even being asserted that we allegedly lured the President into a trap by putting forward 'breathtaking' proposals on the reduction of strategic offensive arms and medium-range missiles and that later we ostensibly demanded, in the form of an ultimatum, that SDI be renounced.

But the essence of our position and proposals is as follows: we stand for the reduction and the eventual complete elimination of nuclear weapons and are absolutely against a new stage in the arms race and against its transfer to outer space.

Hence we are against SDI and for the consolidation of the ABM Treaty.

It is clear to every sober-minded person that if we start the process of radically cutting and then completely eliminating nuclear weapons it is essential to rule out any possibility of either the Soviet or US side gaining a unilateral military superiority.

It is precisely the extension of the arms race to a new sphere and the attempts to take offensive arms into outer space in order to achieve military superiority that we perceive as the main danger of SDI.

SDI has become a barrier to ending the arms race, to getting rid of nuclear weapons, the main obstacle to a nuclear-free world.

When Mr Shultz, US Secretary of State, tells the US people that SDI is a sort of 'insurance policy' for the US this, to say the least, is an attempt to mislead the US people.

In fact SDI does not strengthen the US's security but, by opening up a new stage of the arms race, destabilises the military-political situation and thereby weakens both US and universal security.

The US should know this.

They should also know that the US stand on SDI announced in Reykjavik basically contradicts the ABM Treaty. Article XV of the Treaty does allow a party to withdraw from the Treaty, but only under certain circumstances, namely, 'if it decides that extraordinary events related to the subject matter of this Treaty have jeopardised its (that party's) supreme interests'. There have not been and are no such extraordinary events. It is clear that the elimination of nuclear weapons, if begun, would make the emergence of such extraordinary events even less likely. This is only logical.

Article XII of the ABM Treaty, however, stipulates that the sides should 'consider, as appropriate, possible proposals for further increasing the viability of this Treaty'. The US, on the contrary, is seeking to depreciate the Treaty and deprive it of its meaning.

Each of these quotations is from the Treaty signed by the top representative of the US.

Many stories have been invented to raise the prestige of SDI. One of them is that the Russians are terribly afraid of it. Another has it that SDI brought the Russians to the talks in Geneva and then to Reykjavik. A third is that only SDI will save the US from the 'Soviet threat'. The fourth says that SDI will give the US a great technological lead over the Soviet Union and other countries, and so on and so forth.

Understanding the problem I can say now only one thing: continuing the SDI programme will push the world into a new stage of the arms race and destabilise the strategic situation.

Everything else ascribed to SDI is in many respects rather dubious and is done in order to sell this suspicious and dangerous commodity in an attractive wrapping.

In upholding his position that prevented an agreement being reached in Reykjavik, the President asks the rhetorical questions: 'Why are the Soviets so adamant that America remain forever vulnerable to Soviet rocket attack? Why does the Soviet Union insist that we remain defenseless for ever?'

I must say I'm surprised by such questions. They give the impression that the US President has the opportunity of making his country invulnerable, of giving it secure protection against a nuclear strike.

As long as nuclear weapons exist and the arms race continues he has no such opportunity. Naturally this also applies to ourselves.

If the President counts on SDI in this respect, it is futile. The system would be effective only if all missiles were eliminated. But then, one might ask, why an anti-missile defence at all? Why build it? I won't even mention the money wasted, the system's cost, which according to some estimates, will run into several trillion dollars.

So far, we have been trying to persuade the US to give up this dangerous undertaking. We urge the US administration to look for invulnerability and protection elsewhere – by totally eliminating nuclear weapons and establishing a comprehensive system of international security that would preclude wars, nuclear or conventional.

The SDI programme still remains an integral part of US military doctrine. *The Fiscal Year 1984-1988 Defense Guidance* now in force, which the Pentagon produced at the beginning of Reagan's term in office, directly provides for the 'prototype development of space-based weapons systems' including weapons to destroy Soviet satellites and accelerate the development of the system of the anti-missile defence of US territory with the possible US pull-out of the ABM Treaty.

The document says that the US should develop weapons that 'are difficult for the Soviets to counter, impose disproportionate costs, open up new areas of major military competition and obsolesce previous Soviet investment'. Once again, as you can see, there is, as former President Nixon put it, a chase of the ghost; once again there are plans to wear out the Soviet Union.

It is hard for the current administration to learn lessons.

Is this not the reason why its commitment to SDI is so stubborn? The plans for Star Wars have become the chief obstacle to an agreement on removing the nuclear threat. Washington's claim that we are now moving towards an agreement is of no use.

To eliminate nuclear weapons as a means of deterring US aggression and in return be threatened from outer space can only be accepted by those who are politically naïve. There are no such people in the Soviet leadership.

It is hard to reconcile oneself to the loss of the unique chance of saving mankind from the nuclear threat. With precisely this in mind I said at the press conference in Reykjavik that we did not regard the dialogue as closed and hoped that President Reagan, on returning home, would consult the US Congress and the US people, and adopt decisions logically necessitated by what had been achieved in Reykjavik.

Quite a different thing has happened. Aside from distorting the entire picture of the negotiations in Reykjavik – about which I will speak later – in recent days they have taken actions that, following such an important meeting between the two countries' top leaders, appear as simply wild from any normal point of view.

I am referring to the expulsion of another 55 Soviet embassy and consular staff from the US. We will of course take measures in response, very tough measures on an equal footing, so to speak. We are not going to put up with such outrageous practices. But now, I have this to say.

What kind of government is this; what can one expect from it in other affairs in the international arena? To what limits does the unpredictability of its actions go?

It turns out that it has no constructive proposals on key disarmament issues and that it does not even have a desire to maintain the kind of atmosphere essential for a normal continuation of the dialogue. It seems that Washington is not prepared for any of this.

The conclusion is obvious. It is confirmed by the considerable experience which has been accumulated. Every time a gleam of hope appears in the approaches to the major issues in Soviet-US relations and to a solution of questions involving the interests of the whole of mankind, a provocative action is immediately staged with the aim of frustrating the possibility of a positive outcome and poisoning the atmosphere.

Which is the real face of the US administration then? Is it looking for answers and solutions or does it want to finally destroy everything that may serve as a basis for headway and deliberately rule out any normalisation?

Quite an unattractive portrait is emerging of the administration of that great country – an administration quick to take disruptive actions. Either the President is unable to cope with the entourage literally breathing hatred for the

Soviet Union and for everything that may lead international affairs into calm waters or he himself is this way. In any event there is no restraining the 'hawks' in the White House, and this is very dangerous.

As for informing the US people about the meeting in Reykjavik, the following has taken place, which is entirely in the spirit of what I have already mentioned; facts have been concealed from them. They were told the half-truth of which I spoke earlier. Things were portrayed so as to show that the US, acting from a position of strength, virtually wrested consent from the Soviet Union to reach agreement on US terms.

And the day is not far off when the US will ostensibly attain its goal: it is essential, they say, not to slacken the pace of military preparations, to speed up the Star Wars programme and to increase pressure in all directions.

These days have witnessed the drowning of a great cause in petty politicking and the sacrificing of the vital interests of the US people, allies, and international security as a whole to the arms manufacturers.

A good deal has been said about the openness of US society, about the freedom of information, the pluralism of opinions, and the fact that everyone there can see and hear what he pleases.

In Reykjavik, when pointing out the differences between our two systems, the President told me, and I quote: 'We recognise freedom of the press and the right to hear any point of view.' But how do things stand in reality?

Here is the latest fact.

It has been brought to my attention that a public organisation of ours, the Novosti Press Agency, has published in English the text of my press conference in Reykjavik and of my speech on Soviet television and sent them out to many countries including the US.

Well the fact is that the pamphlets with these texts have been detained at the US customs house for several days now. They are being prevented from reaching the US reader. There's the 'right to hear any point of view' for you!

Or take, for example, the cinema. As I told the President when we were discussing humanitarian affairs, a great number of US films are shown on the Soviet screen. They give Soviet people an opportunity to become acquainted with both the US people's way of life and their way of thinking.

In 'free America' on the other hand Soviet films are practically not shown. The President avoided making any reply and, as usual in such cases, fell back on free enterprise which lets everyone do whatever he wants.

I also told him about the publication of US books in this country as compared to that of our books in the US: the ratio is approximately 20 to one.

I put the question of radio information before the President as well. I said that in this field, too, we are on an unequal footing. You have surrounded the Soviet Union with a network of radio transmitters and broadcast around the clock everything you like in many languages of the Soviet Union from the territories of other countries. The US, availing itself of the fact that we are not its closest neighbour, has isolated itself from our radio information by using the medium wave band – receivers in the US are only of that kind. The President had nothing to say to that either.

Then I suggested to him that we that we take the following approach: we stop jamming the 'Voice of America' broadcasts and you give us an opportunity to conduct radio broadcasts directed at the US on your territory or somewhere nearby so that the broadcasts might reach the population of your country. The President promised to think about it.

It appears that the US is becoming an increasingly closed society. People there are being isolated from objective information in a cunning and effective way. This is a dangerous process.

The US people should know the truth about what is going on in the Soviet Union, about the true content of Soviet foreign policy, about our real intentions, as well as the truth about the state of affairs in the world as a whole.

At the present stage, I would say, this is becoming extremely important.

Now a few words about how the outcome of the Reykjavik meeting is being portrayed in the US. It took only several hours, or days at the most, for everything discussed at Reykjavik to begin dispersing in the fog of inventions and fantasies. Attempts are being made to destroy the seedlings of trust before they take root.

The President stated recently that agreement had been reached only on ballistic missiles, and his assistants said plainly that bombers and all cruise missiles remained untouched.

The Secretary of State presented another version – that our accord dealt with all strategic arms. By the way, the latter was present during my talks with the President, as was our Minister of Foreign Affairs, Eduard Shevardnadze.

Mr Speakes, the White House spokesman, stated that possibly Mr Reagan had been misunderstood and had actually never agreed to the elimination of all nuclear weapons.

Things got to the point of outright misrepresentation.

It is alleged, for example, that during the past meeting the US President did not agree to the Soviet proposal on complete elimination of *all* strategic offensive arms of the USSR and the US by 1996, and that a common point of view on our proposal was never reached.

With all the responsibility of a participant in the talks I state: the President did, albeit without particular enthusiasm, consent to the elimination of all – I emphasise – not just certain individual ones, but all strategic offensive arms. And these are to be eliminated precisely within ten years, in two stages.

The interpretations of the discussion of the nuclear testing issue are a far cry from the truth, too. The US unilateral approach to this issue is pictured in such a way as to lead one to believe that the Soviet Union has given it its full consent. This is not the case, nor could it be.

The issue of the elimination of medium-range missiles in Europe is also being presented in a distorted fashion, to say nothing of the fact that it is being withdrawn from the package proposed by the Soviet side.

But our consent to freeze the number of missiles with a range of under 1,000 kilometres is also being portrayed as the Soviet Union's 'recognition' of the US's 'right' to deploy US missiles of the same class in Western Europe.

With such interpretations I myself will soon be in doubt as to what we really spoke about at Reykjavik – about removing the nuclear threat, reducing and eliminating nuclear arms? Or about how to keep this threat growing, how to diversify the nuclear arsenals and turn not just this entire planet, but outer space, the universe, too, into an arena of military confrontation? For this, comrades, is what is happening.

The prospects of reaching a mutual understanding between the Soviet and US sides so frightened certain people that they began erecting inconceivable obstacles ahead of time and inventing 'preconditions'.

An assistant to the President went so far as to say that before embarking on nuclear disarmament the US must see some changes in the political climate in the Soviet Union.

All this is just not serious, not serious at all.

When similar claims were made 70 or 40 years ago it was still possible to regard them as an inability to think things through, or as historical blindness. Nowadays they can only be the demonstration of a complete lack of understanding of reality.

The issue of conventional arms is also mentioned as one of the 'preconditions'. In and of itself it is serious enough.

To this day there is a well-worn thesis in the West concerning the 'superiority' of the Soviet Union and other Warsaw Treaty states in conventional arms. It is this that is allegedly compelling NATO to continue building up its nuclear potential.

Of course there is in fact no disbalance whatsoever. After Reykjavik this fact was publicly recognised for the first time by Mr Shultz and Mr Reagan. But the crux of the matter does not lie in the maintenance of parity. We do not want the arms race to move from the sphere of nuclear arms to the sphere of conventional ones.

Let me remind you that our January proposal on the elimination of nuclear weapons before the end of the century included also the provisions on the elimination of chemical weapons and on radical reductions in conventional armaments.

We have returned to that issue more than once since January. The proposals of the Warsaw Treaty countries were presented in the greatest detail last summer in Budapest. We sent them to the other side, that is, the NATO countries.

So far we have received no answer.

Every day that has passed since Reykjavik has made it more clear that the meeting in Iceland was that touchstone which determines the true value of the words and declarations of political figures.

So much has been said of the need to be free of the nuclear nightmare, of how we will be able to breathe more easily in a nuclear-free world. Let the USSR and the US get things in motion.

But no sooner had a ray of hope appeared when many of those who had just been cursing nuclear weapons and pledging their allegiance to the idea of a nuclear-free world went back on their word.

Certain quarters in Western Europe even voiced their feeling that it was difficult to part with US nuclear weapons, with US missiles.

Evidently the point is that the policy-makers in the West are thinking of nuclear weapons not in the terms of defence at all. Otherwise it would be difficult to explain why pretexts are now being sought for keeping the missiles in place or why support for the SDI programme is being expressed at government level.

Here is something for both us and the West European public to ponder.

In addition to direct attacks, subtle manoeuvres are being made. Is it not possible to take from the negotiating table what is most advantageous, while ignoring that which is not to one's tasté for one reason or another?

They say that difficulties at Reykjavik arose because we, the Soviet side, put forward our cardinal proposals in a package. But the package contains a balance of interests and concessions, a balance of withdrawn concerns and the interdependence of security interests. Here everything is as if on scales; the two pans must be balanced.

That is why evidently those in the West want to shatter into pieces this logically substantiated and just variant of an overall accord, doing nothing to restore the balance of compromises.

All the proposals we made at Reykjavik are objectively connected with central strategic weapons systems. Our concessions are also a part of the package. No package, no concessions.

This is a reality of our national security. But such an approach ensures the security of the US and all other countries as well.

That is why we attach such significance to strengthening the ABM Treaty. We are not endangering it in any way. On the contrary, we are opposed to having it revised, supplemented or whatever, and we are even more opposed to having it replaced with something else, as the President suggested at Reykjavik. Or maybe this was just a slip of the tongue.

Let me put it frankly: I was very much surprised when during the meeting he began persuading the Soviet side and me personally not to regard the ABM Treaty as gospel. What, then, should one's attitude to treaties be like? Should they be treated as mere slips of paper?

Without strict observance of the treaties, and especially such a fundamental one as this, it is impossible to ensure international order and basic stability. Otherwise the world would be subject to arbitrary rule and chaos.

Let me say once again: when SDI is given preference over nuclear disarmament, only one conclusion can be made – with the help of that military programme efforts are being made to disprove the axiom of international relations of our epoch, an axiom laid out in simple, clear-cut words signed by the US President and myself last year. These words read: nuclear war must not be fought and cannot be won.

Let me say in conclusion that the Soviet Union has put the maximum of goodwill into its proposals. We are not withdrawing these proposals: they still stand! Everything that has been said by way of their substantiation and development remains in force.

Good night, comrades. All the best.

6

Delhi Declaration

Today humanity stands at a crucial turning point in history. Nuclear weapons threaten to annihilate not only all that man has created through the ages, but man himself and even life on earth. In the nuclear age, humanity must evolve a new political thinking, a new concept of the world that would provide credible guarantees for humanity's survival. People want to live in a safer and a more just world. Humanity deserves a better fate than being a hostage to nuclear terror and despair. It is necessary to change the existing world situation and to build a nuclear-weapon free world, free of violence and hatred, fear and suspicion.

The world we have inherited belongs to present and future generations and this demands that primacy be given to universally accepted human values. The right of every nation and every person to life, freedom, peace and the pursuit of happiness must be recognised. The use or threat of use of force must be abandoned. The right of every people to make their own social, political and ideological choices must be respected. Policies that seek to establish the domination by some over others must be renounced. The expansion of nuclear arsenals and the development of space weapons undermine the universally accepted conviction that a nuclear war should never be fought and can never be won.

On behalf of the more than one billion men, women and children of our two friendly countries, who account for one-fifth of mankind, we call upon the peoples and leaders of all countries to take urgent action that would lead to a world free of weapons of mass destruction, a world without war.

Conscious of our common responsibility for the destinies of our two nations and of mankind, we hereby set forth the following principles for building a nuclear-weapon-free and non-violent world:

'A Nuclear Free and Non-violent World': Declaration of the Indian and Soviet Heads of State, Delhi, 27 November 1986.

1. Peaceful coexistence must become the universal norm of international relations:

In the nuclear age it is necessary that international relations are restructured so that confrontation is replaced by cooperation, and conflict situations resolved through peaceful political means, not through military means.

2. Human life must be recognised as supreme:

It is only man's creative genius that makes progress and development of civilisation possible in a peaceful environment.

3. Non-violence should be the basis of community life:

Philosophies and policies based on violence and intimidation, inequality and oppression, and discrimination on the basis of race, religion or colour, are immoral and impermissible. They spread intolerance, destroy man's noble aspirations and negate all human values.

4. Understanding and trust must replace fear and suspicion:

Mistrust, fear and suspicion between nations and peoples distort perceptions of the real world. They engender tensions and, in the final analysis, harm the entire international community.

5. The right of every state to political and economic independence must be recognised and respected:

A new world order must be built to ensure economic justice and equal political security for all nations. An end to the arms race is an essential prerequisite for the establishment of such an order.

6. Resources being spent on armaments must be channelled towards social and economic development:

Only disarmament can release the enormous additional resources needed for combating economic backwardness and poverty.

7. Conditions must be guaranteed for the individual's harmonious development:

All nations must work together to solve urgent humanitarian problems and cooperate in the areas of culture, the arts, science, education and medicine for the all-round development of the individual. A world without nuclear weapons and violence would open up vast opportunities for this.

8. Mankind's material and intellectual potential must be used to solve global problems:

Solutions must be found to global problems such as shortage of food, the growth of populations, illiteracy and environmental degradation through the efficient and appropriate uses of the resources of the earth. The world's oceans, the ocean floor as well as outer space are the common heritage of mankind. A termination of the arms race would create better conditions for this purpose.

9. The 'balance of terror' must give way to comprehensive international security:

The world is one and its security is indivisible. East and West, North and South regardless of social systems, ideologies, religion or race must join together in a common commitment to disarmament and development.

International security can be guaranteed through the adoption of integrated measures in the field of nuclear disarmament using all available and agreed measures of verification and confidence building; just political settlement of regional conflicts, through peaceful negotiations; and cooperation in the political, economic and humanitarian spheres.

10. A nuclear-weapon-free and non-violent world requires specific and immediate action for disarmament:

It can be achieved through agreements on:

- complete destruction of nuclear arsenals before the end of this century;
- barring of all weapons from outer space, which is the common heritage of mankind;
- banning of all nuclear weapons tests;
- prohibition of the development of new types of weapons of mass destruction;
- banning of chemical weapons and destruction of their stockpiles;
- reducing the levels of conventional arms and armed forces.

Pending the elimination of nuclear weapons, the Soviet Union and India propose that **an International Convention Banning the Use or Threat of Use of Nuclear Weapons** should be concluded immediately. This would constitute a major concrete step towards complete nuclear disarmament.

Building up a nuclear-weapon-free and non-violent world requires a revolutionary transformation of outlook and the education of people and nations for peace, mutual respect and tolerance. The propaganda of war, hatred and violence should be forbidden and hostile perceptions with regard to other nations and peoples abandoned.

Wisdom lies in preventing the accumulation and aggravation of global problems which, if not solved today, would require even greater sacrifices tomorrow.

The danger that threatens mankind is grave. But mankind has the power to prevent a catastrophe, and to pave the way to a nuclear-weapon-free civilisation. The gathering strength of the Coalition for Peace embracing the efforts of the non-aligned movement, 'the Six-Nation Five-Continent Initiative for Peace and Disarmament', all peace-loving countries, political parties and public organisations gives us reason for hope and optimism. The time for decisive and urgent action is now.

M. GORBACHEV
General Secretary of the
CPSU Central Committee

R. GANDHI
Prime Minister of the
Republic of India

7

Moscow Forum

Ladies and Gentlemen.
Comrades.

The destinies of the world and the future of humanity have concerned the best minds in various lands ever since man first thought of the morrow.

Until relatively recently these and related reflections have been seen as an imaginative exercise, as the other-worldly pursuits of philosophers, scholars and theologians. In the past decades, however, these problems have moved on to a highly practical plane. The reasons are obvious.

The development and subsequent stockpiling of nuclear weapons and of their delivery vehicles beyond all reasonable bounds have made man technically capable of terminating his own existence. The simultaneous accumulation of explosive social material in the world, and attempts to continue tackling forcefully, with stone-age methods, the problems of a cardinally altered world make catastrophe highly likely in political terms as well. The militarisation of mentality and of the way of life weakens and even removes altogether any moral inhibitions with regard to nuclear suicide.

We have no right to forget that the first step which is always the most risky, has already been made. Nuclear weapons have been used against human beings, and used twice. There are dozens – I repeat dozens – of recorded and acknowledged moments when the possibility of using such weapons against other countries was seriously considered. I am not saying this by way of criticism or condemnation, though they are more than merited. I am saying this to stress once again how close mankind has come to the point-of-no-return.

The First World War shocked its contemporaries for its unprecedented scale of destruction and suffering, for the brutality and technical impersonality

'The Need for International Cooperation': Address to the International Forum for a Nuclear-free World for the Survival of Humankind. Moscow, 16 February 1987.

of the success of annihilation. But appalling as the wounds it inflicted were, the Second World War surpassed its 'records' many times over.

One strategic submarine today carries a destructive punch equivalent to several Second World Wars. There are scores of such submarines and their nuclear systems are far from being the only ones. The imagination is powerless to envision the hell and the negation of the idea of man if any part, however small, of the present nuclear arsenal is used.

The Second World War (like the first) was followed by attempts to arrange the world in such a way as to preclude repetition of the wholesale slaughter of peoples. Although these attempts have not quite lived up to expectations they have nevertheless left some trace. There is the United Nations Organisation. There are regional and other structures for state-to-state and public contacts, structures that did not exist before. In brief, the political search for ways of breaking the world community out of the vicious 'logic' that resulted in the world wars, continues.

A nuclear war would leave no problems, and there would be no one left to sit at the negotiation table, let alone the negotiating tree-stump or stone.

There would be no second Noah's Ark for a nuclear deluge. Everyone seems to understand this. So it is time to realise that we can no longer expect things to take care of themselves. There are still quite a few people in the world who think precisely in this way. International contacts and the policy of governments and states have to be brought without delay into line with the realities of the nuclear age.

The question stands like this: either political mentality is geared to the requirements of the times, or civilisation and life itself on earth may perish.

In all human affairs, and especially in international politics, we should not for a moment forget the currently dominant contradiction betweeen war and peace, between the existence and non-existence for humanity, and we must work to resolve it in good time in favour of peace.

This requires us to seek out, foster and share with each other all the best that history has produced, to look for new creative approaches to chronic problems.

The very survival and not just progress of the human race depend on whether or not we find the strength and courage to overcome the threats hidden in the modern world.

We believe that there are grounds for expecting so. A notable feature of recent decades has been that for the first time in its history mankind as a whole, and not only individual representatives, has begun to feel that it is one entity, to see global relationships between man, society and nature, and to assess the consequences of material activities.

This feeling did not come alone; it has brought with it a struggle to remove the nuclear threat. And it cannot be denied that it has already become a great moral and political school in which the masses of the people and whole nations are learning the difficult but necessary art of living in peace with each other, of striking a balance between general and particular interests, of looking at the present and the future boldly, square on, of comprehending them and in doing so drawing conclusions for action. Your forum is evidence of this.

Before describing the substance of all these problems in detail, I wish, on behalf of the people and the government of the Soviet Union, to extend cordial greetings to you all – participants in the Moscow Forum – politicians and journalists, businessmen and scholars, doctors and people of culture and the arts, writers and representatives of various churches.

We value and appreciate that such a forum is being held and that such a great number of famous and influential people have gathered for it from all over the world. We understand that everyone of you has duties and commitments. Nevertheless you postponed them and travelled the thousands of kilometres here to voice your concerns, to share your thoughts with people worried by the same problems.

This alone is very significant, for the forum includes representatives of various population strata, people from all continents, from dozens of states.

The forum is a true embodiment of world public opinion.

The ideas of the forum, the cares and sentiments that have brought you here are near and dear to the Soviet people. It is in this spirit that I once again address words of greeting and gratitude to you for the work you have done these past days. And I think that the voice of this forum, of each of you, will be heeded.

We are encouraged by the fact that for all the diversity of opinions, views, positions and evaluations, the salient feature of the forum has been a common wish to pool efforts against the nuclear danger, and in tackling other global issues before mankind.

It is very important that the ideas and spirit of the forum should reach the broad public and policitical circles and, more important still, should be reflected in the work of those at the helm of states. The Soviet government will give due attention to what has been stated at the forum. This must be so, because these ideas concern the most vital and most essential thing – how to save a future for mankind.

I have a few things to say on the matters discussed at the forum and I wish to present the point of view of our governemnt. But before doing that I'd like to draw your attention to the following.

You have arrived in the Soviet Union at a time when essentially revolutionary changes are under way here. They are of immense significance for our society, for socialism as a whole, and for the entire world. It is only by understanding their content, meaning and aims that one can form a correct opinion about our international policy. Before my people, before you and before the whole world, I state with full responsibility that our international policy is more than ever determined by domestic policy, by our interest in concentrating on constructive endeavours to improve our country. This is why we need lasting peace, predictability and constructiveness in international relations.

It is often said – we still hear it – that there is some threat stemming from the USSR. A 'Soviet threat' to peace and freedom.

I must say that the reorganisation which we have launched on such a scale and which is irreversible shows to everyone: this is where we want to direct our resources, this is where our thoughts are going, these are our actual programmes and intentions, on this we intend to spend the intellectual energy of our society.

Our main idea is to bring out the potential of socialism through activating all the people's strength. To do so we need full and free functioning of all public and state agencies, of all production collectives and creative unions, new forms of civic activity and restoration of those which were unfairly forgotten. In brief, we want a broad democratisation of all society. Further democratisation is also the main guarantee of the irreversible nature of thee ongoing processes. We want more socialism and hence more democracy.

This is how we are continuing the cause of our great revolution. And our people have welcomed this enthusiastically.

To preclude any idle talk and speculation (we hear a lot of it from the West) I wish to emphasise that we are going about our reforms in accordance with our own socialist choice, on the basis of our notions about social values, and are guided by criteria of the Soviet way of life. We measure our successes and our mistakes solely by socialist yardsticks.

But we want to be understood and we hope that the world community will at last acknowledge that our desire to make our country better will hurt no one, with the world only gaining from this.

Reorganisation is an invitation to any social system to compete with socialism peacefully. And we will be able to prove in practice that such competition benefits universal progress and world peace. But for such competition to take place and unfold in civilised forms worthy of twenty-first-century humanity, we must have a new outlook and overcome the mentality, stereotypes and dogmas inherited from a past gone never to return.

It took time for our society and the Soviet leadership to develop an interest in the new mode of thinking. We pondered a good deal. We criticised ourselves and others and asked ourselves difficult and challenging questions before we saw things as they are and became convinced that new approaches and methods are required for resolving international problems in today's complex and contradictory world, a world at a crossroads.

We came to conclusions that made us review something which once seemed axiomatic, since after Hiroshima and Nagasaki world war ceased to be a continuation of politics by other means. Nuclear war would incinerate the architects of such a policy, too.

We made ourselves face the fact that the stockpiling and sophistication of nuclear armaments mean the human race has lost its immortality. It can be regained only by destroying nuclear weapons.

We rejected any right for leaders of a country, be it the USSR, the US or any other, to pass a death sentence on mankind. We are not judges and the billions of people are not criminals to be punished. So the nuclear guillotine must be broken. The nuclear powers must overstep their nuclear shadow and enter a nuclear-free world, thus ending the alienation of politics from the general human norms of ethics.

A nuclear tornado will sweep away socialists and capitalists, the just and sinners alike. Is this situation moral? We Communists do not think it is.

It may be said that we have come the hard way to the new outlook which is called upon to bridge the gap between political practice and universal moral and ethical standards.

Last year at the Party Congress, the highest forum of Soviet society, we set forth our vision of the world, our philosophical concept of its present and future. But we did not confine ourselves to proclaiming our theoretical doctrine. On its basis we formulated a definite political platform for an all-embracing system of international security. It is precisely a system, and it rests on the principle that one's own security cannot be built at the expense of others. It is a system that organically blends all the main spheres of security – military, political, economic and humanitarian.

In the military and political domain we put forward a programme to abolish nuclear weapons by the year 2000. It was announced on behalf of the Soviet people 13 months ago on 15 January 1986. And we are convinced that this date will go down in the history of struggle to save civilisation from death.

Prior to that we moved that all nuclear explosions be halted, and repeatedly extended our unilateral moratorium. We conceived the idea of the Reykjavik summit and took there initiatives which, had the other side responded, would have signified the end of the arms race and a radical turn towards disarmament and elimination of the nuclear danger. Along with our allies we undertook bold and large-scale steps concerning confidence-building measures and reduction of conventional arms and armed forces in Europe. We expressed readiness to have chemical weapons totally abolished.

In Vladivostok we invited Asian and Pacific countries to search jointly for security for each and all in that huge and rising region of the world, for mutually advantageous and equal cooperation. We signed the Delhi Declaration, in which our philosophical and political approach to the construction of a nuclear-weapon-free and non-violent world merge with the approach of the great India and the billions of people represented by the non-aligned movement.

As firm advocates of a new world economic order, we formulated and submitted for consideration by everyone a concept of international economic security.

Lastly our new approach to the humanitarian problems from the 'third Helsinki basket' is there for all to see, and I must disappoint those who think that this has been the result of pressure on us from the West, that we want to gain somebody's fancy in pursuit of some ulterior motives. No, we do not. This too is a result of the new way of thinking.

Thus in every direction we seek to translate our philosophical vision of the world into practical politics. Naturally enough, it takes confidence for a new edifce of international security to be erected and cemented. We understand: the road to it is not simple, and it's not only we who are to cover it, although we, if you recall our history, have more cause for mistrust.

I will not delve into that. Let me just state that along with a deficit of new attitudes everyone feels a shortfall of confidence. I am not going to look into the reasons for this situation on a wider plane, although a lot might be said. We must now look forward, and not be captives of the past.

Confidence needs to be built up through experience in cooperation, through knowing each other better, through solving common problems. It is wrong in principle to say that first comes confidence and then all the rest: disarmament, cooperation and joint projects. Confidence, its creation, consolidation and development comes from common endeavour. This is the rational way.

And I repeat: everyone must begin with himself. It is not the pose of a self-appointed supreme judge of the whole world but respect for others and an unbiased and self-critical view towards one's own society that international relations need so badly now.

One of the chief results of the reconstructive drive in the Soviet Union is a general and universal confidence boost for our society. This bolsters our conviction that it is possible to establish trust in the sphere of international relations, too. The new mode of thinking is still labouring to break through in world politics. Trust is making ground very slowly. And I think that is why more and more people are realising that the fate of the major cause of our time should not be left to politicians alone. This cause concerns not only politicians. And we are witnessing the emergence and rise of a worldwide mass movement which embraces scientists, intellectuals of different professions, clergymen, women, young people, children (more and more), and even former military men and generals who know full well what modern weapons are. And this is the result of people becoming more and more aware of what a very dangerous point the world has come to.

I believe that your forum is a major contribution to the mass movement for a nuclear-free world and for mankind's survival. I welcome the contribution made by the Moscow Forum.

I would like to say a few words here about the Reykjavik meeting. It was not a failure. It was a breakthrough. That was not just another round of negotiations but a moment of truth when a momentous opportunity was glimpsed to embark upon the path leading to a nuclear-weapon-free world.

The Reykjavik meeting has made a great impression everywhere in the world because we approached the issue of reducing nuclear arsenals in an entirely new conceptual key, as a political and psychological problem rather than just military and technical. And we almost found a solution. But what are we to do with that 'almost' which stopped us from reaching the finish in Reykjavik?

I shall not discuss here why that happened. I hope you know our view. What I want to say is that when, at a certain moment, both sides agreed at Reykjavik to make deep cuts in their nuclear arsenals and then eliminate them entirely, they virtually recognised that nuclear weapons can no longer effectively guarantee security.

What happened in Reykjavik irreversibly changed the nature and essence of the debate about a future world. This is an important political judgement. Some people were scared by the new opportunities, however, and they are now pulling back hard. But hard though the past may tug, there is no returning to it. I am sure mankind can and will quite soon throw off the chains of nuclear weapons. But this will require a fight, a hard struggle.

The new political outlook sets out to raise civilisation to a qualitatively new level. This alone serves to show that it is no one-off adjustment of position but a methodology for international affairs.

There is probably no one in this hall or elsewhere who considers nuclear weapons innocuous. However, quite a few people sincerely believe them to be an evil necessary to prevent a greater evil, war. This viewpoint underlies the doctrine of nuclear deterrence.

Let me say the following.

First, even if we stick to this doctrine, we would have to admit that the 'nuclear safeguard' is not 100 per cent effective aand not termless. It may at any time become a death sentence to mankind. The bigger the nuclear arsenals, the less chance they will be kept 'obedient'. Proliferation, increasingly sophisticated nuclear weapon systems, a greater transportation scale and the constant risk of technical error, human failure or malice are all chance factors on which the survival of mankind depends.

Second, if we look at deterrence from a different angle, we see that it is in fact a policy based on intimidation. Each model of behaviour has its inner logic. When threat is a political means the natural wish is that each such threat should be taken seriously. For that one has to always back up threats by definite action. In this case that means military force. The only conclusion one can draw is that the policy of deterrence, considered in a historical context, does not reduce the risk of military conflict. In fact it further increases that risk. Nevertheless even after Reykjavik, some leaders continue to cling to such a doctrine.

And the most adamant supporters of that doctrine are those who are inclined to teach us morality. But what is their own moral face? They are convinced and make no secret of the fact that threats, force and the use of force are the only language they know in dealing with others. How would you react if you met such a person in the street? How can educated leaders consider behaviour generally considered unacceptable in relations between people, normal for relations between states?

Third, when disarmament is discussed a common thesis is that man is violent by nature and that he has a 'war' instinct and that this instinct is indestructible.

Is war the perpetual concomitant of human existence then? If we accept this view we shall have to reconcile ourselves with continuous development of ever more sophisticated weapons of mass destruction.

Such thinking is unacceptable. It is reminiscent of times when ever more sophisticated weapons were invented and used to conquer other peoples and enslave and pillage them. That past is no model for the future. Man living on the threshold of the twenty-first century knows a great deal and can do a great deal. That is why he must realise the need to demilitarise the world. We believe it possible to build such a world and we shall do everything to ensure success of what is perhaps the most ambitious social goal ever.

The theme of nuclear deterrence has another aspect. In politics one must not forget about the problem of the rational and the irrational. This is particularly so in our complex world where the very content of such notions is most subject to the particular historical experience of the peoples, very different political cultures, traditions and many other factors. It is very difficult to find a common denominator which would seem rational to all. And this confirms the fact that the more nuclear weapons there are, the greater the risk of a fatal malfunction,

Nevertheless the development of more powerful and sophisticated, what are cynically called exotic weapons, continues.

The uniqueness, I might even say drama, of the situation, is emphasised by the threat of the arms race spreading into space. If this happened the very idea of arms control would be compromised. Distrust, mutual suspicion and the temptation of being the first to deploy new weapon systems would increase tremendously. Destabilisation would become reality and be fraught with crisis. The risk of accidental war would increase by several orders.

We regret that the continued US testing has put an end to our moratorium. Yet our initiative has not been wasted.

By our moratorium we showed the world that a nuclear test ban is realistic, provided there is the political will.

I wish to assure this authoritative audience and reply to Dr Lown who urged us to extend the moratorium: the Sovet Union will not relinquish its efforts to get nuclear testing banned and bring about major reduction and eventually entire elimination of nuclear stockpiles.

Now I would like to talk about the passions which flared up in recent days about the deployment of a first phase of SDI. The advocates of deployment insist on 'broader interpretation' of the ABM Treaty. Incidentally, while debates on this subject are going on in Washington and between the NATO allies, the administration has already officially suggested in Geneva legitimising such an interpretation. Whatever the pretexts used to justify this, the aim is clearly to bust the treaty. From the very start the political and philosophic essence of the treaty was to ensure stability through the absence of anti-missile defence and in this way end the eternal competition between the sword and the shield, which is particularly dangerous in a nuclear age. When the treaty is annulled the nuclear missile race will acquire new dimensions and will be complemented by the arms race in outer space, the inevitable consequences of which I have just mentioned.

In November 1985 President Reagan and I made the following pledge in Geneva: 'To prevent an arms race in space and to terminate it on earth, to limit and reduce nuclear arms and to enhance strategic stability.' This was signed in Geneva in the joint statement. By undermining the ABM Treaty, the US administration scorns that pledge and the signature the US put to that termless treaty 15 years ago.

The situation requires stricter observance of international law rather than undermining it or knocking out major elements of it.

Another matter we are considering is why some countries are abrogating a right to invent and develop new weapon systems which, even if not deployed or used, threaten other countries and peoples. This problem transcends the borders of national sovereignty. It is an international problem.

Here is yet another problem. At present national sovereignty of a state extends to the atmosphere above it. And every state has the right to defend it from intrusion. Weapons in space would create a far greater threat. So the aim of the plans to deploy weapons in space is to create a new instrument of blackmail against independent states. Isn't it time to enter in international law a ban on deployment of any weapons in space?

Now allow me to deal with another major reality of our time. It also requires a new way of thinking. I mean the unprecedented diversity and increasing interconnection and integrity of the world. Our world is united not only by internationalisation of economic life and powerful information and communication media but also faces the common danger of nuclear death, ecological catastrophe and global explosion of the poverty-wealth contradictions of its different regions.

The world today is a multitude of states, each having its unique history, traditions, customs and way of life. Each people and country has its own national interests and its own aspirations. This is the most important reality in today's world. It did not exist 30–40 years ago. This is a reality that manifested itself as a result of the choice made by the peoples themselves. They have chosen their path of social devlopement.

However this process has been faster than the ability of some politicians to grasp the meaning of irreversible change. In the sphere of nuclear weapons and in other spheres, they live to old preconceptions.

The way out is also in bridging the gap between the fast pace of events and the realisation of what is going on and what consequences it may have. And this must be done before it is too late.

We know that some leaders still view the world as their domain and declare their 'vital interests' wherever they like. This stimulates the arms race because such views result from a policy of strength designed for political and economic domination. This is the ingrained, antiquated mentality of the time when it was considered 'right' to exploit other peoples, manage their resources and decide their destinies.

These views lead to new regional conflicts and incite hatred. Such conflicts assume dangerous proportions, involving more and more countries as their interests are affected directly or indirectly. Regional conflicts have a very negative impact on international relations as a whole. People are being killed in wars declared and undeclared, at the front and in the rear. Countries suffering from abject poverty and mass hunger are being drawn into a wasteful arms race.

Settlement of regional conflicts is a dictate of our time. And our initiatives on the Middle East may serve as an example of our approach to the problem. It is a major nerve centre on our planet. The interests of many nations, and not only the Arabs and Israel intersect there. It is a crossroads of histories, religions and cultures. Therefore we believe in the need for a very responsible, cautious and even delicate approach. Power politics, piracy and constant threats of force are unacceptable.

We say: let us search and act together. This applies to the Iran-Iraq war, the Central American crisis, the Afghan problem and the situation in the south of Africa and in Indochina. The main thing is to honour the rights of the peoples to decide their own destiny themselves, not to interfere in the internal affairs of other states.

We are against all attempts to artificially destroy historical ties. Yet justice requires regulation of international economic activities so that the rich cannot rob the poor. Can one live content in a world where three-quarters of the countries are deep in debt, while a handful of states are omnipotent usurers? If the situation does not change there will be a social explosion that could destroy modern civilisation.

A fair political settlement of regional conflicts is prompted by the same logic of an interrelated and integral world, logic also requires the solution of other global problems such as food, ecology, energy and worldwide literacy, education and medical care.

Another plight of the modern world is terrorism. It is a great evil. Yet as I have said recently, attempts to wipe it out by state-sponsored terrorism are a still greater crime against humanity. Thie 'method' leads to more deaths and undermines international law and the sovereignty of states, and that's not mentioning moral principles and justice. It creates a vicious circle of violence and bloodshed, and the overall situation deteriorates.

We have already said at the UN and other international forums – and I would like to say it again today – that we are prepared to cooperate with all other countries in fighting every manifestation of terrorism.

All the problems I have spoken of here today are important and with their solution new vistas will open up before human civilisation. Yet their dependence on one another is not identical: without halting the arms race we shall not be able to solve any other problems.

The Soviet Union and the Soviet people consider themselves part of an international community. The worries of all mankind are our worries, its pain is our pain and its hopes are our hopes.

With all the differences between us, we must all learn to preserve our one big family of humanity.

At our meeting in Geneva, the US President said that if the earth faced an invasion by extraterrestrials, the US and the Soviet Union would join forces to repel such an invasion. I shall not dispute the hypothesis, though I think it's early days to worry about such an intrusion. It is more important to think about the troubles which have entered our common home. It is more important to realise the need to eliminate the nuclear threat and accept that there is no roof on earth or in space to save us if a nuclear storm broke out.

Our idea of creating a comprehensive system of international security, and our other initiatives clearly show that the Soviet Union is willing and ready to renounce its nuclear power status and reduce all other armaments to a bare essential.

The USSR does not want anything it would deny others and does not seek even an ounce more security that the US has. However the Soviet Union will never agree to an abridged status or discrimination.

Look at all our proposals. They don't mean leaving any of our weapons outside negotiations. Our principle is simple: all weapons must be limited and reduced, and those of wholesale annihilation eventually scrapped. Should we have any balance to redress, we must redress it not by letting the one short of some elements build them up, but by having the one with more of them scale them down. The historic goal before us, that of a demilitarised world, will have to be achieved stage by stage, of course. In each phase, there must definitely be respect for mutual interests and a balance of reasonable sufficiency constantly declining. Everybody must realise and agree: parity in a potential to destroy one another several times over is madness and absurdity.

It is important, in our view, while scaling down military confrontation, to carry through such measures as would make it possible to lessen, or better still, altogether exclude the possibility of a surprise attack. The most dangerous offensive arms must be removed from the zone of contact. Quite naturally, military doctrines must be purely of a defensive nature.

I have already had occasion to say that now that we are coming to consider major measures for actual disarmament affecting the most sensitive area of national security, the Soviet Union will be pressing for the most stringent system of supervision and verification, including international verification There must be complete certainty that the commitments are honoured by all. Couldn't we take the Soviet-US experiment at Semipalatinsk as a prototype of such supervision?

There is yet another aspect to note as far as verification goes. It is common knowledge that the US has numerous military bases on the territory of other countries. We would like to have an inspection access to them to be sure that there is no activity going on there that is forbidden under any eventual agreement. In this sense there will apparently have to be cooperation of the states that host those bases.

Of course it will be better still to revive the old idea of dismantling foreign bases and bring the troops stationed there back home. We apply this to ourselves, too. We have already taken the first practical steps. As you know we are withdrawing some of our forces from the Mongolian People's Republic, upon agreement with our Mongolian friends. We have brought six regiments back from Afghanistan, and we shall pull out the whole of our military contingent within time-limits as short as possible. But there has to be reciprocity on the part of the US and Afghanistan's neighbours, as well as international efforts to resolve this problem.

We do not claim to know the ultimate truth. We readily respond to proposals made by other countries, political parties, public movements, and just individuals. The Soviet Union has supported the idea of a nuclear-free corridor for Central Europe, and nuclear-free zones for northern Europe, the Balkans, the South Pacific and other regions. We are ready to hold consultations on each proposal to seek the best version, one that would suit everybody.

A promising and noble idea has been expressed at your forum – that of setting up a 'human survival fund'. Such an institution could be used for open discussion of ways to avert the threat of nuclear war. The fund could encourage research on the burning international issues and contribute towards drafting projects of the problems facing humanity, including combating the latest baneful diseases.

We would welcome active participation by the Soviet public – both material and intellectual – in the activities of such a fund.

I do not doubt that the good seeds your forum has planted will produce a good crop. The forces of militarism – and they are synonymous as often as not with the forces of ignorance and intellectual sterility – are not omnipotent.

The movement of scientists for elimination of the nuclear danger, the passionate and most competent speeches by physicians, environmentalists, personalities engaged in culture and the arts, and the various anti-nuclear groups and associations are all unmistakable evidence of the determination of the sound-minded people everywhere to save the precious gift of life on earth, perhaps the only one in the universe.

I see politics and political sciences represented in this audience. And I am wondering whether we can, with the knowledge and the experience we have today, move step by step towards more balanced and harmonious international relations, and towards an all-embracing system of international security, dependable and equal for all. I think we can and must do that.

I think it was the hope and desire to find a positive answer to this question that have brought you to this forum, too.

Our great scientist, Vladimir Vernadsky warned everybody back in 1922 (just imagine, 65 years ago):

> It will not be long before man gets hold of atomic energy, such a source of power as will give him an opportunity to build a new way of life as he wants . . . Will man be able to use that power for his own good, not for self-destruction? Has he learned to use the power that science will certainly give him? Scientists must not close their eyes to the possible implications of their research effort and of scientific progress. They must feel responsibility for the consequences of their discoveries. They must bind their work to better organisation of all humanity.

Just think that over. At one time, the human ambition, without second thought, was to subdue the forces of nature. Now invading nature without considering al the consequences well in advance might turn it into a deadly enemy of humanity. The Chernobyl accident reminded us of that in a tragedy of relatively local proportions. But the nuclear arms race is inexorably pushing us towards universal tragedy.

For centuries, men have been seeking immortality. It is difficult to accept that every one of us is mortal. But to tolerate the doom of all humanity, of human reason, is just impossible.

Unfortunately many of our generation have grown accustomed to nuclear weapons. Many have come to see them as a kind of idol demanding more and more sacrifices. Some even declare the nuclear arms race a guarantee of peace.

Alas nuclear weaons have gone far towards moulding the image of the times we live in. Naturally, destroying them does not mean going back to what was before. Discarding nuclear deterrence must not give free rein to trigger-happy individuals.

This is by no means an idle issue. Some would say the answer is to upgrade other components of military power: conventional arms. That is a bad and wrong way.

Humanity must get stronger and overcome the nuclear sickness and thus enter the post-nuclear age. It will be immune to violence and attempts to dictate to others. Today international relations are made soulless by the worship of force and the militarisation of mentality. Hence the goal of humanising international relations.

Is that possible? Some believe it is, others think not. No use arguing about it now. I think life will have its way. By and large the peoples are coming to realise that. They already realise that nuclear war must never be fought. So let us take the first big step: cut the nuclear arsenals and keep space weapon-free. Let us start from the vantage-ground of Reykjavik, and then move on. And see how that will affect the international atmosphere. My own feeling is that each such step will make for greater confidence and open fresh vistas for cooperation.

And more democratic thinking at international level, equality, and independent and active participation of all nations, large, medium and small, in the affairs of the world community must help in the process.

To 'humanise' international relations there have to be appropriate actions in the humanitarian field too, notably as regards information, human contacts, professional exchanges and so on. That will halp create moral guarantees for peace and hence contribute towards working out the material guarantees. The information aggression practised by some countries leads not only to mental degradation, but obstructs the normal communication of people of different countries, and cultural inter-enrichment. It breeds ill-feeling and alienation between peoples. On the other hand you must agree that a people that knows and values the culture and art of other peoples can have no ill-feeling towards them.

In view of the rising danger of a new spiral in the arms race and of the drastic exacerbation of regional and what we call global problems, we must waste no more time trying to outplay each other and to gain unilateral advantages. The stake in such a game is too high – the survival of humanity. Therefore it is now vital to take the critical factor of time into account.

So let the ideas of this forum reach every corner on earth, hasten enlightenment and broaden mutual understanding. Let your efforts help the advance towards a nuclear-weapon-free and non-violent world – for the sake of the immortality of human civilisation.

Part 2
The Renewal of Socialism

8

Renewing the Soviet Economy

As you know, comrades, the decisions of the April plenary meeting of the Central Committee have been received with great approval by the Communists, the entire Soviet people. This is seen from the results of work of the plenary meetings of the Party committees and the numerous comments sent to the central bodies. The working people are showing everywhere increased concern for the affairs of the state and the society, expressing the wish to advance persistently, to unfold the struggle even more actively for strengthening order in all fields of our life, to be firm and consistent in that effort. In a word, a good, businesslike atmosphere is shaping in Party organisations, work collectives and the country as a whole.

Drawing on the experience of building socialism, the achievements of the Soviet economy and the science-based elaboration of the CPSU's strategy for a long term, the April plenary meeting formulated the concept of accelerating the country's socioeconomic development on the basis of scientific-technical progress.

The decision of the Political Bureau of the Central Committee to hold this meeting in advance of the 27th Congress of the CPSU is motivated by the need for taking urgent measures in that field.

In putting forward the task of accelerating socioeconomic development the Central Committee bears in mind not just an increase in the economic growth rates. The point at issue is a new quality of our development, rapid progress in the strategically important directions, a structural rebuilding of production, switching to intensive methods, effective forms of management, a still fuller solution of social problems.

The need to accelerate socioeconomic development is determined by our internal requirements. We have much to be proud of in the development of the economy. Thousands of plants have been built in this country, the

Report at a Meeting on Questions of Scientific and Technical Progress, 11 June 1985 (abridged)

appearance of our cities and villages has changed, the standards of culture, education and health protection have improved. Much has been done to improve the housing, cultural and everyday conditions of life and the material wellbeing of the people in general. This is another graphic manifestation of the advantages of socialism, of its planned economy. Our successes are indisputable; they have been generally recognised.

Yet it is obvious that since the early 1970s certain difficulties arose in economic development. The main reason is that we did not display in time perseverance in reshaping the structural policy, the forms and methods of management, the very psychology of economic activity.

The Party, the whole people, are faced with the task of overcoming the negative trends, ensuring a sharp turn of things for the better. A different approach is out of the question, since we cannot embark on curtailing the social programmes. Society is faced with the urgent tasks of improving the food supply, increasing the output of commodities and services for the people. It is important to build housing further on a large scale, perfect medical services, develop education, science and culture.

At the same time, the need to accelerate socioeconomic development stems from external circumstances. We are forced to invest the necessary funds in the country's defence. The Soviet Union will further make every effort to put an end to the arms race, but in the face of imperialism's aggressive policy and threats we must not permit military superiority over ourselves. Such is the will of the Soviet people.

In the eyes of the progressive public of the world the Soviet Union has been and remains an embodiment of age-old social hopes of people. Its economy must also be an example of the highest organisational standards and effectiveness. Thus the task of accelerating the country's development has assumed today paramount political, economic and social significance. Its translation into life is an urgent matter of the whole party and of the whole people.

Now that the party is approaching its 27th Congress, and that the programme documents of the Congress are being prepared, it is important to realise that we cannot do without accelerating scientific-technical progress. Therefore all of these documents, above all the guidelines for the country's economic and social development for the twelfth five-year-plan period and up to the year 2000, must contain new approaches to ensure a sharp turn towards the intensification of the economy.

The Political Bureau of the Central Committee has recently discussed the draft of the guidelines and has on the whole supported the target figures and objectives outlined in it. Yet serious criticism was expressed, which necessitates that work on the draft be continued. For a number of industries the draft must include measures ensuring a transition to predominantly intensive growth and the balancing of all indicators. Work on the draft must be continued, and the target figures of increasing the effectiveness of production should be viewed as minimum ones.

The main thing now is to find and commit to action all reserves of increasing the effectiveness of production and improving the quality of products. Our cadres should understand the vital need for reorienting every plant, branch, the whole national economy, towards an intensive way of development.

Many senior officials of ministries wish to 'secure' as much capital investment and resources as possible for smaller plan targets. An enviable persistance in an effort to get additional funds and have the plan target figures reduced is shown by K.N. Belyak, Minister of Machine-Building for Livestock Farming and Fodder Production. No better stand was taken by the USSR Ministry of the Building Materials Industry headed by A.I. Yashin, and some other ministries and departments. I think that we are not fellow-travellers of those executives who hope to draw the country again into vast, unjustified spending.

(*Then Mikhail Gorbachov dwelt in detail on problems of transforming the investment and structural policy. The main emphasis shall be laid on the technical re-equipment of plants, saving of resources and ensuring a drastic improvement in the quality of products.*)

It is important to give up without hesitation the economic management stereotype which was shaped in the past, according to which new construction was considered to be the main method of expanding production, while many operating plans were not modernised for many years. As they say, everything possible was squeezed out, while very little was put in.

Today a considerable part of the production assets has become obsolete, as a result of which the sphere of overhaul has excessively swelled. The return on assets decreases, the number of new work places grows, but at the same time mechanisation of production is introduced insufficiently. The share of manual labour decreases slowly.

No one disputes today that capital investments for reconstruction yield a return approximately twice as great as that in new construction. But the former extensive methods of economic management are unfortunately very tenacious. Fifty billion roubles of capital investments were allocated, for instance, for the iron and steel industry over 15 years. Most of them were channelled into new, non-integrated construction, whereas no attention was given to the technical re-equipment of enterprises. Because of the wrong technical policy of the collegium of the iron and steel ministry and of Minister I.P. Kazanets this industry failed to fulfil the assignments of both the tenth and eleventh five-year plans. The state of affairs here requires cardinal changes.

On the country-wide scale the share of funds channelled into reconstruction in the overall volume of capital investments should be raised from one-third to at least a half already within the next few years. This is not a simple thing. We cannot do without new construction. But projects under construction should be given serious consideration: some of them should be speeded up, others suspended or even mothballed.

At the same time a general stocktaking of production assets should be carried out and a programme drawn up for the reconstruction of every enterprise, every industry. The share of withdrawal of outdated fixed assets, especially of their active part, should be doubled. And it should be emphasised that what is needed is not just any modernisation of production but the kind that involves the introduction of the most advanced technology and has the greatest economic and social effect.

The ratio between capital investments into resource-extracting, processing and consuming industries is a big and acute problem. It is becoming ever more difficult to increase the output of fuel and raw materials. But there is a more rational way, that of all-out economy and a wide introduction of resource-saving technologies. The costs are thus cut in half or to one-third. The Ministry of the Electro-Techinical Industry, for instance, has gained some positive experience in saving resources. As a result the growth of output in this industry in the eleventh five-year-plan period is achieved without increasing the consumption of basic materials.

On the whole our economy remains in many respects an extravagant one. Up to 8 million tons of petrol are unnecessarily burned up every year due to the lag in the conversion of the truck fleet to diesel engines. Because of the imperfection of equipment at thermal power stations we annually overspend more than 20 million tons of reference fuel. There are hundreds of thousands of primitive boiler rooms in this country which are using fuel irrationally. Secondary resources are used poorly. Meantime, resource-saving should be one of the main directions of investment policy. The task is to meet 75-80 per cent of the increment in the requirements of the national economy in fuel, raw and other materials through saving.

Serious consideration, consistency and the need for achieving a quick economic effect are very important in investment policy. Of course a certain order of priorities is inevitable in carrying out these or those measures. But once we have set some tasks they should be solved fully, comprehensively, quickly and energetically. We should not allow capital investments to be spread out thinly according to the principle 'earrings for all sisters'. In the new five-year-plan period we should more resolutely concentrate capital investments in the most economical directions. This refers, for instance, to the agroindustrial complex, where the level of capital investments has reached optimum dimensions while the return from them is so far insufficient.

Machine-building is playing the main, key part in the scientific-technical revolution. Already in the twelfth five-year-plan period its growth rate should be raised by 50-100 per cent. The task is to make maximum use of the available capacities and to modernise this industry as a matter of top priority. For this purpose capital investments in machine-building should be increased, through partial redistribution, by 80-100 per cent and the volumes of supply of modern types of equipment sharply raised.

A task of special importance is to start the mass production of equipment of new generations capable of assuring a many-fold increase in labour productivity and opening the way to the automation of all stages of the production process. It is important to change over to the supply of complete sets of equipment, to organise on a large-scale repair and maintenance service by manufacturers.

Microelectronics, computers and instrument-making and the entire industry of information science act as catalysts of technical progress. They need to be developed at an accelerated pace. No doubt a great deal depends not only on increasing the output of electronic computers but also on a competent use of such computers in the national economy. We have taken major decisions on this score and their fulfilment should be strictly controlled.

In short the task of boosting the Soviet machine-building industry is the highway of our development. A highway that should be firmly followed now and in the future.

The state of affairs in capital construction should also be assessed from the positions of the acceleration of scientific and technical progress. This problem has been on the order of the day for many years but no cardinal improvement has yet occurred here. This reduces to naught in many ways our efforts in the field of scientific and technical progress.

Ineffective tecnological solutions are often provided for in the project designs. Therefore a sizeable portion of them have to be yearly returned for a revision. There is a continued fragmentation of capital investments and the time limits of construction work are incredibly prolonged. As a result even the finest projects become hopelessly outdated. We cannot build this way any longer. It is necessary to establish better order in planning and design construction to ensure a concentration of capital investments, observance of normative time limits for the completion of construction projects, and to make construction work a single industrial process.

The efficiency of the national economy and our growth rates depend in many ways on the structure and quality of materials. In this matter we are so far behind modern requirements. It is known, for instance, that we produce more steel that any other country and yet we are chronically short of metal. The main reasons for this are insufficiently good quality, a limited range of products and, of course, squandering of metal. The share of plastics, ceramics and other advanced non-metallic materials in the overall volume is so far small. In the world today there is a real boom of small-tonnage chemistry and of the production of pure and super-pure materials which determine in many respects the level of present-day technology. Therefore it is necessary to double or treble our efforts to prevent ourselves from falling behind.

The problems of the production infrastructure have come to the fore at the present stage of economic development. The lag of transport, communications, material and technical supplies and other branches leads to great losses. It is necessary to find additional opportunities for solving this acute problem of the national economy.

The tasks of scientific and technological progress require us to take a new approach to all our external economic activities. The country's foreign trade has reached 140 billion roubles. But the rates of its growth can and must be speeded up and, what is most important, the character of our exports and imports should be made more advanced.

Our exports of machinery and equipment have been growing slowly in recent years. There are several reasons for this: both low competitiveness of many of them and insufficient interest on the part of the plants in working for export. We must not put up with this any longer. It is necessary in import policy to use more effectively the opportunities offered by the mutually beneficial international division of labour. This refers, of course, in the first place, to our relations with the CMEA countries.

Then there is the urgent question of the need for establishing better order in the use of imported equipment. As an example of a careless attitude to it mention was made of the work of the Ministry of the Petrochemical Industry of the USSR. Minister V.S. Fyodorov gave assurances more than once that he would rectify his shortcomings. But evidently he does not keep his promises. The CPSU Central Committee has given instructions that the matter should be thoroughly inquired into and the results of inquiry reported to the Political Bureau.

The new technical reconstruction of the national economy will require enormous capital investments.

Where to get them? The principled answer to this question is: the measures planned to speed up scientific and technical progress should recoup themselves. Indeed they are being carried out for the purpose of raising labour productivity and hence speeding up the growth of the national income. But this will take some time, while the funds are needed immediately. So we cannot do here without manoeuvring with resources, concentrating them in key directions.

The top-priority task is to mobilise organisational, economic and social factors, to introduce order in everything, to improve the organisation of production so as to ensure the best utilisation of what the country has. At each amalgamation and enterprise, at each production unit it is necessary to identify the sections where it is possible to obtain the maximum effect for the least outlay, and perhaps without any outlay at all.

It should be firmly established in the mind of every Soviet person that the regime of economy is the road to our wealth and is really the task of all tasks. This is a task of the entire party, of the entire people.

A certain shift towards an improvement of the quality of output, which is the most precise and comprehensive indicator of scientific and technological progress, of the culture and discipline of labour, has taken place in recent years. But one must admit that the quality, the technical and economic standard of products remains a vulnerable element of the economy, a source of many difficulties and problems. All this inflicts serious social, economic, moral and political damage. And it is totally impermissible when newly created equipment turns out to be morally obsolete already at the stage of designing, is inferior to the best standards of reliability, service life and efficiency. By their parameters even products referred to the highest category sometimes compare badly with the best world models. There must be stricter observance of the requirements that are to be met when the state quality mark is awarded to a product. Quality of output should be a matter not only of professional but also of national pride.

The problem of quality, of course, cannot be solved at a single go. But in this work there can be no justification for any procrastination whatsoever. Nobody has the right to remain on the sidelines here – not a single enterprise, not a single designer, production engineer or scientist, not a single worker or collective farmer; in short, not a single honest wage and salary earner. The Party will actively support the struggle for the prestige of the Soviet trade mark and will strictly call to account those who take a passive stand, who put brakes on the solution of this very acute problem.

The frontline of struggle to accelerate scientific and technological progress passes through science. We can be proud of our achievements in space research, mathematics and mechanics, thermonuclear synthesis, quantum electronics and a number of fields of biology. There are very promising development studies along almost every direction of science and technology.

At the same time we must look at the tasks of science through the prism of present-day requirements – requirements that it make a resolute turn towards the needs of social production, while production should turn towards science. It is from these positions that we must analyse and consolidate all the links of the chain combining science, technology and production.

The development of fundamental science should be given priority. It is this science that is a generator of ideas, makes possible breakthroughs into new fields and shows ways of reaching new levels of efficiency. Here we must raise the role of the Academy of Sciences of the USSR. We must sharply turn the Academy's institutes towards expanding research in specific technical directions, enhance their role in and responsibility for the formulation of the theoretical mainstays of fundamentally new types of machinery and technology. The scientific potential of universities and institutes is an important reserve and we are not yet making full use of the possibilities afforded by it. According to existing estimates, establishments of higher education are capable of increasing the volume of research conducted by them by 100-150 per cent.

Exacting demands should be made of the research establishments of the various ministries. Their performance gives rise to serious complaints. Hundreds of research establishments, development and design organisations are subordinated to the industrial ministries. Many of them are isolated from production and are not geared to the attainment of high economic results. The Ministry of the Chemical Industry, for instance, is literally overgrown with a multitude of various scientific establishments and experimental production facilities.

But it is exactly in that industry that major shortcomings have been uncovered in the development of new materials and technologies. The report cites concrete examples of shoddy work by some of the ministerial research institutes.

We aim to perfect the organisational and economic forms of the integration of science, technology and production. For example the creation of comprehensive inter-branch scientific-technical centres within the framework of the Academy of Sciences of the USSR is very effective. Here we draw on the experience of the Y.O. Paton Institute of Electric Welding and other scientific institutions.

In order to overcome the isolation of institutes, development and design organisations from production we should already now make many of them a part of amalgamations and enterprises, thus strengthening the research potential at plant level. It is very important to impart a new impulse to the entire work to expand the network of big research-and-production amalgamations, which should become real advanced posts of scientific and technological progress, as 'Kriogenmash', 'Svetlana' and many other such amalgamations have already become.

While giving priority attention to the strengthening of big research and technical organisations we must at the same time give vigorous support to the work of inventors and innovators, find forms of selecting important technical proposals and ensuring their speediest introduction in production.

Much will have to be done for research and technical development to yield a speedy and weighty economic result. The CPSU Central Committee and the Soviet government hope that the country's scientists, the entire scientific-technical intelligentsia will take to heart the tasks set forth by the Party and will spare no effort in accelerating scientific and technological progress.

Life demands a profound restructuring of planning and management of the entire economic mechanism. In principle we clearly see the main direction of restructuring economic management. It is to ensure a deeper and all-round utilisation of the advantages of the socialist economy. We must advance along the line of further consolidating and developing democratic centralism. The fundamental essence of the restructuring is to raise the efficiency of centralism in mangement and planning, to expand the independence and responsibility of enterprises, to make vigorous use of more flexible forms and methods of management, cost-accounting and commodity-monetary relations, extensively to develop the initiative of the masses.

We should make the economy responsive to scientific-technical progress to the maximum, and ensure that all sections of the economy have a vital stake in that. The Party and economic bodies work vigorously to resolve these problems. Ever new branches are joining in the large-scale economic experiment. But it is necessary to go over from it to the creation of an integral management and control system.

It is necessary to start from the upper echelons. We wil have to implement in practice Lenin's idea of turning the State Planning Committee into a scientific-economic body employing prominent scientists and leading specialists. A leading place in the plans should be given to qualitative indicators reflecting the effectiveness of the use of resources, the scale of renewal of output and growth of labour productivity on the basis of scientific-technical progress.

The Central Committee of the CPSU is being sent numerous proposals on the place and role of the State Committee for Science and Technology. The objective is that the latter be made responsible for exercising control over the scientific-technical standard of the branches of the economy, the correspondence of production to the best achievements, the formation of the network of research institutions and design organisations, and for the coordination of scientific-technical activities in the country.

The main reserves for the attainment of the highest effectiveness are to be found where the branches overlap. To hope that the State Planning committee will be able to look into all the links of the chain of inter-branch interconnections and choose the optimum variant means to indulge in illusion. Neither can the ministries cope with this work. All this places on the order of the day the question of creating bodies for the management of big economic complexes. The role and functions of the ministries should change in the new conditions. They will be able to concentrate their maximum attention on long-term planning, large-scale use of innovations for raising the technical standard of production and products. The administrative staff in the branches of the economy must be reduced considerably and its redundant links removed.

Much has to be done to perfect the structure of the republican management bodies, where the number of ministries and departments is far too great and continues growing. There the problem of integration and concentration of management is even more serious than on the national level.

The role of the main production link – amalgamations and plants – shall be enhanced in order to accelerate scientific-technical progress.

It is necessary to shift to them the centre of gravity of the entire day-to-day economic work, and subordinate them, as a rule, directly to the ministries. The work to be done is not that of 'patching up holes', not simply of merging or splitting organisations, of moving executives from one office into another. The questions pertaining to the perfection of the organisational structure must be resolved boldly, with good substantiation and, what is the main thing, in a comprehensive, and only in a comprehensive manner, from the upper to the lower echelons, both vertically and horizontally.

Restructuring of the organisational pattern of management should be organically tied in with strengthening of the principle of cost-accounting, economic levers and incentives. We need a mechanism genuinely ensuring advantages for work collectives which achieve successes in speeding up scientific and technical progress. We need a mechanism that would make the output of outdated and ineffective products unprofitable. With these aims in view it is necessary, first of all, to take steps increasing the consumer's influence on the technical level and quality of products. Price information should be radically improved to facilitate a successful implementation of economic policy and a rapid introduction of everything new and advanced.

It is necessary to put de facto amalgamations and enterprises fully on a cost-accounting basis, to reduce sharply the number of centrally set plan assignments. It is known to happen, not infrequently, that ministries and even All-Union production amalgamations include many unnecessary indices in the plans. It is time we established a legislative order here. The activities of enterprises should be regulated more and more by economic norms.

Amalgamations and enterprises should be given an opportunity of earning themselves the means needed for raising the technical level of production and the quality of products, for social development and for using these funds at their own discretion and widely drawing on credits. It is very important to establish a close dependence between the performance of work collectives and remuneration of their work. There must be a direct connection between the two. It is important to extend more boldly the principles of the collective contract to the work of amalgamations and enterprises and actively set up enlarged complex teams working on the basis of cost accounting.

Everything outdated must be removed so that the 'cost-conscious economic mechanism', so to say, could operate unimpeded and rap inefficient economic executives over the knuckles – those anxious to secure maximum resources and capital investments from the state and give as little as possible to society.

In short, there is some very serious work ahead to improve the system of economic management. This work cannot be put off because we cannot speed up scientific and technical progress in the real way without creating new economic and organisational conditions.

This task, one of great magnitude, creates the need for deep-going changes in Party work. This work, M.S. Gorbachyov said, has to deal with the human factor, the decisive factor of all changes. The main task of this work today is to bring about by all means a change in the minds and moods of personnel from top to bottom, by concentrating their attention on the most important thing – scientific and technical progress. The present situation calls for diligence and determination on the part of Communists. Life itself is the most acid and uncompromising test, one the Party and all the cadres are undergoing today.

This is a question of a long-term political line, and none of the problems we must solve today can be put off till tomorrow. The demands made on our economic cadres should be raised sharply. There must be no delay, no waiting because there is no time left for warming up: it was exhausted by the past. We should move only forward and at an ever greater speed.

Acceleration of scientific and technical progress calls for a cardinal change of the obtaining situation involving engineering, technical and scientific personnel. It is necessary to think over measures to secure greater public recognition of scientific and engineering work, to strengthen creative principles in it, to stimulate a quality fulfilment of work by fewer persons and on this basis to raise the level of their pay.

We must increase Party influence on the whole course of scientific-technical progress and strengthen the Party strata in the decisive sectors. Systematic work for the education and retraining of personnel, above all in the new professions born of progress in technology, is becoming particularly topical.

The causes of many shortcomings and miscalculations lie also in the fact that the Party committees of the ministries have in some places slackened the political keenness in perceiving and resolving the most important socioeconomic issues, have withdrawn from exercising control, to which they have the right under the rules of the CPSU. Such an approach does not accord with the present-day requirements of the country's socioeconomic development.

A vast field of activities – a concrete and responsible one – is also opening in ideological and propaganda work. People should be helped in becoming convinced that the acceleration of scientific-technical progress is a vital cause meeting the interest of all and enabling all to pursue their abilities and talent. We count on the creative vigour and skill of our working class, peasantry, intelligentsia, engineers and scientists. We expect a great deal from young people in particular, their energy and searching minds, interest in all that is new and progressive.

The working people of the country are faced with the important task of successfully completing the current year and the five-year-plan period as a whole. It is important for the Party organisations to ensure in every way an increase in the production of fuel and other raw materials for industry, to organise timely and high-quality agricultural work, to harvest and preserve the whole of the crop. The point is that the country should enter the new five-year-plan period having the backing of good performance and in an organised manner.

The business at hand is formidable; it is innovative, has possibilities and is difficult. Will we be able to cope with it? The Central Committee is confident that we will. We are obliged to do it. But this will require of each of us intensive thought, determined work, immense concentration, consciousness and organisation. It is not in the Party's traditions, not in the character of the Soviet people to fear the complexity of tasks, to retreat before difficulties, to slacken our efforts and indulge in complacency, especially at turning points, at responsible moments in the country's life.

When the Soviet republic was making the first steps towards socialism in a terribly difficult situation, Lenin wrote with confidence: 'we will extricate ourselves because we do not try to make our position look better than it is. We realise all the difficulties. We see all the maladies, and are taking measures to cure them methodically, with perseverance, and without giving way to panic.'

Today, too, profound faith in the creative energy of the workers, peasants and intellectuals, in the high moral spirit and determination of the people nourishes the Party's optimism. But optimism does not free anybody of the need to work. We will have to work a lot. The CPSU's policy is vigorously supported by the entire society. Soviet people pin great hopes on the ideas, initiatives and plans with which the Party is approaching its 27th Congress.

It is the duty of the Party of Communists to justify these hopes, to show that we are tackling the job in earnest. Relying on the people's creative endeavour and cementing the alliance of science and labour we will have enough energy and firmess to see to it that words are matched by deeds. And this is the main thing in politics, in life.

9

On Socialist Democracy

Comrades,

The 27th Party Congress vested in us, the members of the Central Committee, an immense responsibility – to implement the strategic course of accelerating the socioeconomic development of the country. The Political Bureau understands the situation and the role of the Central Committee at the current stage in the life of Soviet society precisely in this way.

Proceeding from this, the plenary meeting has put on its agenda a matter of paramount importance for the effective implementation of the political strategy drafted by the April 1985 plenary meeting of the Central Committee and the 27th CPSU Congress – the question of reorganisation and the Party's personnel policy. We should consider it in a broad social and political context, with due regard for the lessons of the past, the nature of the current moment and the tasks of the future.

The April plenary meeting and the 27th Party Congress prepared the ground for an objective critical analysis of the situation in society and took decisions of historic importance for the country's future. We have begun reorganisation and will not look back. The first steps on that road have been taken.

Drawing an overall political conclusion, we can say with confidence that major changes are taking place in the life of Soviet society and that positive tendencies are gaining momentum.

Before the plenary meeting I myself and other Political Bureau members and central committee secretaries had many meetings and conversations with members of the Central Committee, public figures, workers, collective farmers, intellectuals, veterans and young people. The overall tenor and meaning of what they had to say was unambiguous: the policies for renovating our society should be firmly pursued and effort redoubled in every area.

Report and Concluding Speech at the Plenary Meeting of the CPSU Central Committee 27–28 January 1987

The Central Committee finds it significant that the policies of the 27th Congress, the practical efforts to implement them and reorganisation itself have been broadly supported by working people and the entire Soviet people. This, comrades, is the most important thing for a ruling party.

At the same time, however, we see that the change for the better is taking place slowly, that the business of reorganisation is more difficult and the problems which have accumulated in society are more deep-rooted than we first thought. The further we go with our reorganisation work, the clearer its scope and significance become; more and more unresolved problems inherited from the past crop up.

The main evaluations of the state of society and the conclusions drawn from them by the Political Bureau have already been presented to the 27th Party Congress and plenary meetings of the Central Committee. They have been fully corroborated. But today we know more, that is why there is a need to examine once again and in detail the sources of the obtaining situation and to sort out the reasons for what took place in the country in the late 1970s and early 1980s.

This analysis is necessary to prevent mistakes from recurring and to fulfil the resolutions of the Congress on which the future of our people and the destiny of socialism depend. It is all the more important since there is still some misunderstanding in society and in the Party of the complexity of the situation in which the country has found itself. Perhaps this also explains questions from some comrades about the measures that are being taken by the Political Bureau and the government in the course of reorganisation. We are often asked if we are not taking too sharp a turn.

We need to be absolutely clear on all the vital issues, including this one. Only a deep understanding of the situation can enable us to find correct solutions to the complex tasks.

By and large, comrades, there is an urgent need to return to an analysis of those problems which confronted the Party and Soviet society in the few years before the April 1985 plenary meeting of the CPSU Central Committee. The experience of the past 18 months has bolstered our resolve to deepen that analysis, to comprehend the causes of adverse processes and to work out measures to accelerate our progress, to keep us from repeating mistakes and to allow us only to advance, proving in practice socialism's organic ability to continuously renovate itself.

The Political Bureau believes that on the basis of this approach we should hold this plenary meeting.

Reorganisation is an objective necessity
Our plenary meeting is taking place in the year of the seventieth anniversary of the Great October Socialist Revolution. Almost seven decades ago the Leninist Party raised over the country the victorious banner of socialist revolution, of struggle for socialism, freedom, equality, social justice and

social progress and against oppression and exploitation, poverty and national discrimination.

For the first time in world history the working man and his interests and needs were made the focal point of state policy. The Soviet Union achieved truly historic successes in political, economic, social, cultural and intellectual development as it built socialist society. Under the leadership of the Party the Soviet people built socialism, achieved victory over Nazism in the Great Patriotic War, rehabilitated and strengthened the national economy and made their homeland a mighty power.

Our achievements are immense and indubitable and the Soviet people by right take pride in their successes. They constitute a firm base for the fulfilment of our current programmes and our plans for the future. But the Party must see life in its entirety and complexity. No accomplishments, even the most impressive ones, should obscure either contradictions in social development or our mistakes and failings.

We talked about all that and must repeat again today that at some point the country began to lose momentum, difficulties and unresolved problems started to pile up, and there appeared elements of stagnation and other phenomena alien to socialism. All that had a most adverse effect on the economy and social, cultural and intellectual life.

Of course, comrades, the country did not cease to develop. Tens of millions of Soviet people were working honestly and many Party organisations and our personnel were working actively in the interests of the people. All that held back the intensification of negative processes but could not avert them altogether.

A need for change was ripening in the economy and other fields – but it did not materialise in the political and practical work of the Party and the state.

What was the reason for that complex and controversial situation?

The main cause – and the Political Bureau considers it necessary to say so with the utmost frankness at the plenary meeting – was that the CPSU Central Committee and the leadership of the country failed, primarily for subjective reasons, to see in time and in full the need for change and the dangerous growth of crisis phenomena in society, and to formulate a clear-cut policy for overcoming them and making better use of the possibilities intrinsic to the socialist system.

A conservative outlook, inertia, a tendency to brush aside all that did not fit into conventional patterns, and an unwillingness to come to grips with outstanding socioeconomic problems prevailed in policy-making and practical work.

Comrades, the leading bodies of the Party and the state bear responsibility for all this.

The extent to which vital problems and contradictions and social tendencies and prospects were understood in many ways depended on the condition and progress of theory, on the atmosphere on the theoretical front.

Lenin's instruction that the value of a theory consists in its providing an exact picture 'of all the contradictions that are present in reality' was often simply ignored. The theoretical concepts of socialism had remained largely unchanged since the 1930s and 1940s, when the tasks being tackled by society were entirely different. Developing socialism, the dialectics of its motive forces and contradictions and the actual condition of society did not become the subject of in-depth scientific research.

The causes of this go way back and are rooted in that specific historical situation in which, because of circumstances that are well known, lively debates and creative ideas disappeared from theory and the social sciences while authoritarian evaluations and opinions became unquestionable truths, that could only be commented upon.

The practical forms of society's organisation became absolutised in a way. Moreover, such ideas were actually equated with the essential characteristics of socialism, viewed as immutable and presented as dogmas that left no room for an objective scientific analysis. An ossified concept of socialist relations of production appeared, and their dialectical interaction with the productive forces was underestimated. The social structure of society was viewed schematically, without the contradictions and dynamism of the various interests of its different strata and groups.

Lenin's ideas of socialism were interpreted simplistically and their theoretical depth and significance were often emaciated. This was true of such key problems as public ownership, relations between classes and nationalities, the measure of work and the measure of consumption, cooperation, methods of economic management, people's rule and self-government, struggle against bureaucratic abuses, the revolutionary transforming character of socialist ideology, the principles of education and upbringing, and guarantees for the healthy development of the Party and society.

Spurious ideas of Communism and various prophecies and abstract views gained some credibility, which detracted from the historical significance of socialism and from the influence of socialist ideology.

This attitude to theory could not but have an adverse effect – and it did have one – on the social sciences and their role in society. It is a fact, comrades, that all manner of scholastic theorising, which had nothing to do with anyone's interests or vital problems, were often even encouraged in the country, while attempts to make a constructive analysis and formulate new ideas were given no support.

This situation concerning theory had adversely affected the solution of practical problems. Outdated methods were perpetuated in the practice of management for decades, while some efficient economic forms, on the other hand, were groundlessly rejected. At the same time relations that did not correspond to society's actual level of maturity and that sometimes came into conflict with its nature were being fostered in production and distribution. Production and labour incentives were actually oriented to quantitative, extensive growth.

Special mention should be made of socialist property. Control over those who managed it and how had slackened. Departmental and parochial attitudes eroded socialist property, it became 'no one's', free, belonging to no real owner, and in many cases was used to derive unearned income.

There was an incorrect attitude to cooperative property, which was viewed as something 'second-rate' and having no future. All this had grievous consequences for agrarian and social policies, bred management by injunction in relations with collective farms and resulted in the abolition of producer cooperatives. There were also grave misconceptions about personal subsidiary holding and individual labour, which did much economic and social harm as well.

Serious discrepancies kept piling up in planning. The authority of the plan as the main tool of economic policy was being subverted by subjective approaches, imbalances, instability, the striving to embrace everything down to trifles, and a host of sectoral and regional decisions, taken in circumvention of the plan and often without due regard for real possibilities. Plans were often short of scientific substantiation; they did not aim at outlining national economic proportions, proper care for the development of the social sphere and the accomplishment of many strategic tasks.

As a consequence the huge advantage offered by the socialist economic system, primarily its planned character, was used inefficiently. In this situation irresponsibility took root, and diverse bureaucratic rules and instructions were devised. Day-to-day practical activity was supplanted by decree-making, a show of efficiency and mountains of paperwork.

Misconceptions about the role of monetary-commodity relations and the operation of the law of value, and sometimes their direct opposition to socialism as something alien to it, led voluntarist attitudes in the economy, to an underestimation of profit and loss accountability and to wage levelling, and bred subjective approaches to price formation, imbalances in money circulation and disregard for the regulation of demand and supply.

Restrictions of the rights of enterprises and associations in the use of profit and loss accountability principles had especially grave consequences. They undermined the foundations of material incentive, blocked the achievement of high end results, and led to a lowering of the people's labour and social activity and to a slackening of discipline and order.

In fact a whole system that weakened the economic tools of government emerged and a mechanism that slowed socioeconomic development and hindered the progressive transformations which make it possible to tap and use the advantages of socialism. That retarding process was rooted in serious shortcomings in the functioning of the institutions of socialist democracy, outdated political and theoretical concepts, which often did not correspond to reality, and in the conservative managerial mechanism.

All that, comrades, adversely affected the development of many spheres in the life of society. Take material production. The growth rates of the national income in the past three five-year plan periods dropped by more than half. From the early 1970s most plan targets were not met. The economy as a whole became cumbersome and little responsive to innovation. The quality of a considerable part of the output no longer met the current requirements, and imbalances in production were aggravated.

Attention to the development of engineering was slackened. Research and development work fell behind the needs of the national economy and did not meet the modernisation demands. Purchases of equipment and many other commodities on the capitalist market were excessive and far from always justified.

Negative processes seriously affected the social sphere. The 27th Party Congress has already appraised its condition. The social goals of the economy in the past few five-year plan periods were obviously diluted and there emerged a sort of deafness to social issues. We see today what all this has led to. Having successfully resolved the employment question and provided basic social guarantees, we at the same time failed to fully realise the potential of socialism for improving housing, food supply, transport, health care and education, and for solving other vital problems.

There were violations of the most important principle of socialism: distribution according to work. Struggle against unearned income was not determined enough. The policy of providing material and moral incentives for efficient work was inconsistent. Large, unjustified bonuses and fringe benefits were paid and figure-padding for profit took place. Parasitic sentiments grew stronger and the mentality of wage levelling began to take hold. All that hit those workers who could and wanted to work better, while making life easier for the lazy ones.

Violation of the organic relationship between the measure of work and the measure of consumption not only warps the attitude to work, holding back the growth of productivity, but also leads to distortion of the principle of social justice – and that is a question of great political importance.

Elements of social corrosion that emerged in recent years have adversely affected society's morale and insidiously eroded the high moral values which have always been characteristic of our people and of which we are proud, namely, ideological conviction, labour enthusiasm and Soviet patriotism.

As an inevitable consequence of all this, interest in the affairs of society slackened, signs of amorality and scepticism appeared and the role of moral incentives in work declined. The section of people, including youth, whose ultimate goal in life was material wellbeing and gain by any means, grew wider. Their cynical stand acquired more and more aggressive forms, poisoned the mentality of those around them and triggered a wave of consumerism. The spread of alcohol and drug abuse and a rise in crime witnessed the decline of social mores.

Disregard for laws, report-padding, bribe-taking and encouragement of toadyism and adulation had a deleterious effect on the moral atmosphere in society. Real care for people, for the conditions of their life and work and for their social wellbeing was often supplanted by political flirtation – the mass distribution of awards, titles and prizes. An atmosphere of lenience was formed, and standards of discipline and responsibility declined.

Serious shortcomings in ideological and political education in many cases were disguised with ostentatious activities and campaigns and celebrations of numerous jubilees in the centre and in the provinces. The world of day-to-day realities and that of make-believe wellbeing were increasingly parting ways.

The ideology and mentality of stagnation had their impact on culture, literature and the arts. Criteria in appraising creative work were reduced. As a consequence quite a few mediocre, faceless works, which did not give anything to the mind or the heart appeared along with works which raised serious social and ethical problems and reflected real-life collisions. Stereotypes from capitalist mass culture with its propagation of vulgarity, primitive tastes and moral bankruptcy began to infiltrate Soviet society to a greater extent.

I must mention here the responsibility of our ideological agencies, editors of art and literary journals, leaders of creative unions, literary critics, men of letters and workers in the arts for the ideological and artistic orientation of the creative process and for the moral health of the people.

There was a lack of principle, punctiliousness and true care for fostering and encouraging talent in the work of the creative unions. Questions of paramount importance relating to the state of affairs in and the condition of culture often failed to get adequate attention from the leaders of the unions. At the same time red-tape and formalism flourished and utter intolerance of criticism emerged. In some cases excessive ambitions took the upper hand over realistic appraisals and self-appraisals.

The situation was aggravated by the fact that the Party approach to art was often supplanted by unwarranted departmental interference in purely creative processes and by likes and dislikes based on personal preferences, while methods of ideological influence and guidance gave way to administration by decree.

Comrades,

The state of the Party and its personnel also affected the socioeconomic and political situation that took shape in the late 1970s and early 1980s. Leading Party bodies failed to timely and critically appraise the danger of the growing negative tendencies in society and in the conduct of some Communists, and to take decisions which life was imperatively demanding.

Although possessing immense potentialities and acting virtually in all work collectives, many primary Party organisations failed to keep to positions of principle. Not all of them waged a resolute struggle against negative phenomena, permissiveness, mutual cover-up, slackening discipline and the spread of drunkeness. Departmentalism, parochialism and manifestations of nationalism were not always properly rebuffed.

Our Party organisations sometimes lacked a combative spirit, showing laxity towards Party members and not fostering ideological and political qualities in Communists. Meanwhile, high ideological standards, conscientiousness, readiness to subordinate one's personal interests to those of society and selfless service to the people, are the most valuable qualities which were always characteristic of the Bolsheviks.

The situation in the Party was also influenced by the fact that in a number of cases the Party bodies did not attach proper attention to strict compliance with the Leninist principles and norms of Party life. This was especially manifest in breaches of the principles of collective leadership. What I mean is the weakening of the role of Party meetings and elective bodies. This denied Communists the opportunity of energetically contributing to the discussion of vital issues and, in the final analysis, of actually influencing the atmosphere in work collectives and in society as a whole.

The principle of equality between Communists was often violated. Many Party members in positions of leadership were outside of control or criticism. This resulted in failures in work and serious breaches of Party ethics.

We cannot overlook the just indignation of working people at the conduct of those senior officials, vested with trust and authority and called upon to stand guard over the interests of the state and citizens, who abused their authority, suppressed criticism, sought gain, and some of whom even became accomplices in, if not organisers of, criminal activities.

Adverse processes related to the degeneration of personnel and breaches of socialist laws manifested themselves in extremely ugly forms in Uzbekistan, Moldavia, Turkmenia, some regions of Kazakhstan, the Krasnodar Territory, the Rostov Region and also in Moscow and some other cities, regions, territories and republics, and in the systems of the Ministry of Foreign Trade and the Ministry of Internal Affairs.

Naturally Party organisations and the Party as a whole were fighting those phenomena and expelled from the CPSU a considerable number of renegades. Among them were people guilty of embezzlement, bribe-taking and report-padding, people who violated state and Party discipline and indulged in heavy drinking.

The overwhelming majority of those who joined the Party are the best representatives of the working class, collective farmers and intelligentsia. They have been honestly and selflessly performing their Party duty. Yet we should admit that in those years there was no strong barrier put up to stop dishonest, pushing, self-seeking people who were intent on benefiting from their Party membership. We deviated to some extent from the rule that the main thing is not the number of new members but the quality of the Party ranks. This told on the combative spirit of our Party organisations.

Everything said above, comrades, shows how serious the situation has become in different spheres of society and how urgent was the need for deep change. This makes it all the more important to stress once again that the Party found the strength and courage to take a realistic look at and the situation, to recognise the need for drastic changes in policy, in the economy and social, cultural and intellectual fields, and to steer the country on to the road of transformations.

In this situation, comrades, the question of accelerating the socioeconomic development of the county, the question of reorganisation was raised. The case in point is actually a radical turn and measures of a revolutionary character. As we talk about reorganisation and associated processes of deep-going democratisation of society, we mean truly revolutionary and comprehensive transformations in society.

We must make this decisive turn because there is no other choice. We must not retreat and there is no place to retreat to. We must consistently and unswervingly steer the course charted by the April plenary meeting of the Central Committee and the 27th Congress, go further and raise society to a qualitatively new development level.

When starting any social change it is important, as Lenin advised, to see 'how is this change to be explained and what are the limits of its practical application'. Criticism of the past – an important element of progress – makes it possible to draw lessons and conclusions for today and tomorrow and facilitates constructive work in choosing the right ways and means for making headway. We have evolved a scientifically valid strategy of acceleration clearly realising that any rashness or spontaneity in shaping the notions of the future are no less dangerous than inertia and dogmatic distortions.

Today it is essential to say once again what we mean by reorganisation.

Reorganisation is a resolute overcoming of the processes of stagnation, destruction of the retarding mechanism, and the creation of dependable and efficient machinery for expediting the social and economic progress of Soviet society. The main purport of our strategy is to combine the achievements of the scientific and technological revolution with a plan-based economy and set the entire potential of socialism in motion.

Reorganisation is reliance on the creative endeavour of the masses, an all-round extension of democracy and socialist self-government, the encouragement of initiative and self-organised activities, better discipline and order, greater openness, criticism and self-criticism in all fields of public life, and full and proper respect for the value and dignity of the individual.

Reorganisation is the ever greater role of intensive growth factors in Soviet economic development; the reinstatement and enhancement of the Leninist principles of democratic centralism in the management of the national economy; the employment of cost-benefit methods of management everywhere; the renunciation of the domineering style of management and administration by injunction; the transition of all elements of the economy to the principles of full-scale profit and loss accountability and new forms of organising labour and production; and every kind of incentive for innovation and socialist enterprise.

Reorganisation is a decisive turn to science, the businesslike partnership of science and practice to achieve the best possible end results, an ability to ground any undertaking on a sound scientific basis, a readiness and keen desire on the part of scientists to actively support the Party's policy of revitalising society, and a concern for scientific advancement, for increasing the number of research personnel, and for making them actively involved in the process of change.

Reorganisation is the priority development of the social sphere, ever fuller satisfaction of the Soviet people's demands for adequate working and living conditions, recreational facilities, education and medical services. It is an unfailing concern for raising the intellectual and cultural standards of every person and of society as a whole. It is also the ability to combine decision-making on the major, cardinal problems of public life with that on the current issues of immediate interest to the people.

Reorganisation means vigorously ridding society of any deviations from socialist morals, a consistent enforcement of the principles of social justice, harmony between words and deeds, indivisibility of rights and duties, the promotion of conscientious, high-quality work, combating the wage-levelling tendencies and overcoming consumerism.

The final aim of reorganisation is, I believe, clear: it is to effect thorough-going changes in all aspects of public life, to give socialism the most advanced forms of social organisation, and bring out to the utmost the humane nature of our system in all decisive aspects – economic, social, political and moral.

This is, comrades, the job we have started. The reorganisation is getting under way everywhere. It is acquiring a new quality, not only gaining in scope but also penetrating the deepest fibres of our life.

The drive for change has stirred all healthy forces in society to action and given people confidence in what they are doing. An objective and self-critical attitude to the state of things, a departure from the cut-and-dried, well-beaten ways of going about their work, and the search for new, uncommon approaches to problems have become typical of more and more Party committees, public organisations and work collectives. We feel the solid and decisive backings of workers and peasants, intellectuals in the arts, science and engineering, of all sections of Soviet society.

A new moral atmosphere is taking shape in the country. A reappraisal of values and their creative rethinking is under way, debates have started on ways of reorganising the economy and social and cultural life and the quest for new methods of organisational and ideological work is gaining in scope. Openness and candour in appraising phenomena and developments, intolerance of shortcomings, and the desire to secure improvements are increasingly affirming themselves as effective principles of life.

A more exacting attitude is developing, discipline and production organisation are improving, and more order is being introduced. The first steps in reorganising cultural and intellectual life are especially important to us, comrades, because we cannot hope to succeed without decisively changing public consciousnes and remoulding mentality, thinking and moods.

We have begun to overhaul the material and technological base and the national economy on the basis of progress in research and engineering, and to update structural and investment policies. Far-reaching goal-oriented programmes have been adopted in the decisive areas of scientific and techno- logical progress. These programmes have been taken into account in drawing up the twelfth five-year plan which is now being fulfilled.

Large-scale measures are being implemented to improve management. From the start of this year all industrial enterprises and amalgamations have been switched over to experimentally tried-and-tested methods of economic management. A number of industries, enterprises and amalgamations have started working on the principles of full-scale profit and loss accountability and self-financing.

The sectors of the economy directly involved in meeting the people's needs such as the agro-industrial sector, light industry, trade and the services have begun operating on principles that give them more leeway, while increasing their responsibility. A fundamental change is taking place in the way the capital construction industry is run. A state quality control system has been intro- duced at 1,500 major factories to improve product quality.

The system of foreign economic activities is being restructured. The rights of enterprises and industries in this field have been extended. New forms of cooperation, including direct relations between enterprises, joint ventures, and specialised-production and co-production schemes with foreign partners, are continuing to gain ground.

With the aim of adopting an integrated economic management system, standing bodies have been set up at the USSR Council of Ministers to manage groups of interrelated industries. A Law on State Enterprise (Amalgamation) has been drafted and work is proceeding to draw up documents on ways of optimising the functions of central economic bodies, ministries and depart- ments to fit in with the new economic mechanism, and to formulate proposals on organising new forms of large production units based on individual and amalgamated factories and operating on profit and loss accountability princi- ples, and on a number of other important matters.

Fundamental measures are being introduced to improve things in the social field. New principles have been worked out, and are being implemented, for raising pay in productive spheres. We have taken a resolute course for abandoning wage-levelling and are consistently adhering to the socialist principle of distribution in accordance with the quantity and quality of one's work. At the same time unwarranted restrictions on individual enterprise have been lifted and favourable conditions are now being provided to promote this kind of activity. People are being encouraged to set up cooperatives in various areas of production and services to meet consumer demand more fully.

On the strength of an analysis of the situation in housing construction and considering the programme task of providing every family with a self-contained apartment by the year 2000, extra reserves have been found to quicken the pace and improve the quality of home building. An additional 10 per cent of capital investments are being earmarked for this purpose, which will make it possible as early as 1987 to increase the amount of housing construction by 9.1 million square metres, or nearly 8 per cent over the five-year plan targets.

The scale of home building undertaken by cooperatives and individuals is growing. Easy-term credits are being offered and the necessary resources made available; and measures are being adopted to promote the cost-benefit method of building homes by factories from their own funds and to increase the capacity of the construction industry.

A programme has been drawn up for building and modernising health institutions, more facilities have been built to produce medicines and medical equipment, and efforts to introduce and promote new forms of health services and develop medical science have been stepped up. Measures have also been taken to improve people's working and living conditions, to extend the system of preventive treatment, eradicate drunkenness and alcholism, and reduce morbidity. The pay of medical personnel is also being increased.

So, even a brief review of the work that has been planned and started, comrades, demonstrates the immense scale of the amount of work facing us is enormous but it cannot be otherwise. The Party does not have the right to reduce its attention to any aspect of the projected changes. All plans must be carried out without fail, to the point and on time.

Certainly some of the measures we're working out and implementing will only yield practical results after some time. But even today the very atmosphere and the public mood are already changing attitudes to work and yielding tangible results.

This is borne out, among other things, by the results of work to fulfil the plan for the first year of the current five-year plan period. National income went up 4.1 per cent as against the planned 3.9 per cent and the annual average of 3.6 per cent in the previous five years. Industrial output grew 4.9 per cent, which is a third more than the average annual increase in the previous five-year period and makes the highest growth rate for the past nine years.

You know that the twelfth five-year plan period is of decisive importance to us as far as modernising the country's engineering sector, updating production assets and accelerating scientific and technological progress are concerned. Those charged with ensuring the priority development of the engineering sector have had to cope with great difficulties, but nevertheless headway is being made. In the past year the production of industrial robots went up 14 per cent, that of flexible automated production systems 160 per cent, production modules 120 per cent, and machining centres 40 per cent. Capital investment in retooling and reconstruction of existing factories grew 30 per cent. The Political Bureau will see to it that the engineering sector programme is being implemented. We hope that machine-builders will cope with the tasks set.

Things are looking up also in a number of other industries. Last year's showings in the iron and steel, coal mining and gas industries were not bad. The lag in oil production is also being overcome.

Labour productivity in industry rose 4.6 per cent over the plan target of 4.1 per cent. This increase accounted for 96 per cent of the gain in annual output. Production costs dropped noticeably for the first time in many years. The turnover rate of material assets went up, while the stocks of uninstalled plant, including imported equipment, were reduced.

Improvements in the agrarian sector are there for all to see. As compared with the average annual harvests in the past five-year period, grain production in 1986 increased by almost 30 milion tons, or 17 per cent; potatoes by nearly 9 million tons, or 11 per cent; sugar beet close on 3 million tons, or 4 per cent; meat by 1.5 million tons, or 9 per cent; milk by 6.5 million tons, or 7 per cent; and eggs by almost 6,000 million or 8 per cent.

As you can see, comrades, agricultural output has begun to grow, something we have not seen in the key indicators for many years. However it must be said that the output growth of such products as vegetables, fruits, sunflower and cotton was either insignificant or nil.

It is also important to note the improvement of the main financial and economic indicators in the performance of collective and state farms. Labour productivity in the socialised economy increased during the year by 6.9 per cent, the profit rate amounted to 19 per cent and profits went up by two million roubles.

While acknowledging the favourable changes in economic development, it should be noted, however, that the target for the growth of national income to be used for consumption and accumulation was not met because of big losses, non-productive outlays and the non-fulfilment of assignments for expanding trade turnover.

The growth of such key figures as real per capita incomes, gross agricultural output, consumer goods manufacture, capital investments, utilisation of fixed assets in production and profit fell short of the plan assignments despite a substantial increase over the previous year. Neither have there occurred serious changes in the investment process. Only two-thirds of the projects of the state plan were put into service.

Changes in the social sphere have begun after all, but with great difficulty. The number of accidents and loss of working time have declined for the first time since the 1960s after the measures taken to strengthen discipline and combat alcohol abuse. The total number of crimes has dropped by almost a quarter and the number of grave crimes by a third. The fight against violations of law and order has been intensified everywhere.

The volume of housing construction has grown, surpassing the 1985 figure by 5.2 million square metres. More kindergartens and nurseries, schools, outpatient clinics and hospitals, cultural institutions and service establishments have been built.

In short, there have been favourable changes. But the weight of the outstanding problems in this important sphere is too great and we are still too timid in tackling them.

As you know it was with great difficulty the reserves were found to expand the construction of housing, cultural institutions and service establishments. But alas, not everyone made proper use of these possibilities. Many construction plans were not fulfilled. The reasons for this should be sought not only in the poor organisation of the builders' work but also in insufficient attention on the part of enterprises, ministries, local Soviets and Party committees.

We still have difficulties with trade in foodstuffs and manufactured goods, with urban transport and the utilities, with institutions of public health care and culture. In short, we have not yet achieved fundamental changes in the development of the social sphere and remain largely in the power of old approaches.

Concluding my description of the work carried out by the Party, by the entire people to implement the decisions of the 27th Congress, I would like to say the following. It is very important that we, members of the Central Committee, take a realistic stand and objectively assess what has been accomplished, that we view the obtained results not just from past positions, but above all proceeding from our announced plans and promises made to the people. This is the only correct Party approach.

We must clearly realise that we are only at the initial stage of the restructuring. The most important and complex work is yet to come. We must advance step by step, persistently and without wavering. We must soberly assess what has been done and not be afraid to rectify mistakes. We must search for and find new ways and means of solving tasks as they arise and definitely achieve progress towards the goals that have been set.

We should absolutely learn from the lesson of the past, that is, allowing no gap to form between decisions and the practical work for their implementation. I am saying this once again because we are still encountering this even now. We must act, act and act again – vigorously, boldly, creatively and competently.

The need to pose the question in this way is dictated by the fact that to this day in many economic, government, state and even Party bodies, and in the work collectives themselves far from everyone is marching in step with the demands being set by life. Many people are slow to cast off the burden of the past, are adopting a wait-and-see attitude and openly putting a spoke in the wheel, impeding the extensive development of the people's political, public and labour activity.

Not everyone has understood that working in the new way means to resolutely give up old habits and methods. In the long run, this depends on the civic stand of every person, on a conscientious attitude to one's job and duties; and we all have a responsibility for this towards the Party, the country and our own conscience.

Meetings and conversations with working people, with Party and economic personnel, show that the reorganisation is receiving ardent support. It can be said that the people are all for it. But what stands out is that many people, while supporting innovations, believe that the reorganisation must take place somewhere higher up, that this has to be done by others – by Party, state and economic bodies, other sectors of the economy, allied enterprises, by others in the factory shop, on the farm or construction site. In short, that this must be done by everybody except themselves.

No, comrades, while justly demanding reorganisation at every level, each of us must begin with himself. All of us – workers, collective farmers, intellectuals, in short everybody, from those in work collectives to the Central Committee of the CPSU and the government must work in a new way – vigorously, creatively and, I repeat, conscientiously.

In the immense undertaking of reorganisation, we Communists rely above all on a high degree of consciousness and organisation, social initiative and the major labour accomplishments of the working class, the leading political force of our society.

While highly appraising the Party's course of reorganisation, the working class and all Soviet people at the same time are concerned about the course of its practical implementation. They call on the Party not to stop, but to act resolutely, to advance and steadfastly follow the adopted course. From this, comrade, we must draw political conclusions.

The existence of this concern in society means that our efforts are still insufficient, that we are not yet acting with the necessary effectiveness and vigour everywhere and in everything. It means that the measures that are being taken and the work that is being done do not always accord with the scope and acuteness of the accumulated problems, that not everything is being done as well as the times demand. This means, comrades, that the Central Committee has enough reason for thinking things over and drawing the appropriate conclusions.

We understand, of course, that the process of overcoming existing stereotypes of thinking and acting is a complex and painful process requiring time and a balanced approach.

It is absolutely clear that this process cannot proceed autonomously, isolated from the transformations going on in political, socioeconomic and cultural and intellectual life.

We must clearly realise that today a whole system of measures is needed. This includes the formulation of theoretical provisions based on the realities of our time and a deeply substantiated scientific forecast of the future; changes in social consciousness and consistent development of democratic institutions; the fostering of the political culture of the masses; and reorganisation of the mechanism of economic management, of organisational structures; and, of course, the pursuance of a vigorous social policy.

This is the only way to remove the brake on progress and give the necessary scope to the forces of acceleration.

I think today's plenary meeting of the Central Committee should tell the Party and the people that a difficult struggle lies ahead, requiring of every Communist and every citizen a high degree of consciousness and organisation, stamina and utmost selflessness.

Comrades, the analysis of the state our society was in on the eve of the April plenary meeting of the Central Committee and the experience of reorganisation have raised an acute and most important question. Do we have guarantees that the process of transformations that we have started will be continued to the end, that the past mistakes will not be repeated, and we'll be able to ensure the comprehensive development of our society?

The Political Bureau answers these questions in the affirmative: yes, we have such guarantees.

These are the united will, the joint actions of the Party and people united by past experience, by awareness of their responsibility for the present and the future of the socialist homeland.

These are the all-round development of the democracy of the socialist system, the real and ever more active participation of the people in solving all questions of the country's life, full restoration of the Leninist principles of openness, public control, criticism and self-criticism, and sincerity in policy consisting in the unity of words and deeds.

Finally, these are the healthy development of the Party itself, its ability to critically analyse its own activity, to update the forms and methods of its work; to determine, on the basis of revolutionary theory, the prospects of society's development, and to work for accomplishing the new tasks life poses.

It is the promotion of socialist democracy, the creative endeavour of Soviet people, the vanguard role of Communists in practical deeds that will ensure both the success and the irreversibility of the revolutionary transformations charted by the 27th Congress.

To Promote Socialist Democracy and Develop the People's Self-government

We now understand better than before the profundity of Lenin's thought about the vital, inner link between socialism and democracy. The entire historical experience of our country has convincingly demonstrated that the socialist system has in practice ensured citizens' political and socioeconomic rights, their personal freedoms, revealed the advantages of Soviet democracy and given each person confidence in the morrow.

At the time of reorganisation, when the task of stimulating the human factor has become so pressing, we must recall once again Lenin's stand on the question of the maximum democracy of the socialist system under which people feel that they are their own masters and creators.

'We must be guided by experience, we must allow complete freedom to the creative faculties of the masses,' Lenin said.

Indeed democracy, the essence of which is the power of the man of labour, is the form of realising his extensive political and civil rights, his interest in transformations and practical participation in their implementation.

Simple and lucid thought is becoming increasingly entrenched in social consciousness: a house can be put in order only by a person who feels that he owns this house. This truth is valid not only in the worldly but also in the sociopolitical sense. And it must be steadily translated into life. I repeat, translated into life, otherwise the human factor will lose its effectiveness.

It is only through the consistent development of the democratic forms inherent in socialism and more extensive self-government that our progress in production, science and technology, literature, culture and the arts, in all areas of social life is possible. It is only this way that ensures conscientious discipline. The reorganisation itself is possible only through democracy and because of democracy. It is only this way that it is possible to open broad vistas for socialism's most powerful creative force – free labour and free thought in a free country.

Therefore the further democratisation of Soviet society is becoming the Party's urgent task. This in effect is the essence of the course charted by the April plenary meeting and the 27th CPSU Congress for promoting people's socialist self-government. The point at issue is certainly not any break-up of our political system. We should use with maximum effectiveness all its potentialities, fill the work of the party, the Soviets and the government bodies, public organisations and work collectives with deep democratic content, breathe new life into all cells of the social organism.

This process is already under way in the country. The life of the Party organisations is becoming more full-blooded. Criticism and self-criticism are broadening. The mass media have begun working more actively. The Soviet people can sense the beneficial effect of openness, which is becoming a norm of society's life.

The congresses of creative unions were held in a principled and critical atmosphere. New public organisations are being set up. The All-Union Organisation of War and Labour Veterans has come into being. The Soviet Cultural Fund has been set up. Work is under way to set up women's councils. All these facts indicate the growing participation of the working people in social affairs, in the administration of the country.

What ways does the Political Bureau see to further deepen democracy in Soviet society?

We will be able to boost people's initiative and creativity effectively if our democratic institutions have a strong and real influence on the state of things in every work collective, be it in terms of planning, labour organisation, distribution of material and other benefits, or selection and promotion of the most respected and competent people to leading positions. It can be said with certainty that the sooner every Soviet citizen experiences these changes for himself, the more active his civic stance and participation in all public and state affairs will be.

Of paramount importance is the development of democracy in production and the consistent implementation of the principles of working people's self-management. The economy is the decisive area of society's life. Tens of millions of people are daily engaged in it. Therefore the development of democracy in production is the most important trend in deepening and broadening socialist democracy in general. This is the lever that will enable us to ensure the broad and active participation of the working people in all areas of social life and make it possible to avoid many errors and miscalculations.

The creation of conditions and introduction of forms of production organisation that will enable all working people to feel themselves real masters of their enterprises are the most important tasks. To be a real master is a lofty and responsible position. While giving extensive rights to actually run the affairs, it imposes great responsibility for all that is happening in one's work collective.

Diverse forms of working people's participation in production management have asserted themselves in the course of socialist construction. The life of work collectives is unthinkable without the Party, trade union, Young Communist League and other public organisations. The role of workers' meetings and collective agreements has been growing of late. New forms of democracy have originated, such as the councils of production teams and workshops. Conditions have become ripe for further steps along the same lines.

Life itself made the need for drawing up a fundamental legal act, such as the Law on the State Enterprise whose draft has already been issued to you, the order of the day. This law is designed to radically change the conditions and methods of management in the main section of the economy, to consolidate the combination of the principle of planning and full-scale profit and loss accountability, independence and responsibility in the activities of enterprises, and to give the new forms of self-administration, born of the creativity of the masses, a legal basis.

The Law is intended to put one of the most important directives of the Party Congress into practice, namely the course towards a more effective use of direct democracy. Under the draft Law, the powers to be given to the general meeting and councils of work collectives in dealing with questions bearing on production, social and personnel affairs, will be a major political measure towards, as V.I. Lenin put it, 'genuine self-government by the people'.

The consistent implementation of the Law on the State Enterprise in combination with the package of measures being implemented in the economic field will, we believe, create an altogether new situation in the economy, will accelerate economic development and lead to the qualitative improvement of many aspects of social life. Considering the tremendous significance of this Law, the Political Bureau proposes that it be submitted for nationwide discussion. I believe that the members of the Central Committee will support this proposal.

Our collective farms and socialist cooperation in general have broad potentialities that are still far from being fully used for democratising management of the economy and the social sphere. The restructuring of the administration system in the agroindustrial complex and the decision to further develop cooperation in other sectors of the national economy create good prerequisites for making use of these potentialities. In this connection we think it would be advisable to convene a congress of collective farmers to discuss the outstanding problems concerning the life of collective farms and make the necessary amendments to the Model Collective Farm Charter.

The Political Bureau energetically supports the practical steps already taken in many republics, territories and regions to introduce more widely other cooperative forms of activity. This will make it possible to meet even more fully the growing demand of the population for many commodities and services, and also create additional conditions for the development of democracy in the economic field and the better realisation of man's possibilities.

It is necessary, comrades, to resolutely overcome the past and present doubts about the cooperative movement. Cooperation, far from having exhausted its potentialities, has great prospects.

Why am I returning to this issue and laying accent on it? Because after the 27th Congress of the CPSU, despite the decisions taken by the Central Committee and the government on the development of cooperation in the field of material and technical supply, everyday services and public catering, the municipal economy, local industry and construction, this matter has not been given proper scope. All sorts of obstacles are being raised in its way, the commitment to administrative-bureaucratic methods of management which are out of tune with the traditional concepts, even if these are vital and stimulate the initiative of working people and enhance their social activeness.

Some comrades apparently find it hard to understand that the enhancement of democracy is not just a slogan but the essence of reorganisation. They must change their views and habits so as not to find themselves aside from the mainstream of life. This is our insistent advice to all who are still doubting and slow.

It is necessary to concentrate on the question of electing heads of enterprises, factories, workshops, departments, sectors, farms and teams, team leaders and foremen. The current stage in restructuring, the transition to new methods of economic management, profit and loss accountability, self-financing and self-repayment make that task a very practical one. This is an important and urgent measure, and it will undoubtedly have working people's approval.

We have embarked in a big way on the path of transferring enterprises to full-scale profit and loss accountability, self-financing and self-repayment; we have introduced state quality control. This means that the profits of enterprises, all forms of incentives for the members of the work collective and the degree to which social demands are met will totally depend on the end results of their work, the quality and quantity of the product made and the services rendered.

Under these circumstances workers and collective farmers will be far from indifferent as to who heads the enterprise, workshop, sector or team. Since the wellbeing of the collective is made dependent on the abilities of the managers, the working people should also have a real say in their appointment and control their activities.

Certain experience in open, public selection of management has been gained in the country. For instance more than eight and a half thousand senior executives have been promoted in the Krasnodar Territory since 1983 with due regard for the opinions of collectives and primary Party organisations. Over two hundred candidates were not approved by the working people and were rejected. The same kind of experience has also been acquired in a number of other places. It has been favourably received by the people and is having a good effect on the results of their work.

Comrades, to sum it up. From whatever angle we may approach this important matter one conclusion begs of itself: the time has come for change, for democratising the process of management selection at enterprises on the basis of all-round application of the electivity principle. This, as you understand, means a qualitatively new situation, a fundamentally different form of working people's participation in production management, an essential enhancement of the role and responsibility of the collective for the results of its activities.

All this should be taken into account in the course of the practical solution of that issue. However I would like to convey one idea right now. The point at issue is one-man management. We think that electiveness, far from undermining, enhances the authority of the leader. He feels the support of the people who elected him. This enhances the feeling of responsibility for the matter on hand, and common discipline in the collective.

The role of the Party and public organisations and economic mangement bodies should be comprehended in a new way. A great amount of work is to be carried out to inculcate in all our personnel a correct understanding of the fact that extension of democracy in production presupposes an organic combination of one-man management and collective effort, promotion of democratic centralism and development of self-government.

The Political Bureau considers the advancement of the Soviet electoral system to be one of the main avenues in democratising our life. Corresponding proposals are being drafted on that issue on the instructions of the 27th Congress.

What can be said here? The existing electoral system ensures representation for all sections of the population in the elective bodies of power. The working class, collective farmers, intellectuals, men and women, veterans and young people, all nations and nationalities in the country are represented in the present Soviets at all levels. The elective bodies reflect the social, professional and national structure of Soviet society and the diversity of the interest of the entire population. This in itself is an immense achievement of socialist democracy.

However, just as all political, economic and social institutions, the electoral system cannot remain unchanged and away from the reorganisation and the new processes developing in society.

What is the essence of proposals and wishes on these matters which people are sending to the CPSU Central Committee, the Presidium of the USSR Supreme Soviet and to other central bodies and the mass media?

From the political point of view it is a question of enhancing the democratic nature of the electoral system and of a more effective and real involvement of the electorate at all stages of the pre-election and election campaigns.

Concretely, most proposals suggest that voters at meetings in work collectives and at places of residence, as well as at election meetings, discuss, as a rule, several candidacies, that elections be held in larger constituencies, and that several deputies be elected from each of them. People believe that this would enable each citizen to express his attitude to a greater number of candidates and would enable Party and local government bodies to get to know better the sentiments and will of the population.

Responding to these wishes we should look anew at the way the elections themselves are organised and at the practice of nomination and discussion of candidacies for people's deputies. It is essential to rid the voting procedure of formalism and to see to it that the election campaign of even this year be held in an atmosphere of broader democracy with the interested participation of the people.

As far as a legislative act on introducing amendments to the electoral system is concerned, it would be useful to publish its draft for nationwide preliminary discussion.

The implementation of these proposals would be the first major step towards the further democratisation of the process of forming the bodies of state power and of their functioning. But obviously it is also necessary to consider deeper changes and further steps in this direction. With due regard for the experience gained and the new tasks we must once again make a thorough and profound analysis of Lenin's legacy on matters of Soviet state development and draw on it in solving the tasks facing society today.

It is quite natural that questions of promoting inner-party democracy should be considered within the overall framework of the further democratisation of Soviet society.

At the 27th Congress a number of important provisions strengthening the democratic principles of Party life were introduced in amending the CPSU Rules. This work should be continued. It appears advisable to confer together on improving the mechanism for forming leading Party bodies.

Many different proposals have come to the Central Committee in this connection. Allow me to report on the conclusions which have been made by summing up the proposals.

To begin with, the formation of elective bodies in the primary Party organisation. The gist of most proposals on this score is to give full scope to the expression of the will of all Communists without exception during the election of secretaries of Party bureaux and Party committees and to enhance their responsibility to those who elect them.

There is also a need to think of amending the procedure for the election of secretaries of district, area, city, regional and territorial Party committees, and the Central Committees of the Communist Parties of the Union republics. Here comrades suggest that secretaries, including first secretaries, could be elected by secret ballot at the plenary sessions of the respective Party committees. In such a case the members of the Party committee would have a right to enter any number of candidates in the voting list. Such a measure would greatly increase the responsibility of secretaries to the Party committees that elected them, giving them more confidence in their work and making it possible for them to determine more accurately the degree of their authority.

Of course the principle of the Party Rules, under which the decisions of higher bodies are binding on all lower Party commitees, including those on personnel matters, must remain immutable in the Party.

The Political Bureau's opinion is that further democratisation should also apply to the formation of the central leading bodies of the Party. I think this is quite logical. It would seem logical to democratise the elections of leading bodies in other public organisations as well.

Comrades, I think you will agree that all these measures will strengthen the principles of democratic centralism in the Party's life and will promote greater unity and cohesion of the Party ranks, tougher discipline, responsibility, and activity of each Communist, all Party organisations and the Party as a whole.

The following questions will possibly arise: shall we not be complicating the procedure of the formation of elective bodies of the Party; to what extent is all this justified, and how much will it help?

Ever since the April plenary meeting of the Central Committee we have been continuously emphasising that the problems which have accumulated in society are connected to a considerable extent with the drawbacks in the activity of the Party itself and in its personnel policy. The Political Bureau believes that the further democratisation of the process of forming elective bodies is one of the important conditions for boosting Party activities, for the infusion of fresh blood, the active work of Party organisations, and a safeguard against repetition of the errors of the past.

Elections within the Party are not a formal act, and we should approach their preparation in a well-thought-out way, in a spirit of great responsibility, proceeding from the interests of the Party and society.

The democratisation of society poses in a new way the question of control over the work of the Party, local government, and economic bodies and their personnel. As far as control 'from above' is concerned marked changes, as you know, have occurred in this respect of late. So-called 'forbidden subjects' for criticism and control are becoming a thing of the past. The Political Bureau and the Secretariat of the Central Committee at their meetings regularly hear reports by the Central Committees of the Communist Parties of the Union republics and territorial and regional Party committees, and consider other fundamental questions of the life of the Party and society profoundly and comprehensively. The Council of Ministers of the USSR and its Presidium have become much more exacting to ministries and departments and to the Councils of Ministers of the Union republics.

Frankly speaking the Political Bureau, the Secretariat of the Central Committee and the government still have a lot to do in this respect. We still have to return to one and the same problem several times over and adopt additional measures to solve it. This has been vividly shown, in particular, by the discussion at the latest meeting of the Political Bureau on the course of implementing the resolutions of the Central Committee and the Council of Ministers of the USSR on accelerating the development of the engineering industry. We take the necessary decisions but, as before, we do not implement them to the full and on time. This happens also because many have not yet got rid of the burden of old habits and an irresponsible attitude to their duties. Discipline is lax. Far from all executives follow the principle of the unity of words and deeds, while others do more speaking than working. We must draw the most serious conclusions from this.

But with all the importance of control 'from above' it is of fundamental importance in the conditions of the democratisation of society to raise the level and effectiveness of control 'from below' so that each executive and each official constantly feels his responsibility to and dependence on the electorate, on the work collectives, public organisations, on the Party and the people as a whole. The main thing in this respect is to create and strengthen all instruments and forms of real control by the working people.

What instruments do I have in mind?

Accountability, first of all. The time has come to observe strictly the rules for systematic accountability of all elected and appointed officials before work collectives and the population. It is necessary that every such account be accompanied by lively and principled discussion, criticism and self-criticism and businesslike proposals, and end with an evaluation of the activites of the person giving an account of his work.

This would be the implementation of Lenin's demand that the work of elective bodies and executives be open to everyone and be done in sight of the people. If we achieve such control there can be no doubt that many causes for complaints and appeals to higher organisations will disappear, and most questions raised in them will be solved at the local level. In the conditions of extended democracy people themselves will put things in order in their work collective, town or village.

The Soviets of People's Deputies, trade unions and other public organisations have immense possibilities for control. In the Supreme and local Soviets it is necessary to strengthen the democratic principles of the work of the sessions, standing commissions and deputies and to raise the efficiency of regular accounts of officials to the Soviets and the practice of inquiries by deputies. Such an approach will even further augment the prestige of the bodies of people's power among the masses.

While perfecting control it is necessary to regulate without delay the flow of all kinds of check-ups and inspections at enterprises, institutions and organisations, inspections which distract people from work and introduce an element of nervousness into the work. The actual value of such check-ups or inspections is, as a rule, negligible. These issues are not new. They have repeatedly been discussed and written about. But the state of affairs has not changed so far. Obviously the Secretariat of the Central Committee and the Presidium of the Council of Ministers of the USSR should straighten out these matters and follow the principle of quality, not quantity, with such inspections.

While normalising the atmosphere in society it is essential to further encourage openness. This is a powerful lever for improving work in all sectors of our developmnent and an effective form of control by the whole people. The experience which has been gained since the April plenary meeting of the Central Committee is good proof of this.

Obviously the time has come to begin elaborating legal acts guaranteeing the openness. These should ensure maximum openness in the activities of state and public organisations and give the working people a real opportunity to express their opinions on any question of social life.

Criticism and self-criticism are a tested instrument of socialist democracy. There seems to be no open objection to this. However in real life we encounter situations indicating that by no means everyone has become aware of the need to support critical-mindedness in society. Matters at times go so far that some officials regard even the slightest remark as an encroachment upon their prestige and defend it in any way they can. Then there are those officials, the more experienced ones, who admit the justness of criticism and even thank you for it, but are in no hurry to eliminate drawbacks, expecting to get away with things as usual.

Such an attitude to criticism has nothing in common with our principles and ethics. At the present stage, when we are asserting new approaches in sociopolitical life, in the cultural and intellectual sphere, the importance of criticism and self-criticism grows immeasurably. People's attitude to criticism is an important criterion of their attitude to reorganisation, to everything new that is taking place in our society.

And here I cannot but say regretfully that we continue to encounter not only cases of non-acceptance of criticism but also facts of persecution for it, of direct suppression of criticism. Not infrequently this assumes such proportions and takes such forms that the Central Committee has to intervene in order to re-establish the truth and justice and to support honest people who take the interests of work close to heart. I have already spoken of this matter, but things are improving only slowly. Take, for instance, the central press reports for January and you'll see that the persecution of people for criticism is far from a rare thing.

In this connection we must support the efforts of the mass media to develop criticism and self-criticism in our society. Their position in the struggle for reorganisation has been appreciated by the Soviet people.

The readership of central newspapers and magazines has increased by over 14 million and Central TV programmes on topical subjects are attracting audiences of many millions. People are impressed by the bold and profound treatment of urgent problems which are involved in the acceleration of the country's socioeconomic development and which cover all aspects of life in our society. The Party believes that the programmes of the mass media will continue to be marked by depth and objectivity and a high degree of civic responsibility.

Many things can be said about the positive changes taking place in the republican and local press. Far from all of them have joined in the work of restructuring. Some lack firmness of principle and boldness in raising questions, and a critical attitude to shortcomings. Many Party Committees sometimes fail to use properly the mass media, a powerful lever in the restructuring process. In some places they continue to restrain mass media activity.

While continuing to count on principled and constructive criticism of shortcomings and omissions, the Party expects the mass media to publicise more widely the experience gained by work collectives, Party, local government and economic bodies, public organisations and top officials in conditions of reorganisation. We badly need answers to many of the burning problems reorganisation has raised or will raise. We must all help in changing our ways more quickly and in the spirit of the time. As V.I. Lenin said, this organising function of the press should be strengthened from day to day and it should learn in practice to be a collective agitator, propagandist and organiser of the masses.

There is one more question that must be made clear. In Soviet society there should be no zones closed to criticism. This refers in full measure to the mass media.

Comrades, there can be no real democracy outside the law or above the law. The 27th Congress of the Party laid down the main guidelines for the development of our legislation and for strengthening law and order. A great amount of work must be done in the current five-year plan period to prepare and adopt new laws connected with the development of the economy, social life, culture, the socialist self-government of the people and the broadening of guarantees for the rights and freedoms of citizens.

The Political Bureau has supported a proposal for drafting new criminal legislation in the near future. The task is to make it more in tune with the present conditions of development of Soviet society. It must defend more effectively the interests and rights of citizens and help strengthen discipline and law and order. We must consider and take measures to raise the role and prestige of the Soviet court. The independence of judges must be strictly observed, the role of the Directorate of Public Prosecutions enhanced and the work of investigating bodies improved.

A draft law has been prepared on the procedure for filing a complaint in court against illegal actions of officials infringing upon the rights of a citizen. This law is soon to be submitted for discussion. Additional steps are planned to improve the work of state arbitration and improve legal education of the population.

Speaking of democratisation of Soviet society – which is a matter of principle to us – it is important to underline once more the main, distinguishing, feature of socialist democracy – an organic combination of democracy and discipline, of independence and responsibility, of the rights and duties of officials and of every citizen.

Socialist democracy has nothing in common with permissiveness, irresponsibility, and anarchy. Real democracy serves every person. It protects his political and social rights and simultaneously serves every collective and the whole of society, upholding their interests.

Democratisation in all spheres of Soviet society is important first of all because we link it with the further development of working people's initiative and the use of the entire potential of the socialist system. We need democratisation in order to move ahead, to ensure that legality grows stronger, that justice triumphs in our society and that a moral atmosphere in which man can freely live and fruitfully work is asserted in it.

Comrades, it is well known that the effectiveness of real democracy depends on how far it reflects the interests of broad numbers of people, how it relies on them and is supported by all segments and groups of society. In this respect, too, the tasks of reorganisation make it necessary for us to analyse again our resources and possibilities for further expanding the social base of democracy. The pertinence of such an approach is obvious.

All our experience has taught us that in periods of change, while tackling the most difficult and boldest tasks, the party has invariably turned to the Komsomol, to youth, to their enthusiasm and dedication to the cause of socialism, to their intolerance of stagnation and their commitment to progress. Today when we speak of the need for democratic changes, for getting the people more fully involved in the process of restructuring, the question of the position taken by the younger generation is assuming tremendous political significance.

I would like again to repeat at this plenary meeting: we can be proud of our youth, we pay tribute to their work – this is actually true and politically correct.

But the times require everyone to display still greater energies. And of course young people, who are interested in reorganisation, should be more active. It is the youth who will live and work in our new society. Party organisations, their committees and the Komsomol should expand the perspective of the younger generation to ensure that young people become active participants in the changes. It is from this position that we should also approach preparations for the next congress of the Young Communist League.

In our work with the Komsomol we should give more attention to the labour, the politico-ideological and moral education of young people. We must act quicker and with greater determination in ridding ourselves of all that is alien to our work with youth and, primarily, of didactic tone and administrative methods. Yes, all this exists and mention of it should be made. Whatever lies behind this approach, be it disbelief in the soundness and maturity of the social aspirations and actions of young people, or a simple desire to play it safe and soften life's difficulties for our children – still, one must not accept such a position.

No, comrades, there is no other realistic way of moulding a personality, of fostering a young person's civic stance, than to involve him in all public affairs. There can be no substitute for practical experience. That is why it is important to alter the present situation. What exactly do I have in mind?

Above all – more trust in young people, combining good assistance and freedom of comradely criticism of mistakes, more independence in organising their work, studies, daily life, leisure, and greater responsibility in their undertakings and actions. This also implies their right to take part in running the affairs of society at all levels.

One important aspect of the democratisation of public life is promotion of non-Party comrades to leading positions. This is a matter of principle. One of the firm guarantees of the health and progress of a socialist society lies in the political and professional growth of the front-rank worker, farmer, engineer, researcher, doctor, teacher, and public services employee. We need constantly to push to the fore and promote talent from the thick of the people.

Sometimes we come across the opinion that promotion of non-Party people is outdated because the CPSU now has over 19 million members. I think it is erroneous. To believe so is to deform the Party's relations with the people. Moreover, coming straight to the point, this infringes on the constitutional rights of citizens and limits our opportunities as regards the employment of personnel.

We have had, and continue to have, quite a few remarkable examples of fruitful work by non-Party comrades who hold leading positions. They head mills and factories, collective and state farms, construction organisations, scientific and pedagogical collectives, engineering services and are actively involved in public activities.

Open selection of workers to be promoted – from among both Communists and non-Party people – will accord with the aims of democratisation and will help involve large numbers of working people in management.

There is also the question of promoting more women to leading positions. There are many women holding Party and state posts and working successfully in science, health care, education, culture, light industry, trade, and public services. In order to meet our country's needs today we must more actively involve women in running the economy and culture on an All-Union or republican scale. We have such possibilities. All we have to do is trust and support women.

Comrades, there isn't one single fundamental issue that we could resolve, now as in the past, without taking into account the fact that we live in a multinational country. There is no need to prove the importance of socialist principles in the development of relations between the nationalities. It is socialism that did away with national oppression, inequality, and infringements upon the rights of people on grounds of nationality. It ensured the economic and cultural progress of all nationalities and ethnic groups. In short, the successes of our Party's nationalities policy are beyond any doubt and we can justly take pride in them.

But we must also see the real picture of the relations between nationalities and the prospects for their development. Now that democracy and self-government are expanding, that there is rapid growth of national awareness of all nationalities and ethnic groups, and the processes of internationalisation are developing in depth, it is especially important to settle promptly and fairly outstanding questions in the only possible way – in the interest of the progress of each nationality and ethnic group, in the interest of their further drawing closer together, and in the interest of sociey as a whole.

In this connection it must be added that negative phenomena and deformities in our society, something we are combating today, have also appeared in relations between nationalities. There have been manifestations of parochialism, ethnic isolation, and ethnic arrogance and even incidents similar to those which took place quite recently in Alma-Ata.

The events in Alma-Ata and what led up to them require a serious analysis and a principled assessment. This has not yet been thoroughly examined. It is clear today that what has occurred should compel not only Communists in Kazakhstan, but all Party organisations and their Committees to deal with the problems of further developing relations between nationalities, and enhancing internationalist education. It is especially important to protect our younger generation from the demoralising effect of nationalism.

V.I. Lenin wrote we must learn to be internationalists in deed. It is our duty to follow this precept.

All of our experience shows: nationalist tendencies can be successfully opposed only by consistent and sustained internationalism. Everything we have accomplished is due to our concerted effort. If one region produces oil, another one provides it with bread. Those who grow cotton receive machines. Each ton of bread, each gram of gold, each ton of cotton, coal and oil, and each machine – from the simplest to the most sophisticated one – contain a particle of labour of all Soviet people, of the entire country, of our whole multinational Union.

The entire atmosphere of our life and mutual work, the family and school, the army, culture, literature and arts are called upon to foster and cultivate in Soviet people of all nationalities, above all the youth, the noblest feelings, those of internationalism and Soviet patriotism.

Acting in the spirit of Leninist precepts, in the spirit of the directives of the 27th CPSU Congress, it is necessary to follow firmly the line of all nationalities and ethnic groups of the country being represented in Party, state and economic bodies, including at a countrywide level, so that the composition of the leading personnel fully reflects the country's national structure.

Natuurally the point at issue is not a mechanical assignment of jobs and posts according to the national principle – this would mean vulgarisation of the very idea of internationalism. Political, professional and moral qualities is what determines in all instances the image of the worker. Besides, one should not disregard the particular delicacy of national aspects in one problem or another, folk traditions in the way of life, in people's psychology and behaviour. All this should be taken into account most carefully.

I ought to mention, comrades, that some leaders at times approach questions of relations between nationalities without due responsibility.

From time to time misunderstandings emerge in relations between neighbouring districts or regions of various republics. At times they flare up into disputes escalating even into litigations while the heads of Party and local government bodies shirk principled solutions rather than prevent or abate the passions. Political workers should act wisely in such situations and cool unhealthy passions.

Our theoretical thought is greatly indebted to the practice of national relations. I mean the clearly insufficient analysis of issues in the nationalities policy that would be in line with the present stage of the country's development. It is a fact, comrades, that instead of conducting objective studies of real phenomena in the sphere of national relations and analysing actual socioeconomic and cultural processes – very involved and contradictory in their essence – some of our social scientists have for long preferred to create treatises reminiscent at times of complimentary toasts rather than serious scientific studies.

One should admit that the errors committed in the sphere of national relations and their manifestations remained in shadow, and it was not accepted to mention them. This has resulted in the negative consequences with which we are now dealing.

At the 27th Congress we stressed the inviolability of our Party's tradition that V.I. Lenin initiated: to display special tact and care in everything that concerns the development of national relations, that bears upon the interests of each nationality and ethnic group and people's national and ethnic group and people's national feelings, and to resolve promptly questions arising in this sphere.

It is in the traditions of Bolshevism to wage a principled struggle against any manifestations of national narrow-mindedness and snobbery, nationalism and chauvinism, parochialism, Zionism and anti-Semitism – no matter what their form might be. We should bear in mind that nationalism and proletarian internationalism are two opposite policies, two opposing world outlooks.

Proceeding from these positions we shall be firm and principled. People's national sentiments deserve respect; they cannot be ignored, but they should not be flirted with either. Let those who would like to play on nationalist or chauvinistic prejudices entertain no illusions and expect no leniency.

Principles, comrades, are principles and we cannot forgo them. No doubt, this position – the principled, Leninist position – will be supported by the entire Party, by the entire multinational Soviet people.

Personnel Policy in Conditions of Reorganisation

I think we clearly understand that success of the reorganisation largely depends on how quickly and deeply our workers realise the need for changes and how creatively and purposefully they implement the Party's policy. What is necessary today is a personnel policy that matches the reorganisation tasks and the need to accelerate social and economic development. When formulating its initial requirements we ought to take into account both the lessons of the past and the new large-scale tasks life poses today.

The years of socialist construction in the USSR saw the formation of a powerful potential of highly skilled personnel, while the immeasurably improved level of education and culture of workers and peasants, of the entire people, creates favourable conditions for its constant replenishment and renewal. Everything that we have accomplished, everything that we have attained, is the result of Soviet people's work and is due to our personnel's selfless effort.

At the same time one should also mention at this plenary meeting mistakes in work with personnel, distortions in personnel policy that have occurred in recent years and resulted in major shortcomings in the activity of several links in the Party, state and economic apparatus, and in negative phenomena in society. Many errors could have been avoided if Party bodies had always consistently pursued a principled, effective personnel policy ensuring high efficiency of all links in Party leadership and economic management.

Of course we should not confine ourselves today to the mere admission of mistakes. In order to avoid such mistakes in the future we must benefit from the lessons of the past.

What are these lessons?

The first is the need to resolve in good time the urgent personnel questions within the Party Central Committee, its Political Bureau – above all from the viewpoint of ensuring continuity in the leadership and the influx of fresh forces. At a certain stage the violation of this natural process weakened the work-capacity of the Political Bureau, the Secretariat and the entire CPSU Central Committee and its apparatus, as well as the entire government.

Indeed, comrades, following the April plenary meeting a large part of the

Secretariat and heads of departments in the CPSU Central Committee have been replaced, along with practically all of the Presidium of the USSR Council of Ministers. This was a forced change since the composition of the Central Committee and the government was not changed or replenished with new members for a long time, as life demanded. All this ultimately affected policy and the practical work of the Party in guiding society.

This cannot and should not be repeated. In order to ensure continuity and prevent a break in the process of renewal, the CPSU Central Committee, the Political Bureau and the Secretariat of the Central Committee, the government, the top echelons of the Party and state leadership should be open to the influx of fresh forces from various spheres of activity. Doing this fully corresponds to the Leninist understanding of personnel policy, to the interests of the Party and the people.

Certainly the Party Central Committee has accomplished a great deal of work and continues to do so. But the level of this work should under no circumstances be allowed to decrease. On the contrary it should constantly grow and meet the demands posed by life, by the development of society and the international situation. Any lowering in the level of the Central Committee's activity is impermissible.

The CPSU Central Committee must be an example of the implementation of Lenin's ideas, principles and methods in work. Our plenary meetings should discuss the really major issues of Party life, the country's domestic and international situation. They should be frankly and openly discussed, with a sense of profound responsibility, in an atmosphere of ideological cohesion and with a wide range of viewpoints expressed.

In this context I want to emphasise the role of Central Committee members, their rights and responsibility. During plenary meetings each Central Committee member should be guaranteed the right to raise questions and participate in their collective constructive discussion. In the Party – and especially at plenary meetings of the Central Committee – there should be no persons beyond criticism or without the right to criticise.

There are many things we will have to rectify here. Let us say honestly: there were many crucial issues of concern to the Party and the people that were not included in the plenary meetings' agendas for several years. Comrades will recall that the plenary meetings of the Central Committee were often brief and formal. Many Central Committee members were never given the opportunity to participate in debates or even put forward proposals during their entire term of membership. Such an atmosphere at the plenary meeting of the Central Committee had a definite effect upon the style of work of local Party committees and organisations.

The second lesson from past experience, comrades, is that we should not underestimate political and theoretical training, the ideological and moral steeling of Party workers. Otherwise very serious disruptions in the activity of Party committees as bodies of political leadership occur.

These criteria in the selection, placement and education of personnel were not always taken into account in recent years. Often the greatest significance was attached to a worker's knowledge of the specifics of one or other branch of production, science, engineering or technology, or his strength of will. Undoubtedly all that has importance, but such qualities in the managerial staff as ideological and theoretical outlook, political maturity, moral standards and the capacity to persuade and lead people should also not be ignored.

It should be directly and honestly admitted that the technocratic 'administrative pressure' style of work caused great damage to the Party cause, especially to work with people which is the main element of the Party's activity. By plunging into economic work and, in several instances, asssuming functions out of their jurisdictions, many Party workers did not pay enough attention to political issues, to socially significant phenomena in the economy, and in social and cultural life.

Certainly objective factors underlie such a style as well. They stem from a number of unresolved issues of economic management and the lack of an effective economic mechanism. In this situation many Party committees, aware of their responsibility and their duty before the people, have to take upon themselves the solution of many economic problems. This has been happening for a number of years and has become deeply rooted in the style and methods of work, leading to a certain warping of the principles of Party guidance and the very composition of our personnel body.

Major measures to restructure management and the economic mechanism open up wide opportunities for improving the work of the Party committees and organisations, enhancing Party influence in all spheres of the life of society and using a political approach to all problems under consideration.

I want to emphasise that no one can relieve Party committees of their concern and responsibility for the state of affairs in the economy. As I have already said, the point is to improve the methods of Party guidance so as to eliminate petty tutelage and methods of supplanting managerial bodies.

The third lesson we must learn is that two opposite tendencies paradoxically coexisted in the personnel policy in recent years. You may wonder what I mean, comrades.

The signs of stagnation have manifested themselves rather strongly in the personnel body. Secretaries of many Party committees and top executives of government and economic bodies at the local, republican and All-Union levels often have not been replaced for decades and there has been no influx of new forces there.

Saying this I do not want to cast the slightest aspersions on many hundreds and thousands of marvellous workers, particularly at the district and city levels, who have always devoted all their energies and knowledge to selflessly serving the Party and the people. Years of honest work and their truly deserved prestige reaffirm their right to hold leading positions. The CPSU and all the people highly appreciate their difficult work, their great services, and give them due credit for that.

I think that the well-known and well-assimilated truth that personnel stability is essential does not need additional proof. This should not be carried to extremes, to the point of absurdity, if you will.

We know all too well what this led to, what price is now being paid for artificial stability which has essentially turned into personnel stagnation.

On the other hand there also existed another no less disquieting tendency in the work with personnel, particularly in the primary units of the national economy. It is excessive personnel rotation, a real reshuffling of managers of industrial enterprises, construction projects, collective and state farms and other organisations.

You know how important the role of highly qualified organisers of production is. The leaders of work collectives – Communists and non-Party people – are the Party's main support in the pursuit of its socioeconomic policy. They shoulder many diverse tasks. So I want to ask one question: how could it happen that the leading personnel of work collectives changed completely within several years in many districts and regions?

This can only happen when actual work with people, a real concern for their political and professional growth, and for rendering them practical assistance is pushed to the background and is replaced by administration by injunction, by hasty and at times rash judgements of their activities and capabilities. I think that Party committees should take this very serious reproach and draw the right conclusion.

Regrettably there are also Party committees and secretaries who cover up their own blunders and, on occasion, failures with ostentatious exigence towards personnel, by pseudo-adherence to principle without regard for either the essence of the matter or the fate of the people involved.

In this connection I want to mention yet another inadmissible quality: the intolerance of some executives of independent actions and thoughts of subordinates. It quite often happens that as soon as workers begin to express independent opinions which do not coincide with those of the secretary of a Party committee, or the head of a ministry or department, enterprise, institution or organisation, attempts are made to get rid of them under any pretext, at times even under outwardly plausible ones. It may appear to be better. But better for whom or for what? For the work? Nothing of the kind. It is always worse for the work.

In this too, we should learn from Lenin. Lenin, like no one else, could bring people together and ensure their concerted effort. He supported resourceful people and attentively listened to Party comrades and, if necessary, patiently helped them to change their minds. We should learn to adhere to principle, and to be exacting and attentive.

The fourth lesson of our work with personnel is to enhance responsibility for the work assigned, to tighten discipline, and to create an atmosphere of mutual exigence. How could it happen, comrades, that many leading positions

at the district, city, regional, republican, and even all-Union levels were held
for decades by executives who could not cope with their duties, by undepend-
able and undisciplined people?

The consequences are well known. For years a number of sectors, among
them the iron and steel and coal industries, railway transport, machine tool
manufacture, agricultural engineering, the meat-and-dairy industry, to name
but some, were headed by executives who were failing to ensure the fulfilment
of the tasks set. Ostensibly everyone knew this. The state of affairs in those
areas was quite often criticised at the sessions of the USSR Supreme Soviet,
at plenary meetings of the Central Committee and even at Party Congresses.
But everything remained unchanged.

Are there not regions, republics, cities and districts where production
targets have not been met for years and where social matters have been
neglected? Their leaders bore no responsibility for failures in work. They got
away with it all.

The same can be said about some managers of enterprises, economic
organisations, health care, educational, scientific and cultural institutions, and
the mass media. They have long neglected their work. They cannot cope with
their duties and instead are masters at throwing dust in people's eyes. They are
complaisant in their attitudes. Until recently they were able to retain their
positions through these subterfuges.

It also happens that an executive finds himself in the wrong position and is
not capable of the job required. His misfortune is that he has got that post and
work that is beyond him. What should be done in such cases? It is essential to
admit such errors and rectify them and, without dramatising them, assign the
person concerned to a job according to his abilities.

We must not and cannot be 'kind' at the expense of the interests of the Party,
society and the people. The interests of the Party and the people are above all.
Such is our immutable law. Real concern for personnel has nothing in
common with complacency and all-forgiveness, philanthropy and flirting. We
should assimilate this lesson well, too.

Finally one more lesson. It is natural to raise this question at our plenary
meeting: why have all these problems that have piled up in the work with
personnel remained for a long time unattended and unresolved? How could
this happen? The question, as you well understand, is very serious.

The Political Bureau's opinion is that the main cause is the weakness of
democratic principles in the work with personnel. I have already spoken of
inner-Party democracy in a principled way as the chief guarantor of the
implementation of the Party's strategic course and the tasks of reorganisation.
Proposals on such a cardinal question of democratisation as the formation of
elective bodies within the CPSU were made as well.

Now I would like to present the question of raising the role of all elective
bodies. It must be frankly admitted that if they acted to the best of their abilities
both in the Party and in the state, trade unions and other public organisations,

many serious omissions in the work with personnel could have been avoided.

Let us look at life with open eyes, so to speak. An excessive growth of the role of executive bodies to the detriment of elective ones has occurred. At first glance everything proceeds as it should. Plenary meetings, sessions and sittings of other elective bodies are held regularly. But their work is often excessively formalised, secondary matters or those decided upon in advance are brought up for discussion. As a result there is a lack of proper control over the activities of executive bodies and their leaders. Let's face it, some comrades began to view elective bodies as a nuisance which give only headaches and create troubles. That's what we have come to.

That resulted in the decreased role of the deputies of the Soviets, of members of Party and other collective decision-making bodies in forming executive committees, selecting personnel, and having control over their activities. Is not the same evidenced by the nature and style of relationships between the permanent staff and members of elective bodies? Quite often one comes across attempts by staff members to command members of Party committees, other public organisations and deputies to the Soviets. It turns out in fact that democratic mechanisms for the formation and functioning of the elective bodies are proclaimed but far from always work and consequently are not sufficiently effective.

That is why, returning to what was said about the development of socialist democracy as the reorganisation proceeds, I want to re-emphasise the topicality and immense importance of the formulated proposals on these matters. We should work out and implement measures to ensure a decisive role of collective, elected bodies. No executive body, still less so any of its officials, is allowed to supplant an elective one or domineer it.

The necessary political and legal prerequisites should be created for the elective bodies to exercise effective control over the executive staff, its formation and activities. This will be a reliable safeguard against many errors, including those in the work with personnel.

I think the participants in the plenary meeting realise well the fundamental importance of putting the question in this way and of the need urgently to solve it.

One of the causes of serious omissions in the personnel policy is the weakening of the role of control bodies within both the Party and the state and public organisations. They did not heed many reports about abuses and violations in a number of regions and branches of the national economy, in regional, territorial and republican Party committees. The work of control bodies was often confined to superficial checks and formal financial inspections, to examination of various complaints and minor human conflicts. These matters certainly need attention, but confining ourselves to them would be impermissible, especially now.

The 27th Congress of the CPSU has given a new direction to the activities of the control bodies. It is important that all of them, from the district to the central ones, should live up to their lofty mission and set an example of adherence to principle and justice.

Comrades, summing up, we cannot and must not repeat the mistakes of the past. What is more, I think, nobody will allow us to do so.

Such are the main lessons of the personnel policy about which, in the opinion of the Political Bureau, it is necessary to report to the plenary meeting.

The main conclusion from them is that we must radically update our personnel policy, free it from distortions and oversights, make it truly modern, more vigorous and purposeful, inseparably link it with the key trends in the effort to accelerate socioeconomic development.

I repeat that the point at issue is not just one of improving the organisation of work with the personnel, but of formulating a personnel policy that accords with the tasks of reorganisation. It is only with such a broad approach that work with the personnel will expedite profound, in effect, revolutionary, changes.

Lenin taught us to approach the work with personnel from a political angle, first of all, to view it in the very context of the problems being tackled at the given stage and to select personnel 'by the new standards, according to the new tasks'. What does this mean as applied to the present stage of social development?

The personnel's attitude to reorganisation and the ongoing acceleration of the country's socioeconomic development, their attitude not in words, but in deeds, is today the decisive criterion in personnel policy. We must certainly take into account the fact that the selection and work of the personnel continued for a long time in far from optimum conditions. That is why change does not come easily. We must work painstakingly and persistently if we are to reorganise the personnel body.

We have decisively taken the course of supporting enterprising, thinking and energetic people, who can and wish to forge ahead boldly and who are capable of winning success. We have many of them. The decisions of the April plenary meeting and the 27th Congress have lent them wings and opened broad vistas for creative activities. Just look how strikingly fresh and powerful are the talents of such managers as Vladimir Kabaidze from Ivanovo, Boris Fomin from the Leningrad 'Electrosila' Works, Anatoly Parshin from the Taganrog 'Krasny Kotelshchik' Works, Ivan Frantsenyuk from the Novolipetsk Steel Works, Raisa Roshchinskaya, director of the Novocherkassk Clothing Factory, Yuri Baranov, Director of the Donetsk Mine Administration 'Sotsialistichesky Donbass', Nikolai Travkin, Head of the 'Mosoblselstroi' Trust No. 18, Alexander Duduk, Director of the Byelorusssian 'Mir' State Farm, Mikhail Klepikov, a well-known team leader from the Kuban, chairmen of collective farms – Vasily Gorin from Belgorod Region, Nikolai Tereshchenko from Stavropol Territory, Mikhail Vagin from Gorky Region and Yuri Bugakov from Novosibirsk Region, and many, many others.

We must learn to support such workers in every way and to appreciate their independence and initiative. It is important to build in every Party organisation, in every work collective, an atmosphere that would stimulate all to search for effective solutions, and encourage the most open and frank exchange of views. Certainly we must vigorously renounce such methods as dressing down which are often used even to this day. We are for reorganisation but not for a shake-up of the personnel. It is necessary, comrades, to respect people and trust them more.

Today everyone has the opportunity to display his abilities and we must assist those who wish to work with both advice and comradely criticism. But we part company with those who cling to old ways and who remain indifferent to the current changes, sometimes even opposing them.

Thus the attitudes to the reorganisation and real contribution to its implementation are decisive in appraising the personnel. We must certainly take into account other basic qualities as well. I mean first and foremost intolerance of shortcomings, conservative ways, indifference and passivity, and commitment to all that is advanced and progressive.

Reorganisation requires that the workers be competent and highly professional. Today one cannot do without a modern and broad background, without a profound knowledge of production, science and technology, management, economics, labour organisation, incentives and psychology. Generally speaking we must put the country's intellectual potential to maximum use and considerably increase its payback.

Organisational standards and discipline are assuming increasing importance. They are indispensable everywhere but are especially vital in conditions of modern production with the extensive use of the latest technologies. In recent years, consequent upon things being set in order and carelessness being dealt with, there has been a noticeable increase in the economic growth rates.

Yet the task remains here. Poor discipline and negligence are too deeply rooted and are felt painfully to this day. It was criminal negligence and lack of responsibility that stood behind such tragedies as the accident at the Chernobyl nuclear power station, the wrecking of the *Admiral Nakhimov* and a number of air and railway accidents which claimed a toll of human lives.

An atmosphere ruling out any possibility of a repetition of such tragedies must be created everywhere. Discipline, promptness and efficiency should become the law for everybody.

And finally, the most important quality is the high moral standard of our personnel – honesty, incorruptibility, modesty. We now know, not only from the past, but also from our recent experience, that we would not be able to carry out the reorganisation tasks without strengthening our society's moral health. It is therefore only logical that we have come to grips so uncompromisingly with negative phenomena precisely in the moral sphere. I mean the struggle to eradicate drunkenness, embezzlement, bribery, abuse of office and protectionism.

Society reacts most keenly to all that is associated with the moral image of

Party members, primarily senior executives. Our paramount duty is to rehabilitate the untarnished and honest image of a Communist leader, an image somewhat degraded by the crimes of certain renegades.

In general, comrades, considering the imperatives of the times, we are to readjust radically our work with the personnel in all branches of the national economy, in all areas of social life, in all echelons of leadership, both at the centre and in the provinces.

The Political Bureau sees the essence and main objective of the present personnel policy first and foremost as developing a more exacting attitude to the Party and its workers. To carry on reorganisation in society is to reorganise the activities of the Party and its workers at all levels – from the Central Committee to primary organisations, to creatively assimilate and consistently implement the Leninist principles and rules of Party life at all levels.

How is reorganisation proceeding within the Party? What example is set by the Party committees, Party leaders and activists?

Today we can say that most Party committees and their leaders have got down to work with a great sense of responsibility and a sincere desire. They are not yet able to cope with many things, but they are gaining experience and confidence with every passing day. These changes create reliable prere-quisites for accelerating our advance.

All the Party workers are going through the test of reorganisation. But they cope with it differently. A visible gap has formed between those who are decisively forging ahead and those who are marking time. Reorganisation does not come easy to some Party leaders. They cannot yet give up the controller functions so unnatural for Party committees or get rid of the tendency to decide all questions for others and keep a tight grip on things. But this, as before, prevents a sense of responsibility for the entrusted job growing in the workers and hampers the development of their initiative and independence.

Instead of developing innovative quests Party workers often morbidly react to the initiative and activity of people and view them as something short of a natural calamity. The paramount duty of the Party committees at the time of reorganisation is to guide the creativity of the masses to help people rapidly eliminate shortcomings and get things going properly.

It is necessary at the same time to warn comrades against artificially speeding up events and putting the cart befre the horse. Reorganisation and the acceleration of our advance are based on the objective laws of social development. As in any social movement the role of the subjective, personal element is sufficiently great here. Its influence may be either favourable or otherwise. It is therefore highly important that the process of revitalisation, which affects human lives rather tangibly, be reliably protected against relapses of administration by injunction and a mechanical approach to matters in hand. A devaluation of the idea of reorganisation cannot be allowed anywhere, not in a single sector of our social and production system. One must see and react immediately, when time-serving and self-seeking are appearing under its banner, when real work is replaced by high-sounding phrases.

I wish to repeat that without developing democracy, without the broad involvement of the working people, we will not be able to cope with the tasks of reorganisation. The Party committees and all workers should learn to operate in conditions of greater democracy and growing political and labour activity on the part of the people.

We have had ample opportunity to see that the reorganisation proceeds faster where the district and city Party committees are more energetic and work in the new manner. This is only understandable. They are the closest to the primary Party organisations and work collectives and consequently to the frontline of the struggle to accelerate the country's social and economic development. Most of these committees have taken the right stand and are pursuing the Party's policy of reorganisation resolutely and consistently.

Yet an analysis of the situation at the local level, press reports, and working people's letters to the Party Central Committee indicate that there are still quite a few city and district Party committees which keep to the old ways, act in the old fashion and remain on the sidelines of the movement for renewal. Even if this concerned just one city or district committee, it could not be ignored. But this is something widespread and so we must, comrades, be concerned. In many cases this situation in the city and district Party committees is explained by the style and methods of work and the attitudes of their secretaries.

I think we will do right if we pay more attention to these important Party units – city and district Party committees. We must help them adopt a more active attitude towards reorganisation as soon as possible. The primary Party organisations will then also work better and guide the work collectives in accomplishing their tasks. We are witnessing the steady growth of Communists' activity. We see inertia and formalism gradually disappearing from the work of Party organisations. But there is still a great deal to be done. The primary Party organisations need effective aid and support.

Comrades, immense responsibility for putting into effect the strategic policy for accelerated social and economic development devolves on the managerial personnel. A changeover is currently under way across the country from administrative to cost-benefit methods of management and to a responsible and creative manner of running affairs.

Today the work collectives of factories and amalgamations are being provided with vast financial, material and technical resources to modernise production and solve social problems. The managers are granted wide latitude, not only to make whatever tactical economic manoeuvres are expedient, but also to pursue long-term aims within the five-year plan period and beyond; in short, a new economic, social and political situation is developing, in which an energetic and competent executive can fully use his abilities.

Most executives welcome the far-reaching measures being implemented by the Party and the government to reform the system of management. They are becoming more active in their implementation.

We can already see a good start of many useful initiatives. The experience of Leningrad and Kharkov in converting factories into working in shifts is catching on and bringing the first benefits.

In Leningrad and in the entire region virtually all leading factories have been switched over to two- or three-shift operation. This has allowed an increase in the number of afternoon-shift workers by almost 50,000. Fixed assets are now being used more efficiently and updated more quickly. It has become possible to release 350,000 square metres of shopfloor space for other uses and slash the need for new construction by 120,000 square metres. According to preliminary estimates all this will help save over 100 million roubles in capital investment, most of which could then be spent on housing construction and on other social projects.

The managers and specialists of the factories and amalgamations which have followed the example of the VAZ Auto Factory and the Frunze Engineering Amalgamation in Sumy by changing to a profit-and-loss accountability principle and self-financing at the beginning of this year have been initiating many new things.

Interesting experiences in mastering new managerial methods have been gained by the Byelorussian and other railways. These experiences have helped to improve the performance of the rail service in general and raise labour productivity. Work collectives in a number of regions in the Ukraine have displayed a business gumption and enterprise by launching a large-scale drive for resources. The initiative of miners and metalworkers looking for and tapping new reserves to meet their targets ahead of schedule also deserves to be supported. Work collectives in Sverdlovsk, Lipetsk and other cities have been setting a good example of how to tackle housing and other social problems.

The acreage of grain and a number of other crops cultivated by means of industrial technology has been on the increase. Teams working on the basis of contracts and the profit-and-loss accountability principle are being formed at collective and state farms. This has helped to increase quickly agricultural production and make the economy more efficient.

Yet it must be said frankly that the process of workers and office personnel mastering up-to-date approaches to work and modern methods of economic activity is proceeding with difficulty, in a manner full of contradictions, and not without painful phenomena and relapses into past practices. The introduction of state quality control is a good example. Realising the immense importance of this measure, many work collectives have prepared well for work in the new conditions. Though there are difficulties progress is being made. Labour discipline and production quality are improving.

But there are also those who could not meet the high requirements. Instead of rolling up their sleeves and getting down to improving quality they began scaring themselves and others by dwelling on the possible complications, conflict situations and even factory shutdowns.

Comrades, I am far from simplifying the situation. But one thing is clear: we Communists, all Soviet people, can no longer put up with a situation in which many enterprises have for years been manufacturing products that are hopelessly obsolete, are seriously criticised by consumers and hold back the country's scientific and technological progress. We are tackling a big task and must see it through to the end.

The transition to the cost-benefit methods and the expansion of the rights of amalgamations and enterprises create a new situation for ministries and departments. We already discussed the questions concerning change in their style and methods of work at the June 1986 plenary meeting of the Central Committee. What has been done since?

Changes in the work of ministries and departments are taking place, even though slowly and painfully. Headquarters of various branches of the economy are directly participating in drafting proposals for enterprises' operation in new economic conditions. They are giving more attention to questions of scientific and technological policy, the restructuring of enterprises and starting the production of goods meeting modern requirements.

We have reinforced some branches and their subdivisions with capable people. As a rule energetic specialists who want to run things in a new way and ensure the introduction of modern methods of work have been placed in key posts. This policy should be continued, the performance of ministries and departments actively improved and their staff replenished with highly-qualified personnel capable of initiative.

At the same time there are still instances of red tape and irresponsibility in the work of ministries and departments which carry out the Party and government resolutions. The staff of ministries and departments appear to be captive of old regulations and instructions, act by inertia and refuse to give up their prerogatives.

It is not the first time, comrades, that we have drawn the attention of the heads and staff members of ministries and departments to the need for a radical reorganisation of their activity. In this way everyone gets the opportunity to join in this work and master new approaches to the business at hand. But it is impermissible for a ministry or its staff to be idle or, even more so, to impede the restructuring process. This warning from the rostrum of the plenary meeting is necessary because this concerns the interests of the state of the people, questions of big-time policy. It is appropriate to recall here Lenin's words that an apparatus exists 'for policy and not a policy for the apparatus'.

Workers are being placed in new conditions by the restructuring of external economic activities, giving many ministries and amalgamations direct outlet to the foreign market and granting all enterprises the right to set up direct ties of cooperation with partners in socialist countries. This is something the branch ministries have sought for years.

But it should be well understood that success in external economic activities is possible only if active use is made of scientific and technological achievements, if personnel is adequately trained, new markets are developed, etc. The main condition for utilising the new opportunities is to start producing goods whose quality meets world standards.

After the decisions were adopted much time and effort were spent on various organisational matters, on specifying rights and duties, and the relations between foreign trade organisations and the branch managerial bodies. But the organisational period has already ended. Now it is necessary to direct efforts towards practical actions and actively to start the development of ties with all foreign partners, especially in the socialist countries.

I have already said that the success of the strategy of acceleration depends above all on how we are fulfilling the tasks of scientific and technological progress, on how skilfully we are combining the advantages of socialism with the achievements of the scientific and technological revolution.

The real accomplishments here are determined by the level of scientific knowledge, by the advancement of original ideas that can be embodied in fundamentally new machines and technologies that make it possible to forge ahead in the leading areas of science and technology. Such is the strategic task the restructuring process sets before science.

Everything is important in accomplishing it – from enrolment of students at institutions of higher learning and the standards of training specialists, to replenishing the Academy of Sciences with talented scientists; from the work of scientific student societies to the research programmes of the leading academic and branch institutes; from a creative atmosphere in scientific collectives to the most effective forms of organising and promoting science.

Integration of science with production has now acquired a special importance.

A significant role in this matter is assigned to intersectoral scientific and technical complexes. By now over 20 of them have already been established. We have great hopes that the activity of these complexes will accelerate the development of new ideas and in particular the introduction of scientific and technical achievements. Therefore it is necessary to give more attention to the work of intersectoral scientific and technical complexes. The Presidium of the USSR Academy of Sciences and appropriate ministries and departments should provide them with all the necessary facilities, give them the help they need and do everything to facilitate their effective work.

Such major issues as the proper coordination of academic, higher-school and sectoral science; the integration of efforts by natural, technical and social sciences; comprehensive research; the profundity of treatment of fundamental problems; and the enhancement of the effectiveness of particular projects in many respects remain unsolved.

Addressing our scientists and all scientific workers on behalf of the plenary meeting, I want to say that for science to be actively involved in the process of restructuring it should be reorganised in many ways. Life forces us to quicken our pace. He who is not in the lead in scientific ideas is running the risk of falling behind in everything. That is the way the question is posed by our time, a time of profound changes in science and technology, yet unseen by mankind.

This makes it necessary for Party committees, ministries and departments and economic bodies to meet the needs of science which should always feel effective support. We know that the Presidium of the USSR Academy of Sciences and its president, Academician G.I. Marchuk, have interesting ideas and proposals on this score. I can assure you that these ideas will find support in the Central Committee and the government.

Prospects for socioeconomic, scientific, technological and cultural progress depend in many ways on the educational system and the quality of education. We have begun a reform of general and vocational schools. As you evidently know this reform is not a simple thing and therefore demands unflagging attention all along the line – from building up education's material and technical base to improving the content, forms and methods of the teaching and educational process. Decisions have been made to reorganise higher and specialised secondary education, raise the salaries of the higher school staff as well as grants for post-graduate and undergraduate students. All this will create favourable prerequisites for the accelerated development of science and production and for the fulfilment of the decisions adopted by the Party Congress. We must implement them and see to it that high end results are achieved as soon as possible.

The system of advanced training and retraining of specialists will be built on a new basis. Present-day production demands that the knowledge and skills of workers should be continuously increased and improved. The establishment of a state-run system of life-long education was set by the 27th Congress as one of the main tasks for us to accomplish. This is the only way to maintain the competence of personnel at the level of present-day demands, especially in the new and newest fields of technology and engineering. There is hardly any need to prove how important it is to hasten the preparation of proposals on this issue.

And finally, a few words about the tasks facing our planning, financial and other economic bodies. In their effort to radically reorganise their work they should take into account the provisions of the economic reform.

The economic departments of this country have submitted quite a number of proposals for restructuring management and the economic mechanism. But frankly speaking, the personnel of these departments are slow to reorganise and I would say even fall behind economic transformations in the sphere of production. What is happening there requires considerable changes in the functions of general economic department and their local bodies.

The political directives formulated by the 27th Congress should be taken by them as a guide in their work. The aim of the economic reform in the country is both the extensive development of independence of the lower echelons in the economy and further consolidation of the principles of centralism in management while simultaneously freeing the centre from petty tutelage of sectors, amalgamations and plants. All personnel, particularly the leaders of economic departments, should now act precisely in this key and give up the old approaches to work.

One more question directly relating to the activities of economic executives. Special attention in the twelfth five-year plan is given to the development of the social sphere. This is dictated by the state of affairs in this sphere.

We must close more quickly the existing gap between the development levels in the productive and social spheres.

The Party Congress made serious corrections in the political guidelines on these matters and came to the conclusion that insufficient attention to the social sphere had become one of the factors behind the lag in scientific and technological progress and the growth of production efficiency, and had hampered the utilisation of the existing potential.

The fact that over many years economic executives were not strictly asked to account for social matters seriously affected their attitude to work. This situation must be resolutely rectified. It will be difficult to accomplish without Party committees taking a firm position on the matter and without consistent practical steps on the part of the government.

Let us take the latest example. The first stage of the Astrakhan gas complex was commissioned late last year. Over 1.5 billion roubles were invested in that project. Eight thousand workers and specialists work there but only three thousand of them have permanent housing. Moreover the lag in building housing, outpatient clinics, canteens and other social and cultural facilities was a planning fault from the very beginning. Such is the deplorable outcome of the incorrect, mistaken approach to social matters by planning bodies. The situation is to be rectified as soon as possible.

All leading personnel from top to bottom are responsible for pursuing a vigorous social policy. Life itself has demanded that man's interest be given top priority in the activity of leading executives. Their ability to cope with social matters has now become one of the chief criteria of their business and political maturity.

Comrades, a great role in implementing the decisions of the 27th Congress is assigned to Soviets, trade unions, Komsomol and other public organisations and their workers. They too are facing the task of restructuring their activity. In effect the restructuring has already begun.

In what direction should it be continued? This is a question of immense political connotation since the points at issue are very important institutions of our political system. In carrying out reorganisation one should bear in mind both the current situation and trends in the development of Soviet society in general, of the political system, socialist democracy and the economic mechanism.

I want to reiterate: the course towards democratisation and the establishment of a new mechanism of administration and management offers an opportunity to combine correctly the Party's political guidance with the active role of government bodies, trade unions and other organisations.

We have already adopted fundamental decisions on improving the activity of the Soviets under the present conditions. These decisions enable them to act as true bodies of authority on their territory. Changes in the activity of the Soviets are taking place, but they cannot as yet satisfy us. We are all interested in seeing the Soviets starting work as soon as possible in earnest, in the spirit of the times.

Party committees must firmly steer the course towards enhancing the role of the Soviets and must not permit unjustified interference in their affairs, let alone supplanting them. It is of no less importance that the heads of the Soviets and the Soviet apparatus start to work at full capacity and overcome inertia, the habit to look back all the time at someone and wait for instructions. It is necessary to enhance democratic principles in the activity of the Soviets and their executive bodies.

As we said at the 27th Congress there are many issues bearing upon the vital interests of the working people that no one will resolve for the Soviets. They concern social policy, the improvement of services. The Soviets, however, have not fully realised their new rights, and are not making due demands on economic managers. This is also one of the reasons why last year's plans were not fulfilled as regards many indicators in building social and cultural facilities.

Let us take communal services. The way they operate, especially in the condition of freezing temperatures, is giving rise to much criticism at present. But that is the direct and proper business of the Soviets. They should drastically alter the work of improving trade, services, the organisation of recreation for working people and consumer goods production, and use more broadly the reserves for replenishing food resources.

We are planning major measures in the field of health services and public education. They are linked most closely with the activity of Soviets at various levels. The tasks are building up, so the Soviets ought to act with greater efficiency and persistence. This is what we have the right to demand from the people working in the Soviets and their apparatus. This is what Soviet people expect from them.

Reorganisation and all its facets concerns trade unions. Their rights are substantially expanded with the growth of the economic independence of enterprises and amalgamations. At the same time their responsibility is considerably growing in connection with more powers given to work collectives and the development of self-government. And, certainly, no one is relieving the trade unions of their obligations to accomplish tasks of social policy, to defend working people's interests.

In brief the demands on trade union workers have sharply increased. It is necessary to help them adopt an active stand in reorganisation, to create conditions for their broader participation in decision-making at all levels of management.

Now that the review and election campaign is drawing to an end in trade union organisations and the scheduled Congress of the Soviet Trade Unions is approaching, it is important that the entire complex of topical problems related to reorganisation be placed in the focus of attention of the delegates to the Congress. Work collectives make up the central link of reorganisation. It is there the trade unions should reveal their potential, appraise in a new way their capabilities and rights and thus increase their contribution to the national cause of socioeconomic acceleration.

In launching the struggle for improving the health of society the Party has proceeded since the very beginning from the premiss that this immense work should be based on the solid foundation of persuasion. Shaping the consciousness of millions of working people in the spirit of restructuring is one of the key areas of ideological activity.

We have succeeded to a certain extent in bringing ideological work closer to life, to the processes under way in society today. It is largely thanks to Party organisations, to our propagandists, that the ideas of renewal are becoming truly attractive for the masses. Work on the ideological front has not yet been launched in earnest in many areas. This includes political and economic education, lectures and foreign policy propaganda, atheistic education and so on.

The Central Committee is steering Party organisations into drawing all Party leaders, all Communists, into ideological work. But this in no way removes the task of stengthening the ideological sectors with highly skilled, educated people who feel the essence of the tasks set, who are capable of lucidly explaining the policy of the Party and of leading and organising the people.

The present-day conditions persistently demand that the Party's ideological army be reinforced with people who are well versed in economics, law, philosophy, sociology, literature and the arts. These are people who are deeply convinced that the decisions adopted by the 27th Congress and the course for restructuring are vitally needed.

Comrades, the need for strengthening socialist legality and order in the country confronts the Soviet courts, procurators' offices, militia and other law-enforcement agencies with new crucial tasks.

The Central Committee attaches great significance to these issues which are of concern to society. It recently adopted a special decision on further strengthening socialist legality and order and increasing protection for the rights and legitimate interests of citizens. It has given law-enforcement agencies and their personnel important and more challenging tasks. The Party committees and government bodies are to make every effort to increase the authority of those working in the courts, procurators' offices, judicial bodies, militia, courts of arbitration and notary offices, and see to it that these legal workers must be true to principle. The Party committees and government bodies must support voluntary patrolmen maintaining public order and help disseminate legal knowledge.

This position held by the Party places high demands on those standing guard over the law. Letters from working people and complaints from localities indicate that there are still a number of breaches in law-enforcement agencies themselves. In some areas, to use a popular idiom, they 'use cannons to shoot at sparrows', while leaving grave crimes against the interests of our society and citizens unsolved.

We set the law-enforcement personnel the task of abiding undeviatingly by this decision and learning persistently to work in the setting of greater democracy and public openness, relying on the trust and backing of all people.

Now a few words about diplomatic personnel. The activities of the Foreign Ministry are currently being reorganised. The structure of its central apparatus and foreign missions is being readjusted. Senior personnel are being renewed. This line should be pursued consistently and care should be taken to increase the efficiency of the diplomatic services. We must make certain that diplomatic work is fully in line with the vigorous international activities of the CPSU and the Soviet state.

The state security bodies staffed by ideologicaly steeled and professionally well-trained personnel dedicated to the Party and the people, vigilantly guard the Motherland's interests. We are convinced that the Soviet security bodies will continue uncovering hostile intrigues against our country quickly and cut them decisively short.

Finally, the tasks of the military personnel. The Party never slackens its efforts to build up the country's defence capability and assigns to servicemen a special role in fulfilling this vital task. This determines their immense responsibility to the people.

The Soviet armed forces are deeply involved in reorganisation as well. They are reliably protecting the peaceful work of our people and the country's security. They are discharging their internationalist duty with honour.

The Central Committee strongly relies on the military personnel and the Soviet officer corps in strengthening the country's defence capability. I am positive that in the complicated international situation today the Communists and all army and naval personnel will act with utmost responsibility, upgrade their skills, and increase the combat preparedness of all arms of the service.

The Soviet people and our Party rely on our armed forces and are doing everything to strengthen them. They have every reason to hope that no aggressive forces will be able to catch us unawares.

Comrades, in conclusion I would like to speak briefly about the goals for 1987. This year, which marks the seventieth anniversary of the October Revolution, holds special significance for us. The Soviet people are looking forward to the forthcoming anniversary as they thoroughly reorganise all aspects of public life. This year the Political Bureau believes it would be well to issue an Address to all Party members and all working people in the USSR.

The Central Committee calls on Communists and all Soviet people to display a still greater understanding and sense of responsibility for what is to be accomplished, for the destiny of the country and for the future image of socialism. We have achieved a lot in the decades of socialist construction. But time is putting new and ever greater demands on us. In these new changed conditions Soviet society is passing a test of dynamism, of the ability to climb the steps of progress rapidly.

Our economy is passing the test of high efficiency, of receptivity to advanced technologies, of ability to produce first-class goods and compete on the world markets. Our morality and the entire Soviet way of life are being put to test for an ability to develop steadily and enrich the values of socialist democracy, social justice and humanism. Our foreign policy is being tested for firmness and consistency in the defence of peace, for flexibility and self-possession in conditions of the frenzied arms race fuelled by imperialism and the international tension fanned by it.

In its innermost revolutionary essence, in the Bolshevik boldness of the plans, in its humanistic social orientation, the work being done today is a direct continuation of the great accomplishments started by our Leninist Party in October 1917.

Today the whole world is looking at the Soviet people. Will we be able to cope with the task? Shall we hold out? Will we be able to meet worthily the challenge thrown to socialism? We must give a worthy answer by our deeds, by our persevering work. And we cannot put it off.

As you well understand, comrades, the year 1987 has a most important role to play in the implementation of the Party's acceleration strategy. The success of the whole five-year plan period, of our major undertakings and the fulfilment of our long-term plans will depend on how well we do it. Hence it is of utmost importance to concentrate from the very beginning on specific deeds, on the implementation of the decisions taken. In short, it takes work – painstaking, routine but extremely important – on the part of Party committees, organisations, and all work collectives to implement Congress decisions.

Not only must we consolidate and develop our achievements of the first year of the five-year plan period in all sectors of the economy and in all spheres of life, but we must also advance further and make greater use of long-term growth factors. Along these lines it is imperative to achieve noticeable changes for the better and to make them irreversible.

While orientating the personnel to tackling the current tasks and fulfilling the assignments of the twelfth five-year plan period by all means, we must, as Lenin taught us, not lose sight of our perspective. We must specify and finalise ways of economic and social progress. The drafting of the plan for the thirteenth five-year plan period will begin shortly. It will be based on the new system of management making it possible to utilise socialism's potentialities and advantages to a greater extent.

Since the ongoing radical reform of economic management concerns fundamental questions of the functioning of the socialist economic system, as well as many aspects of political and social life and the style and methods of work, it would be expedient to examine the entire range of these problems at the Central Committee's next plenary meeting.

In view of these mounting tasks we turn to our personnel. What is required of them is good organisation, efficiency and the ability to mobilise the creative energies and resources of work collectives to the utmost. Everyone should learn to be able to react promptly and in a businesslike manner to the arising problems and difficulties, which naturally may emerge since the tasks being tackled are new and in no way easy. As a matter of fact all of us have to pass the test of political maturity in mastering new methods of work and guidance in all areas of socialist construction.

In short the new year has brought forth new and quite responsible tasks in implementing the general line of the 27th Congress. The Political Bureau is convinced that the ideas of the Congress, which have been profoundly understood by all our personnel and which have taken hold of their minds and thoughts, will more and more persistently and on a growing scale make their way into life. They will determine the course of our development and guarantee that the country will make fundamentally new advances in the economic, social and cultural spheres.

It is possible to sum up what has been said as follows: we all, and every one of us, should improve our work. The mobilising role of our Party, of all its organisations and of all Communists should manifest itself with particular force in the new situation. It is important to continuously keep in touch with the pulse of life and do everything for the projected plans to be implemented.

In this connection I would like to take counsel on this fundamental issue. Perhaps it is advisable to convene an All-Union Party conference next year on the eve of the report-and-election campaign within the Party, and extensively to review the course of the implementation of the decisions of the 27th CPSU Congress and sum up the results of the first half of the five-year plan period. It would also be in line for the conference to discuss ways to further democratise the life of the Party and society as a whole.

The discussion started at this conference could be continued at report-and-election Party meetings and conferences, at which the results of the restructuring work of each Party organisation should be analysed in an exacting way.

The very fact of convening an All-Union Party conference in accordance with the CPSU's Rules would be a serious step towards making our Party life more democratic in practice and developing Communists' activity.

Comrades, by formulating a personnel policy in the conditions of the reorganisation and acceleration of the country's social and economic development, the plenary meeting of the Central Committee thereby determines the most important areas of our work for many years to come. At the plenary meeting today we have repeatedly referred to Lenin, his thoughts and ideas. This is not just a tribute of great respect, not only an acknowledgement of Lenin's authority. This reflects the pressing desire to revive in modern conditions and to the fullest possible extent the spirit of Leninism, to assert in our life the Leninist demands on personnel. You will recall, comrades, how passionately, how tirelessly Lenin taught us that the success of revolutionary struggle, the success of any cardinal restructuring of society is largely determined by the tone set by the Party.

We wish to turn our country into a model highly developed state, into a society with the most advanced economy, the broadest democracy, the most humane and lofty ethics; where the working man feels he is real master, enjoys all the benefits of material and intellectual culture, where the future of his children is secure, where he has everything that is necessary for a full and interestng life. And even sceptics will be forced to say: yes, the Bolsheviks can accomplish anything. Yes, the truth is on their side. Yes, socialism is a system serving man, working for his benefit, in his social and economic interests, for his cultural elevation.

Concluding Speech at the Plenary Meeting of the CPSU Central Committee 28 January 1987

Comrades,

Our plenary meeting is finishing its work – the discussion of the main item on the agenda. The atmosphere in which it has taken place and the speeches made to witness the complete unanimity of views on all issues which the plenary meeting of the Party's Central Committee had to consider and decide. This has not been a formal unity but a unity based on the awareness of the Central Committee's responsibility for the success of the strategy formulated by the April plenary meeting and the 27th Congress of the CPSU.

Now that we have finished the discussions and are to adopt a decision it would be appropriate to ask this question: has our plenary meeting come up to the expectations of Communists and of all Soviet people? How is this question to be answered? Even by the highest standards, this plenary meeting has been a major political event in the life of both the CPSU and Soviet society.

I believe we have every reason for saying that this plenary meeting is taking the Party, the country and all society perceptibly further along the path of reorganisation. However, its significance can only manifest itself fully on this indispensable condition: all that we have agreed upon here must be consistently translated into reality by the CPSU plenary meeting's Political Bureau, the Central Committees of the Communist Parties of the constituent republics, the Party committees at territorial, regional, city, district and area levels, and all Party organisations throughout the Soviet Union.

This is why I put it this way: the plenary meeting will live up to the expectations if we continue in the same vein after it. This plenary meeting has laid a solid foundation for making further, steady progress along the path of acceleration, change, and improvements in personnel policy meeting the needs of the present stage of historical development.

The extensive discussions, in which 34 comrades took part out of the total 77 who had entered their names on the speakers' list, have given us a unique opportunity to look once more from different levels and angles of Party and state work, at the drive for reorganisation, to reflect on its purpose, assess the very process of reorganisation again, and hear first-hand opinions about it.

What is of paramount importance to us, and I think we have the right to say this, is primarily the political confirmation by the plenary meeting of the fact that the Party and all healthy forces of society stand for reorganisation. And since this is so there can be no other path at all. And this should mark an end to the debates on whether we need reorganisation or not. I fully agree with Comrade D.K. Motorny who stated here that reorganisation is no longer an idea; it is a reality.

The Soviet people are associating their own plans as well as the future of their country and its international prestige and authority with the reorganisation effort. Should we permit any wavering in pressing on with it? No, comrades, we should not.

Certainly, reorganisation is already a reality. Today we realise ever more clearly and profoundly that from the standpoint of both internal development and external conditions, the international situation, we must ensure the country's more rapid social and economic progress. But there will be no acceleration without society's renovation. Nor will there be any change in all spheres of its life without its renovation. The new tasks cannot be tackled by taking the old approaches, especially the historic tasks facing us today.

Reorganisation is not strolling along a well-beaten path. It is going uphill, often by untrodden ways. As the Central Committee's plenary meeting has shown once again, quite a few problems have accumulated in our society. Immense creative efforts and a long, selfless struggle are needed to carry out the great cause of reorganisation as our people and the time demand.

We are just at the start of the road. This must be made plain by the Central Committee's plenary meeting, since knowing where we are enables us to realise what we must do and how. If some people have decided they have already changed their ways, they must be reminded that we have only just started our reorganisation. The most important work is yet ahead. This is another important conclusion drawn by the plenary meeting of the Party's Central Committee.

While pursuing our reorganisation we must not run to extremes in our judgements. We must stand firmly on what is the only stable base – reality. Overestimating our achievements would be detrimental, but I would also like to stress with equal force that we must not fail to take note of even the slightest progress, even the tiny modicums of experience, since that would be just as harmful. All this is inadmissible, first of all, for the following reason.

We are just getting into our stride, finding concrete approaches in our political line and mapping out ways of attaining the targets we have set ourselves. We are just turning on the mechanism and means of reorganisation and making our first steps in having them swing into action and yield results. But already today as we reviewed the results of 1986, we saw that the headway had been made.

How has progress been made? It is the direct result of our people's support for the line towards reorganisation, towards acceleration.

How can we fail to see this or say that nothing has happened or nothing is taking place? The revolutionary is not the one who uses revolutionary phrases, but the one who can view things in perspective and rouse the people and the Party to protracted and persistent effort, taking note of every step of progress and using it to find another fulcrum for a new and broader stride.

Today at the plenary meeting of the Central Committee we must express the Party's immense gratitude to our people for realising and feeling that they are called for a difficult struggle for such changes and such goals which will bear fine fruit to our entire society, to every family and every person.

The Soviet people have believed us and supported the Party. This is why the good changes achieved in 1986 are so important to us. They are of importance because they reflect our people's powerful support for the Party's policy and for its course for acceleration.

I want to emphasise some other points mentioned at the plenary meeting. To my mind it is quite legitimate that the subject of serious in-depth democratisation of Soviet society has been put as the major one in the Report of the Political Bureau.

This is, comrades, the lever which will make it possible to draw into the reorganisation its decisive force – the people. If we do not do this we will never accomplish the tasks of acceleration, nor achieve reorganisation. There will be just no reorganisation at all.

On the other hand, while developing and furthering socialist democracy and bringing its potential into play we must create most reliable guarantees that will prevent a repetition of the errors of the past. But the point is not only in that.

We need democracy like air. If we fail to realise this or if we do realise it but make no real serious steps to broaden it, to promote it and draw the country's working people extensively into the reorganisation process, our policy will get choked, and reorganisation will fail, comrades.

That is our main idea, and as all the members of the Political Bureau – we exchanged opinions on the course of the plenary meeting during each interval – I am very much satisfied with the fact that this major line in the CPSU's activities at the present stage of the drive for attaining the goals of acceleration has been fully supported by the Central Committee's plenary meeting.

The Communist Party is firmly of the opinion that the people should know everything. Openness, criticism and self-criticism, and control exercised by the masses are the guarantees for Soviet society's healthy development. Since the people need them, this means that they are really needed. This is all the more important since the CPSU is the ruling party. It is also interested in openness, in criticism and self-criticism, for these are real and reliable forms of the normal functioning of the CPSU. These are the means which can protect the Party from errors in politics. The price of these errors is known to all of us.

Today we all are arriving at the same conclusion: we need openness, criticism and self-criticism as effective forms of socialist democracy. In our state, a state of workers and peasants, everything concerns the people, because it is a state of the people. They should know everything and be able to consciously judge everything. These words, as you know, were said by Lenin. The people want the truth. While on this point I would like to remind you of Lenin's standpoint expressed in a letter to the newspaper *Iskra*. 'Indeed, it is high time to make a clean sweep of the traditions of circle sectarianism and – in a party which rests on the *masses* – resolutely advance the slogan: *More light!* – let the Party know *everything*,' Lenin wrote. As never before we need now more light so that no dark nooks are left to become overgrown with mould again, something we are resolutely fighting, but have yet a long way to go in our struggle. This is why we need more light.

Can it possibly be that with such a powerful Party and patriotic people, loyal to the ideals of socialism and their Motherland, we will fail to rise to the occasion if someone tries to take advantage of wide openness and democratic processes to pursue selfish and anti-social purposes and to slander?

I want to share an observation I made from analysing my trips. Before, more often than not, demagogues came to the fore, showing off their 'courage'. The demagoguery was mainly along such lines: in what direction are the top officials, especially those in Moscow, looking? The situation is different now. I draw this conclusion from scores of meetings. Today mature, serious people engage in frank conversations, often in most unexpected, unprepared audiences and places. They raise issues in a businesslike manner, ask questions about what is unclear to them, and find out how particular issues are to be solved.

It is the openness and democracy that have allowed the working class, the peasantry, our intelligentsia and all healthy forces to hold up their heads. Once a demagogue appears, they put him down. I have seen this dozens of times. People will always see which is which.

Openness, criticism and self-criticism are vital for us. These are major requisites of the socialist way of life. If someone believes that we need these only for criticising past drawbacks he is making a big mistake. The main point is that openness, criticism and self-criticism, democracy, are necessary for our advance, for accomplishing immense tasks. We shall not be able to accomplish these tasks without the people's active involvement. This is why we need all this.

If some one finds that it is not easy to work in such a situation I want to recall that six months ago I urged people to begin learning how to work in conditions of widening democracy. Let all of us learn that.

The press must promote openness of information in the country and keep our people informed about everything. But it should do this responsibly: such is the wish we are expressing. Don't indulge in sensationalism. We need the press as an active participant in reorganisation.

We should add work efficiency. Remarks by many comrades on this score have already been sounded right here.

This concerns all, including the press. At present it is very important for us to see all that is positive and constructive and adopt that for further use, to make it the asset of the entire Party and all people, and to cherish the sprouts of new approaches in the process of reorganisation. Greater openness and the popularisation of everything advanced are necessary in this field, too.

With this January plenary meeting of the Central Committee we are entering – I do not want to be accused of inventing another stage – but we are now entering a new stage of our movement, our reorganisation. I shall explain this. The situation has been reviewed, a political course has been set, and the main decisions for implementing the course have been adopted. Now what is needed is deeds and only deeds.

The people will judge our policy and our efforts of reorganisation and they will do this ever more strictly, by the tangible results we achieve in securing real improvements in the working and living conditions of the millions: how much has been done to make the organisation of production more efficient or labour remuneration more fair, to step up housing construction, improve trade, services, municipal transport and the work of outpatient clinics and hospitals, and to build a healthier atmosphere in Party organisations and within work collectives.

In short we Communists must prove the correctness of our policy and the vitality of reorganisation on thousands upon thousands of facts of daily life. This places especially high demands on the personnel and concentrates their attention on attaining practical results. This is why it is so important now, as has already been said in the Report, to quicken the step, move into a higher gear, and for everyone to put in an even bigger effort at one's workplace.

I especially would like to stress the significance of the tasks to be tackled in this year 1987. These tasks are stupendous in terms of their scope and of the frontiers we shall have to reach in coping with them. They are especially important from the standpoint of mastering new methods of management, of switching the entire economy, including its numerous sectors, on to new rails of management.

Reorganisation, comrades, is a great school. It sets formidable tasks and we must pass through this school with flying colours. I would like to repeat once again: we must act, act and act – energetically, boldly, creatively and competently! This is, if you will, the principal task of the moment. Everybody, all Party organisations, all Party committees, all leaders, all Communists should regard this task as their own.

On behalf of the Central Committee of the CPSU I would like to address all comrades in the Party and all Soviet people: the cause of reorganisation, the cause of the revolutionary revitalisation of society, and the country's future, are in the hands of the people. The future will be what we make it, by our common labour, our intellect, and our conscience.

Reorganisation is the frontline for every honest person, for every patriot. There is enough work for everyone and the road ahead is long.

We are firm in our desire to carry out the decisions of the 27th Congress. We shall press on with bringing Soviet society to a qualitatively new peak in life. We are confident that reorganisation is irreversible.

Members of the Central Committee have spoken in favour of a countrywide Party Conference. For the Party such a conference would be a political event of great magnitude. I understand that those who did not participate in the deliberations also share this proposal which the Political Bureau put forward at the plenary meeting.

Comrades, we remember from history more than one conference which at crucial stages helped open up new ways and means for achieving the set aims, and solved problems transcending far beyond the framework of tactical ones.

We consider it necessary, and I am putting this to you for consideration, that the Political Bureau prepares proposals ready for one of the nearest plenary meetings of the Central Committee on the date and procedure of holding such a conference. We think that the All-Union Party Conference will impart a mighty charge to the report-and-election campaign and give a new impetus to the reorganisation activity of the Party and all its organisations.

These are, briefly, considerations which I wanted to express in conclusion of the discussion that took place at the plenary meeting of the Party's Central Committee. I thank you all for your active participation in the work of the plenary meeting and wish all great successes in our common cause.

10

Revolutionary Transformations

Trade Unions and Workplace Democracy

Comrades,

On behalf of the Central Committee of the Communist Party of the Soviet Union (CPSU) I greet your Congress and in your person all the working people of the land of Soviets.

Exactly a year ago, on 25 February, the 27th Congress of the CPSU began its work here in the Kremlin Palace of Congresses. The Congress has proved a turning point in the destiny of our homeland and for the future of socialism. It broadly and boldly reviewed the experience gained in building a new society and worked out a mobilising policy for accelerated countrywide socioeconomic development and for work toward the ideals of peace and humanism.

A month ago we had the January plenary meeting of the Party's Central Committee. That plenum substantially deepened our awareness of the situation that has developed, specified the tasks in reorganising all the political activities of the Party and the people, elaborated a detailed concept for the democratisation of social life, and gave a powerful impetus to the process of throwing off everything that still hampers revolutionary transformations.

A meeting with the participants in the forum: For a Nuclear Weapon-Free World, For the Survival of Humanity, was held in the Kremlin slightly more than a week ago.

As you know, the political and ethical principles of the foreign-policy strategy of the Soviet Union and its approach to the global problems of mankind, notably the priority of preserving life on earth, were set out before an authoritative and widely-representative audience.

These events reflect the mighty rhythm of our times – a period of great undertakings, re-evaluation and growing hopes, social enthusiasm and uncompromising struggle between the new and the old. This is a difficult time but an unusually interesting one, a time when society is gaining confidence in

Speech at the Eighteenth Congress of Soviet Trade Unions, 25 February 1987 its strength, a time of civil maturation and patriotic non-complacency of people.

We are confident that the practical work of your Congress and the decisions taken by it will be likewise imbued with the spirit of our times.

A year is on the whole a brief period but the year past saw very much from the viewpoint of social meaningfulness. And at the same time we now realise: only the very first steps have been made.

The main thing, and hence the most difficult still lies ahead. Up to now we have been mostly preparing for reorganisation: we were working out its strategy, mapping out the main ways, identifying everything that was a hindrance and called for adjustment, and determining positions of departure.

It is now time to get the reorganisation actually moving. The year 1987 will be determinant in many respects, for the fate of the reorganisation is effectively being decided now and the foundation for acceleration is being laid.

The reorganisation, as was emphasised at the January plenum of the Central Committee, is reality, and not an idea any longer. It is getting hold of the minds of people and that means it works. It works for socialism, for the renewal of our society.

We are building not from scratch, and one cannot build anything worthwhile starting from scratch. We have got something to be proud of and to rely upon. We have got great values which we place above everything else.

Behind us we have a vast and diverse experience, which has not yet been assessed to the full, in building socialism in practice, experience which one must constantly turn to, learning to solve in the Leninist way problems as they arise.

Behind us we have tremendous economic, scientific, technical and intellectual potentials created and multiplied by the energies and talents of all peoples of our great country.

Yes, comrades, we have traversed a long path, a difficult and heroic one.

But through all the ordeals we have carried the revolutionary spirit of the people, faith in socialism and its supreme justice.

We have coped with and overcome eveything. We have managed unprecedented advance from the wooden plough and the light-giving flint to space flights, and we have experienced an incomparable joy – the joy of great accomplishments.

The indissoluble connection between work and civic concern for the common weal, which brings together all generations of Soviet people, our patriotism, working-class pride, labour enthusiasm, and the sacred feeling of belonging to the great cause of the October Revolution – all these are the mammoth gains of our system without which it is simply inconceivable.

It is precisely the working man and first of all the working class with its devotion to revolutionary traditions that is the principal motive force in today's tranformations.

Industriousness has always been the supreme ethical value of our people, and mastery has invariably belonged to man's chief virtues.

Today, too, we have got true experts, people to look up to and to live up to. these are the likes of Vladimir Matveyevich Gvozdev, team leader at the Raspadskaya mine of the Yuzhkuzbassugol Association of the Kemerovo Region, Nina Nikolayevna Shcherbakova, a weaver at Moscow's Tryokhgornaya Manufaktura cotton mill, Vajno Alexandrovich Saar, team leader at the Tallinnstroj Building Trust, Razifa Salikhanovna Khanova, a milkmaid at the Karl Marx Collective Farm in the Bashkir Autonomous Soviet Socialist Republic, Valeri Makarovich Kolesnikov, a rolling-mill operator at the Kuznetsk Metallurgical Complex, and Yevgeni Petrovich Razmyatov, leader of a multi-skill team at the Petropavlosk-Kamchatsky commercial port.

These and thousands of other names have been brought forth by our times of revolutionary acceleration. The country refers to them as Stakhanovites of reorganisation, and fair enough, I should say. We have such people everywhere, in many work collectives.

It is essential to secure that the number of those working for the renewal of society, for the reorganisation, and doing so through innovatory and conscientious labour rather than by means of words and assurances, swells with every passing day.

Of course we all want changes for the better as soon as possible. The lofty goals which the Party has put forward and the growing changes in the economy, social and political spheres have resulted in what may be termed a 'revolution of expectations'.

Many want a speedy social and material return. I can judge this from recent meetings with the working people of Latvia and Estonia.

Let us be frank, comrades. We can achieve acceleration and better quality for our entire life in only one way: through effective and highly productive work.

No mechanisms of distribution or redistribution create anything by themselves.

Yes, we need to refine much in the national economic management system, in the social, political and ideological spheres.

Such work, as you know, is being conducted and will be conducted in the future as well. But there has to be more emphasis on labour ethics as a whole.

The January plenary meeting of the Central Committee directly mentioned the responsibility of the Party and of its leading bodies for the state of affairs in the country.

But, for sure, this is only one aspect of the matter, although a very important one. Yet there is another aspect too.

It is no secret to anyone that many were content and some still remain happy to work in a slipshod manner, with unearned pay, undeserved bonuses, with a mutually undemanding atmosphere, with lack of control, and with irresponsibility.

It must be clear: time, efforts and practical actions are needed for our legitimate material and social expectations to come true.

Reorganisation implies an increase in everyone's efficiency in one's work, be it worker, collective farmer, office personnel, engineer, scientist, teacher, government minister or Party official. By no means everywhere and always do things stand in precisely this way.

When evaluating at the January plenary meeting of the Central Committee the positive changes achieved last year, we said that they reflected the Soviet people's powerful support for Party policy and for the Party's course towards reorganisation.

But the beginning of the year has shown that the positive changes have not become a steady tendency of economic development.

Difficulties in metallurgy and the chemical and electronic industries grew from the second half of last year but that was not given proper attention in ministries, in the USSR State Planning Committee and the USSR State Committee for Material and Technical Supply. The workers at many enterprises in these sectors did not set about correcting the situation in time.

The results of January showed that both in the centre and provinces many people did not prepare themselves properly for work in the conditions of enhanced demands on the activity of enterprises and amalgamations given full-scale transition to new methods of economic management.

The situation is being rectified now, but the process is slow. The Central Committee of the Party counts on understanding from the working class and all working people of the significance of the moment, of the importance of successful implementation of the projected plans for the cause of acceleration, and on the growing contribution to economic development.

We want today to radically alter the atmosphere in society, for we cannot be pleased with how we lived and worked previously.

Nothing will come of it if we do not fully break the forces of inertia and deceleration which are dangerous in their ability to draw the country back again into stagnation and dormancy and the menacing congealment of society and social corrosion.

Here I would like once again to touch upon the report of the January plenum.

We had an April plenary meeting in 1985 and of course it was not a fortuitous phenomenon. That plenum succeeded in expressing what was being thought and welling up in the country. It critically analysed the state of affairs in society and called for the elaboration of a concept of acceleration.

When we saw the reaction by the Party and by the people to the ideas of the April plenum, we became convinced that we had taken the correct path.

Following the April plenum we held a large-scale meeting in June on matters concerning scientific and technological progress. As a result of that meeting we worked out important programmes for machine-building and a number of other branches of the national economy, and planned out measures to refine the management machinery, including those for running groups of interconnected sectors of the economy.

All that was the starting point for giving shape, on the basis of the April plenum, to the concept outlined by the 27th Congress. The concept is known to you, comrades.

Following the Congress there arose the task of putting the strategic line towards the acceleration of the country's socioeconomic development on the plane of practical work. Previously, as you know, quite a number of good decisions aimed at advancing the economy had been taken, but they often remained unfulfilled.

The Central Committee of the CPSU was aware that there would be no acceleration if we did not start to reorganise societal life and make healthier the entire atmosphere in the Party and community.

It was at that time that there arose a question of preparing a plenary meeting of the Central Committee to work out a theory of reorganisation and determine the tasks of the personnel policy at the new stage.

Such was the main thrust of the January plenum.

To prepare it proved a difficult matter. Suffice it to say that we postponed the start of the plenum three times, for we could not hold it without having a clear idea of the main issues.

We were to deepen the analysis of the situation which had preceded the April plenary meeting and to draw lessons from it.

The most important thing was to suggest what should be done for the reorganisation to proceed vigorously and not peter out.

If we at the plenum had limited ourselves only to statement of deficiencies and difficulties and had not suggested specific directions for reorganisation, such a plenum would have been of little benefit.

We must provide an answer to the main question which is uppermost in the minds of people: how we are to make the reorganisation irreversible and to make sure that errors are not repeated.

The Political Bureau of the Central Committee arrived at an unambiguous conclusion: the reorganisation would get stuck if the main character – the people – did not join it thoroughly in all the spheres – economic, social, political, spiritual and in the sphere of management.

Everything should be placed under the control of the people so as to make the reorganisation irreversible and to prevent a repetition of what happened in the past. There is only one way to resolve these tasks, namely through broad democratisation of Soviet society.

Prior to the January plenum everyone asked the question: will not this process come to a stop?

The January plenum strengthened the conviction within society that reorganisation is assuming an irreversible character. This has greatly invigorated the attitudes of many sections of the population. There were quite a few people who stuck to a wait-and-see policy. Now they are joining the ranks of activists. But this process is not easy, is not without pain.

What is the matter? Until now we were at the stage of developing a concept of social and economic development – the April plenum, the 27th Congress and the June plenum. At present the process of reorganisation has started to move deeper, into practice, and it turned out that it was affecting the interest of many: in one case – through product acceptance by state-appointed inspectors, in a second – through self-repayment and self-financing, in a third – through election, in a fourth – through control, openness, criticism and so on.

Nothing is surprising here. The process of reorganisation affects increasingly new spheres of societal life and the interest of all social groups. And typically of truly revolutionary changes, reorganisation encourages and lends fresh vigour to some; others are perplexed; still others simply do not like the ongoing changes. These changes are particularly against the liking of those who got used to working without much effort, to do everything on the off-chance, who are indifferent and inert. These changes are also not to the liking of those who until now ran the affairs of an enterprise, district, city or laboratory as if it were his own patrimony, with least regard for the opinion of the collective, of the workforce. Among them are also people who used the atmosphere of total licence for embezzlement and gain, cynically disregarding our laws and morality. Here lie the sources of resistance to reorganisation: sluggishness and the desire to wait things out.

I will say again: in principle, this is no surprise. On the contrary it would be strange if the reorganisation suited all – honest and dishonest, hard-working and lazy people, activists, principled persons and high-handed functionaries. This would mean that something in our policy had not been well considered, that something did not work, was faulty. There is here a political nuance which should not be disregarded. I mentioned selfish opponents of reorganisation. There is, however, dramatism in the situation when selfless, honest people who so far remain captives of outdated notions are among its opponents. These are people who have not realised the acuity and critical character of the problems facing society.

We ought to persuade them and win their confidence through the correctness of our cause, through success of the reorganisation. It is our duty to help such people understand their true interests and find their place within the common ranks.

In general the reorganisation is affecting all: Political Bureau members, central committee secretaries, government members, workers, farmers and intellectuals. It is affecting the whole of society, the interests of all and everyone. At this point I want to recall Lenin's instruction concerning the need to distinguish between short-term and vital interests of the working class.

Yes, indeed, the reorganisation is affecting our short-term interests. But it meets the vital long-term interests of the working people. We ought to understand that. This understanding is of principled significance.

This is a very important provision.

The reorganisation ought to reveal socialism's potential, advance society to new frontiers, ensure a new quality of life in all spheres – economic, social and intellectual – and consolidate socialism. As I have already said it meets the vital interests of the working people. And if it is affecting us in some way today we should consider everything calmly, objectively assess the situation and adopt practical measures to abate outstanding problems.

We possess necessary political experience and theoretical potential to resolve the tasks facing society. One thing is clear: we should advance without fail along the path of reorganisation. If the reorganisation peters out the consequences will be far more serious for society on the whole and for every Soviet person in particular.

Our choice of the path is correct. We are not moving away from socialism. Through reorganisation we are developing the potential of the socialist system. We are moving not away from democracy, but towards unfolding democracy in the working people's interests.

So shall we abandon all that? Abandon reorganisation to oblige those whom it affects and whom it compels to think, act and live in a new way? This would be no policy. this would be serving someone's interests and ambitions. The CPSU Central Committee and the government shall not agree to that. I want to assure you of that, your Congress, and in your person the country's working people of that.

We are convinced that this view is shared by the delegates to the Trade Union Congress and all Soviet people. This is what we take into account in our activity.

I will make one point anew. We must consistently and perseveringly broaden socialist democracy. The Soviet people have immense social and political experience. A great intellectual potential has been built in the country. The generations which are in action today and which are taking upon themselves responsibility are generations who were born and have grown up under socialism.

Socialism is a system of the working people. Everything taking place in the socialist state is a cause of the people. That is why we stand for openness. It should be the norm rather than a campaign. We stand for criticism and self-criticism, which also should be the norm in our life. We need such forceful forms of democracy as openness, criticism and self-criticism radically to change every field of social life.

This is a guarantee against repetition of the errors of the past, and hence a guarantee that the reorganisation process is irreversible.

Greater democratisation might prompt some people to ask if we are not disorganising society, if we shall not weaken management, lower standards for discipline, order and responsibility.

This is an extremely important question and we must have complete clarity on it.

I will put it bluntly: those who have doubts about the expediency of further democratisation apparently suffer from one serious drawback which is of great political significance and meaning – they do not believe in our people. They claim that democracy will be used by our people to disorganise society and undermine discipline, to undermine the strength of the system. I think we cannot agree to that.

Democracy is not the opposite of order. It is the order of a greater degree, based not on implicit obedience, mindless execution of instructions, but on fully-fledged, active participation by all the community in all society's affairs.

Democracy is not the opposite of discipline. It is a conscious discipline and organisation of working people based on a sense of really being master of the country, on collectivism and solidarity of interests and efforts by all citizens.

Democracy is not the antithesis of responsibility. It means no absence of control, no mentality that everything goes.

Democracy means self-control by society, confidence in civic maturity and awareness of social duty in Soviet people. Democracy is unity of rights and duties.

The deepening of democracy is certainly no easy matter. And there is no need to fear should not everything proceed smoothly at once, should there be pot-holes if not gullies.

But our society is mature, our Party strong. The socialist system relies on the firmest foundation of the people's support and draws strength precisely from democratism of our lifestyle.

The more democracy we have, the faster we shall advance along the road of reorganisation and social renewal, and the more order and discipline we shall have in our socialist home.

So, it is either democracy or social inertia and conservatism.

There is no third way, comrades.

I have already said recently that we need democracy not to show off and not to play democracy. We need democracy to rearrange many things in our life, to give greater scope to creativity of people, to new ideas and initiative.

Comrades, reorganisation opens up new prospects, advances new tasks to be handled by the Soviet trade unions.

What is the view of the priority tasks of trade unions in this connection? As far as I can see, precisely this question, central to your debate, was raised in Stepan Shalayev's report.

Let me express some opinions, too.

These tasks and the ways of working towards them lie in two interconnected routes.

One of them is the place of trade unions in society as a whole, their constitutional rights and obligations, relationship with the Party, with the state and its agencies, the ministries and departments and with other public organisations.

The other route is the activity of trade unions directly in work collectives, their daily varied ties with the masses, with individuals.

The new conditions in whch the country lives and acts, and the tasks we are working toward, make us re-evaluate also the role of trade unions in the life of society.

I see the new role of trade unions in conditions of reorganisation above all in their becoming a counterbalance to technocratic aspirations in economy that one should say have become widespread recently, and in pressing for the enhancement of the social trend of the economic decisions taken.

And this means that trade unions must vigorously participate in working out social sections of the plan and advance their own alternatives when necessary.

More than that, trade unions must vigorously act on a nationwide scale to prevent a gap in the solution of production tasks and development of the social sphere. This has happened in our country, this still causes us great losses, and immense effort is required to rectify the situation.

This work must be joined actively, comrades.

And if there are problems that need to be solved legislatively, well, there are no blocks for trade unions there either.

The proposals made by trade unions on this score invariably receive the most sincere attention and interested support of the Party and state leadership. Well I will say straightforwardly that we have an interest in the more active work of the trade unions. But if some trade union officials may have been offended or stung by my criticism – and you must remember that I said while visiting the Kuban area that some trade union officials were dancing cheek to cheek with economic managers – I think you understood the message of that criticism: one has to have one's own firm stand and firmly pursue a line protecting the interests of the working people.

I believe many useful and valuable things can be learnt also by studying the experience of the work of trade unions in the fraternal socialist countries and of international trade union organisations.

The main thing here is the aims to which this work, its ultimate result, and its usefulness to people and society, will be subordinate.

This means that in solving vital questions of the work, health, daily life, rest and recreation of people, the trade unions should act energetically, efficiently and in a businesslike manner.

Take, for instance, one of the most burning of our problems – housing.

It is known that the Party has set the very important task of providing in effect every family with an apartment or house to itself by the year 2000.

We are building up efforts along all lines, involving both the state and the work collectives. In 1986 we built 5.2 million more square metres of housing than in 1985 and that increment is not the limit.

Housing complexes are being made for young people and enterprise housing investment is being expanded.

The state has decided to grant privileges to workers who want to build houses with their own money. It has been said at your Congress, for instance, that house-builders in the Far East have decided to increase by 50 per cent their ready-made construction parts without expanding production areas.

Such an initiative can only be welcomed and the builders in the Far East should be wished success in going about this initiative.

As you know I visited the Far East last summer and saw with my own eyes the acuteness of the housing situation there.

Housing is just as urgent an issue in other regions of the country as well. And this came home once again during my visit to the Baltic area.

The main thing here is not so much money as the capacity of building organisations, the provision of housing construction with the necessary material resources.

Local bodies should do a lot here. And this already is being done in a number of republics, regions, towns and districts.

Housing is a national issue and it should be tackled accordingly.

All the work collectives should act as energetically as the auto-workers in Gorky and Minsk, the chemical workers in Voskresensk and the steel workers in Kuibyshev. The trade unions jointly with the economic management bodies should unfold this public initiative broadly throughout the country. It is an immense reserve, comrades, and people understand that all the efforts of the country should be pooled to tackle this task as speedily as possible.

Putting the concrete individual in the focus of attention, the trade unions are called upon to take more care about their most valuable asset, human health, about efficient health care and safety at work.

Efforts to combat drunkenness must not be slackened either. This fight has brought about substantial positive change, primarily as regards public health and order in our society. But there are still many problems.

For the time being, losses of worktime through temporary disability are 'conscientiously' put on record from one year to the next. In industry alone they have been more than ten times those caused by absenteeism, idle time, and absences with official permission.

Important decisions have now been prepared on these matters. The trade unions should make a contribution to this matter of importance to the state. A complex of resolutions have been drawn up on further improvements in health care in the country.

One more point. We have already talked a good deal about formalism in socialist competition, but there is almost no change.

Yet today we need emulation first of all to develop worker creativity, initiative, competitiveness of mind and talent, the art of organisation and the mastering of front-ranking experience.

It is time to actually do something we have been talking about for years – reorienting the system of socialist emulation to indices of quality, resource saving and strict fulfilment of contracts. These are the three whales, so to speak, on which socialist competition should be based first and foremost. It is precisely that area in which the priority role of the trade unions is beyond doubt. No special instructions to this effect should be waited for. Every precondition has been provided. Now tackle these matters and you will bear the most responsibility for them.

Since this is so I must say at once that the trade unions have grown accustomed to an absence of genuine competitiveness, to eyewash, to abundant forms of emulation which are so confused that a normal person simply fails to understand what this is all about.

At times one even begins to think that some 'paper motor' has been put into the sphere of emulation with the help of trade unions and revolves regardless of whether anybody is emulating drive or not.

It is time to bring socialist emulation back down to earth, to the production shops and teams, to subordinate it to real pressing tasks, to make it a matter of the working people themselves who are interested in mastering the best experience, in perfecting their work and themselves.

In short, comrades, you have more than enough concerns. In conditions of consistent democratisation of society, the role of trade unions will steadily rise, as will their responsibility for the economic and social policies. Their cultural and educational targets will become more complex and diverse.

Continuing the theme of what the role of trade unions should be in the present conditions I would like to say the following. The fate of the restructuring is being decided not in offices but by the actual deeds of work collectives.

The work collective is the central cell in the restructuring effort and everything in the long run depends on attitudes in this cell, on the new way work develops.

In effect this is a problem of a person's real position in his collective and thereby in our society as a whole.

How is his work organised? How productive is it and how is it remunerated? In what measure are a person's performance at work and satisfaction of his needs interconnected? How are the relations between allied trades, between accessory manufacturers, between officials and subordinates at all levels built?

Here the dependence is simple and clear: as things go in the work collectives, so shall they go in the whole of society. If we manage to organise highly productive work and ensure a high quality of output, then the country's economy as a whole will advance.

If there is order and organisation in the collectives there will be order and organisation everywhere else in society.

If we learn all together to build normal human relations in the collective and if we make the moral and psychological climate healthier the entire social atmosphere in the country will be just as healthy.

The Party's Central Committe attaches much importance to the law on the state enterprise (Amalgamation). A draft has been submitted for nationwide discussion.

In effect the draft law is invested with a new ideology for economic management. We do not think that it is truth in the last instance, that it is a finalised document. If we approached it in this way there would be no need to put it to a countrywide discussion. We think that this document provides a good basis for a broad discussion in our society, for a thorough analysis of all the views and remarks and for the writing of a good law on the state enterprise.

The law is called upon to change cardinally the conditions and methods of economic activity in the main link of the economy; to formalise juridically combination in the performance of enterprises of planning and full cost-accounting, independence and responsibility; and to legalise new forms of self-management.

I will name such measures of a fundamental nature as the creation of the first 20 inter-branch scientific-technical complexes: the introduction of new principles for increasing remuneration of work in the productive branches; the introduction of state quality control of output at 1,500 leading enterprises; second and third shifts in a number of production collectives; the extensive development of cooperative forms in the spheres of production services, and the spread of the system of collective and family contracts.

And this list could be continued.

As you see the reforms are proceeding extensively and steadily. Yet the work in a new way is actually only beginning.

If we take the production life of a work collective I believe the most important changes there will be determined by the transformation of the economic mechanism that has been started, by the transition to cost-account-ing, self-financing, self-repayment and self-management.

But these measures, comrades, will really begin to work only when each work collective will take them as something that is its own, as close and vital to it and not something from above.

Generally speaking, who needs cost-accounting and who stands to gain from it? Those who work honestly. It is needed by the country and in the final analysis by every working family, by every working man and woman.

To whom does cost-accounting pose a danger? To the windbag because it immediately exposes his untenability. To the idler and shoddy worker because it hits out at the very mainstays of his parasitical wellbeing achieved at the expense of society and of all honest working people.

We must approach in a new way the role of the work collective both in society, including in the economic sphere, and in the life of every Soviet citizen.

Who besides the work collective can really discern the social countenance of every person, determine the measure of social justice, not in general and on the whole but, so to say, on a roll-call basis?

Who knows best where possibilities have been exhausted and where considerable reserves remain untapped?

Who has done everything and where, and where has work in a slipshod manner become a norm?

Finally, where can a man exercise his rights and fulfil his obligations of really being in charge if not in his own collective, right in his workplace?

It appears that the experience of recent times has demonstrated with the utmost clarity that one's renunciation of an active stance in life costs dearly both society as a whole and every person.

And let me tell you straight we will not be able to change that situation until everyone feels a personal need for it, personal responsibility. Until he feels that he is in charge.

Comrades, I would like to emphasise specially the following aspect. In the current 'cost-accounting' situation the work collectives and trade unions are becoming a strong partner of the state in furthering social programmes.

I should think that the AUCCTU and the republican trade union councils could make a broader use of the right of legislative initiative in the interests of the working people and when and where necessary oppose more forcefully attempts by economic bodies to infringe on the prerogatives of the work collectives.

It is wrong when production plans are changed without the consent of the trade unions, when money is taken from the economic incentive funds and when other violations are tolerated. The trade unions must not put up with such a situation. And we shall support them.

Evidently attention should be devoted to the AUCCTU's proposal on giving the trade unions the right to suspend any decisions taken without their knowledge where such decisions affect terms of payment for work, and the work-rest relationship, and to be actively involved in shaping policy for pricing diverse goods and services.

They should have the possibility to act as resolutely where social welfare establishments and environmental protection facilities are omitted at enterprises under construction.

Speaking about that, one must not neglect the following phenomenon – many trade unions as yet remain in the second echelon of the reorganisation, as it were, and that holds for such a vital matter as protection of the interests of the working people and upholding social justice.

Take the matter of pay. We have started a serious reorganisation in that sphere. And it should be said that the matter at hand is not a campaign or some once-only undertaking, but a principled policy line towards eliminating levelling.

This is a serious political matter, comrades. Work and work alone should be the criterion for determining a man's value, his social prestige and his material status.

It should be noted that in the conditions of cost accounting, self-financing and self-profitability the sources of payment for work and the provision of financial incentives depend on the profit of an enterprise, on the funds earned; and the work collective in essence takes charge in distributing them.

But let us ponder the following matter: are trade unions doing everything they can to actively influence the policy of payment for work? You know better than I – certain enterprises are still in no hurry to part with wage levelling.

The management is in no hurry because it is a bothersome matter that requires changes in the organisation of production and calls for good order in work quota setting; and a trade union committee, too, often wants to go on living without treating anyone badly.

No, comrades, it is high time we did away with this kind of 'timidity'. Some will have to be treated badly, the slacker, the drunkard and the slovenly. Let them take no offence: they are getting what they deserve.

And we will elevate – both materially and morally – the diligent man, the one who is working tooth and nail. And the trade unions should defend his interests might and main.

I must say that the trade unions have as yet not joined in earnest in the important undertaking of getting two- and three-shift rotas.

This is a badly needed and economically important matter – in our industry alone fixed production assets worth 100 billion roubles are not loaded properly and in essence are idling.

The trouble is, however, that at many enterprises the introduction of work in many shifts has often been approached in a bureaucratic fashion, without due regard for production organisation, catering, public transport, or many other vitally important problems.

I had many meetings in Latvia and Estonia. And among the issues raised the problem of getting two- and three-shift rotas was one of the main problems taken everywhere. In Yurmula, where working people from practically all over the country from Sakhalin to the western regions are vacationing, those questions were also put to me. What did people say? There are enterprises where one shift is divided into two just to fulfil an order from either the respective branch ministry or from local authorities. Fifty per cent work during the first shift. And 50 per cent during the second. So it turns out that during the first shift 50 per cent of the equipment is used and the other 50 during the second. But this is a mockery of common sense and of an undertaking of state significance. For the Leningraders' plan approved by the Political Bureau was to concentrate two or three shifts on the advanced and progressive equipment and to get a maximum return from it, to improve labour productivity and at the same time to accomplish the planned tasks, to remove the old equipment and to open up the road for speeding up the modernisation.

At the same time this enables an enterprise to do without expansion, without building new premises, to release funds and channel them into building housing, social and cultural establishments. Such is the major plan of state significance contained in that idea. Instead some managers just go through the motions and profanate that very important undertaking.

Trade unions should pay special attention to this. If one enterprise changes it is unlikely that the entire city will alter its normal rhythm in the sphere of transport, organisation of trade, education and work of pre-school centres, and consumer services. Therefore the transition should be carried out by the city or basically by the entire city.

This seems to be so clear that no discussion is required. Nevertheless transition to two- and three-shift rotas is often carried out without restructuring the operation of city services which I have just mentioned. This is a mistake. This is done in haste that no one needs and which discredits the important state undertaking.

We said this recently in a resolution of Central Committee and the government. We made a first analysis of the work in this direction and defined a number of major measures of which you already know. Anyway, we decided to provide incentive for those working on second and especially third shifts. This, I think, is correct. We ought to do that. This is an extremely important state task that is to be resolved.

I think that in the conditions of growing economic independence, work collectives will demand from trade union activists that they be more principled and energetic in using the rights enjoyed by trade unions. You have these rights. The Soviet trade unions possess great and material force. These are the right to monitor how the administration fulfils its agreements and contracts and the right to criticise economic managers for actions contradicting the legitimate interests of the working people.

Naturally, in putting higher demands on trade union functionaries, it is necessary to display maximum attention and tact and extend support for them.

Trade union committees should become genuine, I would say, rather than a convenient partner of the administration and consistently defend workers' interest. To be frank, substandard working conditions at many enterprises, insufficient health care and inadequate rest rooms are something that trade union organisations have got used to in many places.

This still occurs very often. The legitimate rights and interests of working people imply using boldly the trade unions' great potentialities and acting, as necessary, to have wrong decisions corrected.

In closing my remarks on domestic affairs I want to remind you of V.I. Lenin's words: 'We must see to it that literally every member of the trade unions stands to gain from production, and remembers that only by increasing production and raising labour productivity will Soviet Russia be in a state to win.'

This is the way V.I. Lenin put the question in 1920; this is the way we put it today in the conditions of new revolutionary changes.

A time has come when unprecedented opportunities are opening up for better work for greater results and for vigorous endeavour to build a better future with due account for all our rich experiece and with all our considerable potentialities being tapped.

Let us act, comrades, in this direction.

And now to international affairs, since enough has been said lately on this account, I hope. Such issues are directly linked to the course of our domestic development.

These affairs take much effort, while the world situation, as you are aware, has remained complex over the past years.

What is most essential is that imperialism and reactionary forces are doing their utmost to hinder, come what may, our onward development and compel us to remain on the tracks of military confrontation.

The 27th Congress emphasised that the Party saw its principal internationalist duty in leading the country successfully along the trail blazed by the October Revolution.

Such is the strict criterion by which we ought to measure each step; such is the viewpoint from which we should assess the tasks that are being advanced and the choice of policy, both inside the country and in the international arena.

The words 'perestroika' (reorganisation) and 'glasnost' (openness) are viewed everywhere abroad, especially since the January meeting of the Central Committee, as synonymous with 'progress' and 'peace'.

Naturally, some – our allies, friends and democratically minded people – are following with hope, confidence and great expectations the changes in our society, the style and atmosphere of our everyday life.

Others – political and ideological opponents – are watching these processes not without certain apprehension and at times even hostility.

Characteristically, despite these differences, the main thing has been correctly noticed abroad: the new way of thinking which the Party has placed as the basis of its policy is the CPSU's response to the challenge of the time, a challenge calling for a fundamentally new approach to the tasks that have come before mankind at the end of the second millennium.

There are in fact two fundamental tasks, that of saving the world from nuclear catastrophe and that of placing at man's service the immense potential of knowledge, material and spiritual possibilities he possesses.

They are indeed immense, urgent and closely interrelated. The Party, in working out its strategy for acceleration and reorganisation, has set an example by approaching them from humanist Marxist-Leninist positions.

The Soviet proposals aimed at eliminating weapons of mass destruction and establishing a comprehensive security system have evoked a special response.

Some of them are already 'working' – they have become the subject of dialogues and negotiations, both bilateral and multilateral.

Properly speaking we have tried to give an impetus to the reorganisation of inter-state relations as well, to align them with the real tasks and requirements of our times.

As a result international life has become more dynamic, and the tendencies towards the search for forms and means of deepening cooperation, political, economic, scientific, technical and cultural, have grown stronger.

True, sometimes we can hear such an opinion: all this is correct, we do support the Party's foreign policy, but the world is still an intranquil place, the arms race goes on and on, the nuclear threat remains a reality and US imperialism is not only unwilling to disarm, but is also building up its offensive capability.

Such an assessment of the situation is on the whole correct. But I believe it is still incomplete.

Yes, the situation on the international scene is dangerous, the Soviet-US negotiations on nuclear arms limitations are making no headway through the fault of the US rulers, and acute conflicts in various regions of this planet are fraught with grave complications.

One should not disregard another aspect either.

A dramatic change in the very atmosphere of international relations, in public sentiment, in the attitude of both ordinary people and many statesmen to the choice of stance on the principal question of today – the question of war or peace – has made itself felt and is becoming ever more pronounced.

This had been manifestly confirmed by the Moscow Forum For A Nuclear-Weapon-Free World, For The Survival of Humanity.

It was a very representative meeting of authoritative scientists, writers, artists, musicians, businessmen, public and religious figures from very many countries.

A meeting of people who are mostly far from having a socialist world outlook and even people holding conservative views on major political and social issues. It is also a fact, and quite meaningful.

However, the people were brought together by the one conviction: only affirmation of a new mode of thinking in international relations can put up an obstacle to nuclear war, can make peace not only possible but inevitable.

The forum has been an important event in international life, I would say a barometer of the sentiment of world public opinion. And the needle of that barometer is pointing firmly and plainly to peace.

There have been debates, heated ones, too, as to how to proceed in that direction, how to resolve certain problems, and substantial differences in approaching them have cropped up.

Well, debates, criticisms and comparison of views are all quite natural and the surest of roads to the truth. And the truth, that is, the need to avert a catastrophe, to survive and to learn how to live in a manner befitting human beings, has never, as far as I know, been called into question by any of the participants in the Moscow meeting.

It seems to me that the results of the forum demonstrate that a new, very broad, heterogeneous and yet momentous movement – the movement for the survival of humanity – is taking shape in the world.

This is a good, favourable sign. It gives rise to confidence in the victory of the forces of reason over the forces of war and militarism.

Trade union organisations in different countries are becoming even more active in combating the nuclear threat. The trade union movement is a major force in the contemporary world and one of the most important components of the movement for the survival of humanity.

The coupling of the fight for the interests of the working people with the fight for peace and disarmament means that the masses' awareness of the danger looming dark over humankind is ever more clear and profound. This is why it is so important that the trade unions join in that fight.

I am glad at the chance to greet at your congress here numerous envoys and representatives of trade unions from different countries, of their international associations.

I am convinced that the right to live and work in peace is a primary and inalienable right of every man. Nothing can set working people at odds with their like. The arms race and war bring workers neither profits nor dividends. Peace, cooperation and work provide the conditions for worker wellbeing and social progress.

The peace and security of a country is not the concern of diplomats and politicians alone. Peace and security of the homeland is the concern of every one of us, of all Soviet people.

Comrades, I would like to make this a point. Peace is to be achieved primarily by our everyday work at the factory, in the field, and at the research institute.

The better and more successfully we cope with our tasks at home, the louder and more forcefully will resound the voice of the Soviet Union in defence of peace internationally.

Comrades, today we know and understand full well that the all-out offensive – economic, political, psychological and militarist – launched by the forces of reaction at the end of the 1970s and the beginning of the 1980s was dictated, among other things, by our internal state of affairs.

Today the enemy's stake on our lagging behind having suffered a serious setback, imperialism is shifting the emphasis to prevent us from enacting the plans for reform, to hamper, slow down and frustrate them through the arms race.

To this end they exert every effort to keep up international tension and preserve conditions in the world in which to continue to describe the USSR as a source of all evils and misfortunes.

All this is as outdated as imperialism itself. There is nothing unexpected as principally new in such behaviour by the reactionaries. Our answer is clear.

We have been and will keep doing everything necessary to guarantee absolutely our security and the security of our friends and allies, so that no one is tempted to test out our borders. But we shall not make a single step in excess of the demands and requirements of sensible, sufficient defence.

Let us not repeat – without thinking and automatically – what imperialism is seeking to impose on us in the arms race.

We are keeping and will continue to keep all doors open for any honest steps to limit and reduce arms, to secure dependable verification over this process and to strengthen international mutual security.

Our every step along the path of socialist renewal is both a victory for the forces of peace and progress and a setback for the forces of aggression and militarism.

This is, comrades, how the issues we are advancing in domestic policy merge with the matters to be resolved in the international arena.

The tasks of acceleration, reorganisation of socialist society, prevention of nuclear catastrophe, demilitarisation of the world and humanisation of international relations form the core of the strategic course of the 27th CPSU Congress, a course confirmed and particularised by the January plenum of the Central Committee.

Let me assure you, comrades, that the Party shall not depart from the course it has taken.

Relying on your support, on the support of the workers, farmers and intellectuals and all Soviet people, the Party shall advance – resolutely, boldly and purposefully – along the path started 70 years ago by the Great October Socialist Revolution.

I wish the Congress successful work, and the delegates and guests big new accomplishments, health and vigour.

11
A New Revolution

Comrade Young Communists,

The Twentieth Congress of the Young Communist League is now in its second day, an organisation with which the combat and labour youth of almost all Soviet people is linked and which has given all of us a start in a new, socialist life.

Never have I so wished to participate in a debate as today, at the current YCL Congress. I know that my comrades in the Party Central Committee and the government feel the same. I think this is clear. Those who represent the today and morrow of the Soviet State are now present in this hall, and everything said here has a great sense not only for the present but for the future. There are no, and nor can there be any indifferent people here because everyone feels – this cannot but be felt – your revived Young Communist fervour and fighting spirit and your proprietory concern for the present and your thrust into the future. We share your mood, and we also feel younger these days.

The Communist Party and all society are maximally interested in your Congress truly marking a new stage and opening a new chapter in the USSR's youth movement. Both the report and the debate show that the Young Communist League understands its responsibility to its country and people and that the young people enthusiastically want to participate even more actively in the process of deep-going change, the renewal of all aspects of the society in which we live. This is a good mood, and no other mood can fill your work and life with inspiration.

The exacting atmosphere of your Congress cannot but gratify us. It is consonant with the current stage of the USSR's development, with the pressing character and great significance of the issues which our society is tackling now. We are sure that this atmosphere expresses the aspirations of all

Mikhail Gorbachev's Speech at the Twentieth Young Communist League Congress, 17 April 1987 the Soviet young. Everything here at the Congress shows that young people regard themselves as part and parcel of the revolutionary processes now taking place in our country. This is most significant because it concerns the stand taken by the Young Communist League. On behalf of the CPSU Central Committee I welcome Viktor Mironenko's statement to the effect that the Young Communist League unequivocally stands for reorganisation. We regard this, comrades, as the stance of all young people in our country because you are their representatives.

Furthermore, the attitude adopted by you is of immense political importance for the Party. The YCL Congress is being held at a crucial time – a time of daring initiatives and intensive work. From the standpoint of the scale of social transformation it certainly goes beyond the limits of everyday life. And you, dear friends, shall take part in the revolutionary renewal of socialist society.

You hold in your hands the giant economic potential of a great power, the unique riches and beauty of your native land, the immense scientific achievements, and the humanist values and traditions of our culture and ideology. You shall continue the cause of the October Revolution and safeguard peace on the Earth.

Immense responsibility for our country, for the destinies of socialism, and for a peaceful future for human civilisation as a whole lies on young people. And as Party members and your comrades we wish you to spare no effort to attain great and lofty aims. This is the main thing in people's lives.

The present day is a fine school of civic attitude and political and ideological maturity. Do your best to comprehend as deeply as possible the essence of the changes which are afoot and their innovatory spirit and to understand better their significance for our generation and for society as a whole. Only such understanding of the depth, scale and novelty of the changes linked with reorganisation will become a real incentive to constructive work and will help you get a clear idea of your own place and role at a crucial stage in the history of our socialist state.

We want you to be active, conscious participants in the readjustment. I would even risk telling you: do not take anything for granted. Please, understand everything and draw, on the basis of this understanding, conclusions necessary for your life and work. Only such a clear and conscious stand is needed to accomplish the tasks of reorganisation.

Each generation of Soviet people tackled the main objective of its life. Before speaking about the task which is facing you I would like to quote Vladimir Ilyich Lenin who said: 'I am deeply concerned over the future of our young because they are a part of the revolution.' This was right at the time when it was said by Lenin and this is no less important, significant and right now because the revolution continues.

Viewing our history from the most unbiased positions, we see all the victories and achievements, errors, bitterness and disappointment. And we can say proudly on this score that the young, having taken the road of the October Revolution, have fulfilled their mission and thereby justified the hopes of the revolution fighters.

For one generation it was the revolution, the civil war and the first five-year plans, for another the Great Patriotic War and the youth of still others coincided in time with the heroic years of the postwar rehabilitation. You and your coevals are now taking the baton from those who developed the virgin lands, discovered the oil wealth of the Tyumen area, laid the Baikal-Amur trunk railway, built the power stations in Siberia, and reached the heights of scientific and technological progress. Great deeds which make our people and our country great stem from the selfless day-to-day work.

The young of the Soviet State have always been worthy of their people and their Homeland which has nurtured them and brought them up. It was so and we Communists are sure that it will be so in the future, too.

Permit me, on behalf of the Party and the Young Communist League, to express from the Congress rostrum deep respect and wholehearted gratitude to your glorious predecessors, to those who accomplished the greatest revolution in the life of mankind, built and defended socialism, and consolidated the might of the Union of Soviet Socialist Republics.

Their deeds are a prized, invaluable possession of history. They will always live in the people's memory. They are the heroic destinies of the great biography of our country!

Comrades, the essence of the party line for modernisation and reorganisation can be expressed in the brief formula: more socialism. Here lies the answer to the main question about the viability of the society in which we are living.

The 70 years that have passed since the October Revolution have revealed the powerful, vital resources of the socialist system. To its record socialism has enormous social victories, generally recognised economic and cultural achievements and inspiring historical prospects. We take well-justified pride in all that and treasure the great values of the society in which we are living.

Another question is: are we satisfied with the present state of affairs? What we must reply here in all honesty is no, we are not satisfied. We are faced with the task of unfolding and using in full measure all the advantages and opportunities of socialism, its extremely rich material and moral arsenal, and its powerful revolutionary potential.

When we say more socialism, we stress that what we need is an ever self-renewing and developing socialism capable of staying in the vanguard of human civilisation in the economic, cultural and moral sense.

More socialism means more thrust and creative efforts, more organisation and order, more science and initiative in the economy, and more efficiency in management.

More socialism means more democracy, greater openness and collectivism in our society, more culture and humanitarianism in relations among people, more dignity and self-respect in the individual.

More socialism means a stronger push for the high patriotic goals and more civic concern about the country's affairs and about the future of peace.

Our common duty, a duty of all generations of the Soviet people, is to lead our Homeland into the twenty-first century as a mighty and prospering power.

Comrades, it is two years now since we started reorganising all spheres of life in our society. It is only natural that people are thinking about these developments, evaluating the current and future changes, comparing them with what came before and noting the successes and failures of this reorganisation work. Many people are asking where we have succeeded and where not. Let me give you the basic facts. Over a short period we have traversed what is in historical terms a considerable distance. It was the road of truth and critical analysis of the realities, a difficult road of development of new ideas and of the concept of social renovation. That work is already producing its first results.

In-depth analysis of the situation in the country, sharp criticism of negative aspects and increasing democratisation of life have become the beginning of moral cleansing of society, emancipation of people's consciousness and growth of their social activity.

In other words, the period under review was not easy but, in the long run, certainly fruitful. We achieved at that stage the most important thing: the idea of modernisation and revolutionary change came to the minds of milions and won to their side the overwhelming majority of our people. There is every sign that the tone in our social life is set by the proponents of 'perestroika', and we think that this process and this trend will grow broader and stronger. That is the most important thing, comrades.

We have passed far-reaching decisions on the main directions in the materialisation of 'perestroika' and of our political line worked out by the 27th Congress of the CPSU. They embrace all spheres: economics, culture, the social sphere, the life of Party and public organisations and work collectives.

I might say that today we have an accurate compass with a proven azimuth, and the past two years have given us more confidence in the correctness of our choice, the choice of policies of acceleration and reorganisation. The main thing now is to keep advancing and place the emphasis on implementing the decisions passed. I don't mean: wrap up all the discussion. We will still need a good deal of debate to clarify the new questions and problems continuously posed by 'perestroika'. And yet the decisive role now belongs to action.

We have no right to forget the lessons of the past. I have already said this, but will repeat it now once again: we had quite a few good decisions even before today, but they did not always lead to serious changes that were expected by society. That was first of all because they were not backed by action.

The CPSU Central Committee is once again urging everyone to action. Action is the guarantee of success for 'perestroika' at the present stage. We must have less cracking words and more practical deeds that would speak for themselves.

That is why, dear comrades, all of us who represent here at your Congress the Party Central Committee and the Soviet government are strongly rejoicing over the businesslike spirit of the YCL congress and over your determination to promote 'perestroika' and to assert its spirit with practical involvement and young energy. So, the fact that Lenin's words 'Only by working together with workers and peasants one can become a real Communist' have sounded here is very natural and indicative. In fact, this is the principal task of the political organisation which the YCL is.

Both in the report and in their addresses delegates repeatedly turned to this idea of Lenin's. When we are saying that it is high time for action, we are urging the YCL to be always in the right place at the right time, to work to put through all the 'perestroika' targets, to combat stagnation and to be an active proponent of changes for the better in all spheres of the life of soceety. I welcome the active position of the Congress delegates, including those who have spoken from this rostrum!

Sometimes people ask: are there opponents of restructuring, and, if so, who are they? Sometimes even letters contain the request: 'Mikhail Sergeyevich, please give at least a few names.'

I think that we must clarify this question. We have no political opponents, there is no opposition to restructuring. There are the initial-stage difficulties of these revolutionary changes. These difficulties affect us all one way or another. For we all, let us say so, are the children of our time. The braking mechanism did not exist by itself. Its specific bearers are at the Central Committee and government level and in the ministries, republics and regions. They are also in work collectives, and even in the Komsomol, though it is hard for you to get infected with conservatism yet.

The point is that we must now think in a new way, act in a new way, work in a new way and master new approaches to tackle the new tasks. This is what constitutes the difficulty and complexity of restructuring.

I probably must add that there are people who have got used to the old way of life, do not want to change it or are changing it but very slowly. Their position objectively does not meet the spirit of restructuring. Not everybody, for example, likes the higher demands, the strict responsibility for the job entrusted to them. When it was firmly declared: each must get reward for the work done – this displeased certain people. But tell me, didn't we raise the issue fairly? Doesn't it stem from the very course of our development? I think you will agree that this is not an armchair fantasy. Life demands it.

Of course, to overcome such attitudes is not easy because many have over long years got used to unearned pay, 'guaranteed' bonuses and so on and so forth. To wipe out the parasitical, consumerist sentiments, serious economic and educational work is needed. In our society the material and social position of an individual must be determined by work, and work alone. And, for these principles to remain immutable, it is necessary to work for this both on a national scale and in each work collective.

Especially in the work collectives. It is they that are the mainstay of restructuring. It is here that the struggle of working people's awakened initiative against everything stagnant, rejected by life itself now goes on.

And, of course, we particularly underscore such a problem as bureaucratism. An understanding of the importance of combating it has resounded at your Congress. Has society any guarantees of a successful fight against bureaucratic evil? Yes, it has. And we all know what has to be done for this. Above all, we need openness, criticism and a further promotion of the democratic principles of our society.

And this is not a temporary or utilitarian need, as some people believe. It's a fundamental issue. Openness, criticism and democracy are the driving forces of renovation, and their absence will again bring us back to stagnation.

You know that the debate on whether there is too much criticism, whether we need such broad openness and whether democracy might lead to undesirable phenomena, is still going on. We do not regard this controversy as something negative: concern for the stability of our society is present in it in its own way. But we must not allow democracy to be watered down. There are people who seem to be advocating the new, but when it comes to practice they hedge the extension of democracy, criticism and openness with all kinds of conditions and reservations.

I do not know which in succession will be my statement on behalf of the CPSU Central Committee on this question, but I shall say once more: Comrades, criticism and openness must stand guard on the political and moral health of our society. As to democracy, it is time for all to understand that there simply can be no socialism without a real democracy. Socialism is the system of working people, socialism is democracy.

At the same time I feel I must stress forcefully that democracy is not at all anarchy and all-permissiveness, not personal account squarings or a possibility to vilify someone for mercenary ends. By the way, such facts are there, even though they're isolated cases. We must not allow a magazine, a newspaper, the mass media, a public platform to be turned into a means for squaring personal accounts. Genuine democracy is inseparable from honesty and integrity, from responsibility, frankness in judgements and respect for the opinion of others, and from strict observance of the laws and rules of socialist society.

As to the behaviour of people who are trying to 'capitalise' on democracy for personal purposes, here too the best instrument of struggle is openness, the creation of such a public opinion as would reveal egoism, demagoguery and attempts to use democracy for selfish purposes. The opinion of the Party's Central Committee is as follows: openness, criticism and democracy are vital if we are decisively to advance the cause of restructuring.

And if someone tries in the new conditions to revive the unsuitable tendencies and phenomena we condemned at the Party Congress before the entire country and received full approval from our people, then I think we must not tolerate this. What do I mean? Much of the negative trends of the past were due to the fact there were whole restricted zones for criticism, for contol by the people, for control by the Party and the Central Committee. How this came about has already been stated and there is now no need to go into it once again. Another thing is essential. Now we have no right to let new areas of the life of our society, new organisations, new persons, whatever officials, district- or union-level figures appear that would eventually get beyond criticism and beyond control. I believe that we have drawn the right conclusions and must strictly guide ourselves by them today.

Your opinion? That applause of yours has a special value: it shows support for our Party line.

Indeed, you understand very well the need to carry it on, since you have come from all parts of the country and know real life – you face it directly in its entirety. You can now realise both from work experience in your collective and from the situation in the country that the new stage of extending socialist democracy is just beginning. It's just gathering strength. And therefore we need an atmosphere of activeness and openness that is becoming ever more vibrant in the country today, because this is a working and businesslike atmosphere without which, I repeat, restructuring is impossible.·

The reorganisation, comrades, is for people. They will judge it on its merits, on how the ideas and designs are translated into the flesh and blood of the things we do, on what changes result in the everyday life of millions. It is a test of the good faith of our policy.

The worst thing now would be to indulge in wishful thinking, anticipate events, claim success and achievement where there are none so far, portray changes that have not yet taken place. Faith in the reorganisation will be damaged if we don't get the better of window-dressing, perhaps our most dangerous enemy; unfortunately, we put up with it too much. The most pressing task is to make the reorganisation work. Those who would like to reduce the whole thing to mere talk about reorganisation must be cramped. We must yield no ground in this major issue. That is the question!

We can understand that some people will take more and others less time to make out the situation in this society and in this country, and change tack. And we must give everybody his chance. Evidently, the time taken to readjust depends on personal qualities, frame of mind, and political maturity. This process will be individual in every case. That we can see. But we cannot accept or justify the position of those pretending to go along with the reorganisation and trying to reduce it to a talking point. We must be watchful. We do not need lip-service, we need reorganisation in substance, for our life-style, for the sake of the people, for socialism.

Comrades,

The Party's supreme concern, speaking of the problems of our youth movement today, is to offer the greatest-ever prospect for the young people, to throw the doors wide open for them everywhere – in every area of economic, scientific and technological progress, social creativity and intellectual development. To do so means to give our young men and women full scope for individual action, to free them from petty tutelage and supervision, and to develop them by letting them do real things and bear real responsibility, and by trusting them.

Appeals and slogans are not enough, as we understand, to rally young people for the most complex tasks. Youth enthusiasm has to be backed up with effective concern for the destinies of young people.

What do we mean? How do we, in the CPSU Central Committee, see the main lines in youth work at the present stage?

First. It is necessary to create all conditions for full-scale youth involvement in renovating society and making it more democratic. We must help young folk come to the political culture of socialism in actual practice.

The future of socialist democracy is connected with the development of the instruments of competition in the economy, science, cultural and intellectual life; with the extension of self-government at all levels; and with an enhanced role of personal initiative by all. You must learn to apply all the instruments of popular rule and breathe your youthful energy into making the nation's life more democratic.

On the other hand, only by the actual experience of working for greater demoncracy, that is, by doing something practical about it, difficult at times though it might be, can you cultivate a public spirit in yourself and people of your age plus a Communist outlook, patriotic pride and a sense of co-responsibility, principle and mettle.

Of course, snags and setbacks can crop up along your way. Today all of us, and not only the young, must learn to live and work in obedience to the laws and standards of advancing democracy and to develop immunity against all 'infantile disorders' connected with deepening this process.

There is no reason to fear that. Social experience, practice and the very realities of life will put everything where it belongs and judge it on its merits. It is important for all of us today to learn and to teach the young social creativity, for without it there can be no progress. Now, without progress, there can be no acceleration, and no attainment of the objectives that we have set ourselves.

Second. We must take care, indeed, to renew and build up the intellectual potential of society all the time. This is essential if we are to achieve our social, scientific and technological prospects. We all, in the Central Committee of the CPSU and in the Soviet government, have a feeling of profound satisfaction and great approval as we see how thoroughly and seriously your Congress is debating the Young Communists' contribution to the nation's economic and social development.

Yes, comrades, there are truly mammoth targets for our economy to hit – in terms of both magnitude and novelty. The hardest of problems have to be resolved under the current five-year plan. You and we have to brave another two or three most difficult years, when we shall have to resolve all at once, on the go, our major problems, create all prerequisites – political, economic, organisational, legal, psychological, intellectual and moral – for the reorganisation. And we have to move ahead in all directions at once. This is perhaps the most demanding, yet clearly the most interesting time.

Over the current five-year-plan period we must modernise practically all our mechnical engineering so that its main parameters are up to world standards. When last year, before the June plenary meeting of the Central Committee, we studied the situation there, it was found that many branches of our mechnical engineering turn out at best 50 per cent of its output at the world level and sometimes only 25–30 per cent. How shall we reach new targets in labour productivity, how shall we tackle problems of automation, mechanisation, how shall we ensure fast rates of transformation?

We must get answers to many questions in the economy. The prerequisites for implementing the strong social policy we have worked out are being created there. We need real breakthroughs in industry, especially in mechanical engineering and in scientific and technological progress. We are laying the groundwork for such breakthroughs today.

That is why the extremely complex, innovative targets of the current, twelfth, five-year plan are making quite new demands of all, and primarily young people. Your generation should be ready to take part in the major modernisation of our economy based on the organic fusion of the achievements of the scientific and technological revolution and the advantages of socialism. What shall be done by us in mechanical engineering and in science under the twelfth five-year plan must then be transferred to the national economy, thus changing its entire nature.

At the same time, we are mastering the new mechanism of management, the profit-and-loss accounting system, self-support and the output of top quality goods. I would like to welcome the clear-cut public-minded stand of young workers and engineers who have resolutely come out in support of the Party's line towards raising quality and who have supported the establishment of the state quality control service. They have backed this policy despite the fact that it has greatly affected work collectives and has given rise to acute problems.

In two years this is perhaps the most essential practical fact which has deeply revealed the stance of our working class, of all working people. You know that in the first few months of this year at some enterprises workers earned less than usual and bonuses were not paid. The Party's Central Committee learnt the workers' opinion: we shall not get wages for substandard goods any longer. This stand is simple and deeply meaningful. It has shown the working class's support for the requirements of the restructuring process and for the tasks of the acceleration of development in this country.

From this rostrum I would like to welcome young workers and engineers who are worthily representing the working class and all working people of our country at the Congress.

Comrades, we value the fact that our people understand the Party's policy. The policy will beneficially influence the present and the future of society if it is wholeheartedly and practically supported by the people. If this does not happen, the policy is dead, and there will be no progress. That's why I think it is so important to underline this point.

The report and delegates' speeches have presented a vast panorama of the practical deeds of the YCL, of the young. Relying on the experience of my trips across the countrry, I would like to confirm the young people's contribution. Young people are in fact active in the most difficult sections of our economic construction, in the vanguard of the drive for scientific and technological progress. Even now young people are shouldering the enormous burden of responsibility for economic development. Comrades, we see and appreciate this. I am sure that our whole nation sees and appreciates this.

In recent times I have seen what young people are doing in the Far East, Siberia, the Ukraine, Moscow, Leningrad and the Baltic republics. And I could say much on this score. The Central Committee and the government have every reason to count on young people's assistance towards the key targets of our economic strategy.

I want to cite just one example reaffirming that young people are doing much as it is, grappling with perhaps the most important problems whose solution will have great consequences for scientific and technological progress countrywide. Not long ago I learned about the activities of a team of young workers who, I would say, are accomplishing a supertask for science and economy by developing supercomputers.

We need such production complexes today to get modern systems to control major projects and automate designing and modelling, improve global weather forecasting, assist space exploration, technology and defences. Remarkably, young people, YCL members, and young graduates of higher educational establishments are elaborating most complicated systems. Experts in various branches, they have set up special youth teams and worked selflessly and enthusiastically. These people do not think of earnings or work time, they are driven by their idea.

This unlimited devotion and high qualification have helped the young break through in a vitally important field of our development. And we believe in the success of this vast work. Full-scale production has been launched of all-purpose computers which perform 125 million operations a second, and in some cases much more. In the next few years this body of workers will create a computer performing over a billion operations a second. This concerns the twelfth five-year-plan period. In the period 1991–5 a computer performing more than 10 billion operations a second will be created. From the rostrum of your Congress I want to mention Sergei Tarasov, Fyodor Gruzdov, Vladimir Volin, Shamil Alyautdinov, Valentina Khrapova and Vladimir Grebenshchikov. I will also mention their mentors – K. Valiyev, G. Ryabov, B. Babayan and A. Nazaryan.

Let me heartily welcome them!

Some in the West have been reckoning on a Soviet lag technologically, notably in supercomputers. Let them hear and heed this information from the rostrum.

A team of young Novosibirsk scientists led by Doctor of Sciences Kotov also gave a good account of itself in the same priority field. It is working on a state-of-the-art supermini computer and has produced good results. At an early stage the Novosibirsk specialists were joined by a young team from Minsk's integral production association. This is helping the project along and making it live up to modern economic requirements.

The above achievements concern only one direction of economic reorganisation and progress. I am sure, dear comrades, that the Young Communist League and young people in general will make a vast contribution to scientific and technological progress and economic modernisation.

The new technical retooling of production and accelerated technology advance pose unprecedented demands on the general education and polytechnical fitness of workers, and particularly the young. People coming to work should be intelligent, well versed in computer technolgoy, and have been trained for efficient and disciplined work from an early age.

The new tasks, naturally, call for a new system of education by work. Scientists and executives of respective branches are actively tackling these matters at the Party Central Committee and in government bodies. Important decisions have been taken on reforms at general educational and vocational schools, on development of higher and secondary specialised education with due regard for latest developments. I would even say that in this direction the most important task is being accomplished and conditions created for accelerated advancement and successful restructuring. People come first in the current restructuring. The process calls for clever, competent and professional people dedicated to socialism.

Efforts in this field will have to be pooled and coordinated. We take into account your self-criticism concerning the YCL's work at general, vocational and technical schools and at higher educational establishments. This shows that the YCL is aware of its responsibility in tackling a very important nationwide problem. Sadly, there is little self-criticism on the part of the government executives who are responsible for this vital matter.

Let us not lull ourselves with talk of reform in general education and vocational training. Let us say frankly: the reform is so far producing no results. This means that the work of the Ministry of Education of the USSR and all its agencies is ineffective.

But what is the stand of Party and government bodies? Where is their influence and authority? This must also be said today. We think that the Party organisations and staff of the Ministry of Education, the system of vocational technical training, our higher schools and, indeed, of the sectoral ministries should be determined in readjusting their work. The way in which they readjust will influence the reorganisation countrywide. This influence will be very strong. That is why we shall not tolerate stagnation, futile attempts at being over-subtle and ineffectiveness there, as has been the case in education where clear questions long decided in practice have at times been clarified over decades.

There is a tremendous scientific potential, including many competent people, concentrated in the ministries responsible for the training of personnel in the country, for education. And we hope that they will draw conclusions from today's debate and apply them in their work.

For its part, the Young Communist League can and must be the leader of a campaign for knowledge. And I welcome this on behalf of the Central Committee and the government. In my view, this was stated precisely that way in Viktor Mironenko's report.

You don't have to assume the duties of ministries and departments. You simply should give no peace to anyone. And you can do this. All the more so since new opportunities in this respect will offer, when the Congress decides on amendments to the Rules of the Leninist YCL. A wide sphere of activity will appear for Young Communists to take and develop the initiative in both general and higher education.

Third, the intricate knot of problems of social development for the young demands the closest of attention. We, comrades, have taken to heart the sharp, disturbing speeches at the Congress on these matters, particularly on the provison of good working and living conditions for young participants in building projects and residents of new towns, on improvement of hostel life and other matters. We have already tackled some issues mentioned here in the report and during the debate and are busy solving them. Other questions are new to us, and they will be considered.

We, the Central Committee and the government, have agreed to this: everything of nationwide importance from what has been stated at the Congress will be analysed by the Central Committee of the Leninist YCL and submitted for the consideration of the CPSU Central Committee and the USSR Council of Ministers. We shall do our best attentively to consider all this.

We are aware that the general social condition and the social mood of the young depend on solutions to these questions. These are housing, necessary conditions for young families and opportunities to display ability. In a word, everything with which the young link the very notion of social justice.

Work with young people cannot be separated from the general programme of cultural, ideological and moral education to develop personality. We cannot allow a discrepancy between material well-being and spiritual maturity. Today we clearly see that many obstacles to reconstruction and society rejuvenation are brought about by lack of culture in the broad sense. Sciencewise, high technology cannot exist and develop without a corresponding cultural infrastructure, without further development in the culture of work and life. A gap between them creates social tensions.

The historic task of socialism is to improve man and create conditions for all-round realisation of his abilities. We stand for consistent implementation of a system of measures by the Party, the government, economic bodies and mass organisations so that each young man and woman becomes aware of his or her involvement in all developments and concerns of society.

So we see the idea, voiced at this Congress, about a law on youth as justified. Let us ponder it. Obviously, a law on youth will even more fully guarantee the rights of young people in all spheres of society's life. Even if we only include in the law the acting guarantees and the rights and duties of young people, this alone will be highly significant. But we can add new provisions taking into account everything that has been said at the Congress and that life prompts.

I want to say at your Congress that the CPSU Central Committee and the government wil persistently work for the line of the 27th Party Congress of strict adherence to the principle of socialist justice. The socialist way of life knows only one superiority – of personal advantage based on abilities, knowledge, experience, will and aspiration for lofty social ideals. These should be the criteria.

The task of the Young Communist League is to safeguard the social awareness of young people. I think your organisation would be right to launch a broad-based and open competition of young people. I am calling on you to make Komsomol the soul of competition in all spheres – education, work, cultural activities, research work and recreation organisation. But, comrades, this should be a new type of competition, which would reveal talents and create conditions for realising the merits and abilities of young people. More than that, there should be a competition for the right individuals to advance to managing posts.

The Central Committee sees the task of the Party in resolutely and everywhere fighting a consumer attitude to young people and assuring care of good working and living conditions and recreation for them. It was rightly said yesterday that many managers remember the young only when they are in difficulty and often forget them when social issues are discussed. We condemn this approach. Active social policy implies improving the way of life of young people, making it even more interesting and meaningful.

Comrades,

Your Congress is busily involved in an important and committed discussion of the role which the Leninist Young Communist League is playing at the current stage of the development of society and its place in our democracy – a discussion of what we expect of the Young Communist League at present and in the future. It is a matter of tremendous and cardinal significance not only for youth but also for the whole society. Life has shown quite vividly that many of the Young Communist League committees have found themselves blighted with bureaucratic practices. Instead of taking effective action, they are tied up in rhetoric and redtape; instead of establishing broad and open contacts with young people, they organise gaudy campaigns, give boastful reports and put forward far-fetched initiatives. There are very many organisations within the Young Communist League which can be described as organisations of unrealised initiatives. This disease is grave and dangerous, and must be combatted. Sometimes, in analysing the work of the YCL leaders, one gets the impression that the masses of young people are moving on one side of the street and their leaders on the other – and, what is more, in the opposite direction.

I think that this largely results from the general situation and atmosphere in our country. So, we shall not lay the blame for everything on the young alone.

Yet, you know, in the YCL, too, an 'elite' has formed which causes much discontent among young people. Is it acceptable for a student of a higher educational establishment to be allowed to attend lectures when he feels like it merely because he has become active in the Young Communist League? Such practices arouse much astonishment among students. Activists should set an example in their work. Now what work do young people do in their student years? They learn. When exam-time comes the deans and even rectors get lists of such students with the implication that they should be given a passing mark. This is a disgrace for the Young Communist League! Where does this privilege come from? the Young Communist League activists have only one privilege – to be truly worthy of the moral right to be a leader of students or schoolchildren if it is school we are talking about. Such things which poison the healthy atmosphere in the Young Communist League should be resolutely done away with.

I would like to say once again that all this has not come about through the fault of the Young Communist League alone. That is the price of the negative phenomena in our society in the past decades, of errors in the upbringing of youth and of formalism in the party leadership of the Young Communist League. However, the Young Communist League has no right to relieve itself of the responsibility for such a state of affairs. In my opinion, this is the correct way to present the issue, too.

It impresses us that the Congress is discussing aspects of the YCL's internal life precisely from these standpoints. Reorganisation has stirred up the whole of our society today. It is good to see young people refusing to reconcile themselves to what it would seem people had got used to long ago. We Communists regard this intolerance as a norm of the life and activity of the Young Communist League. The YCL must be intolerant of everything that contradicts the values and ideals of socialism. We in the Central Committee appreciate the Young Communist League's discussions and endeavours. It is our closest ally. We want to see our younger generation interested in everything, critical and exacting.

What should be done to this end? What targets of your activity should be brought to the foreground? In this case, too, we should consult Lenin.

Vladimir Ilyich never felt the slightest doubt that the Young Communist League was a political organisation, above all.

Involved as it is in resolving all kinds of problems in the life of our country, the Young Communist League must always remember Lenin's behest that it lead the younger generation, stand at its head organisationally and ideologically.

Vladimir Ilyich believed it obligatory for the youth movement to have broad organisational independence and to develop initiative. Without this 'the youth will be unable either to train good socialists from their midst or prepare themselves to lead socialism forward'. These are Lenin's words. The Young Communist League is a school of civic courage and political maturity, a school of moulding man on socialist principles, a school pursuing the aim of fostering devotion to our ideals. Today the Young Communist League is called upon to be the young guard of reorganisation.

Reorganisation needs people with firm civic principles, socialist ideological devotion, equal to their high moral duty and capable of staunchly upholding the truth, people not infected with toadyism and hypocrisy.

The social significance of brave people, ready to uphold the decisions taken, of clever and conscientious advocates and devotees of socialism is greater today than ever before.

Reorganisation needs people capable of taking independent decisions, of not waiting for instructions from above on every trifle, of taking the responsibility and of carrying all matters, big or small, through to the end.

You can now often hear people complain that the Young Communist League does not display much initiative and independence. But you must not forget that beginning with the Young Communist League at school and all the way through to higher schools and enterprises when its members are grown-up mature people, they are in fact deprived of independence. There are guardians everywhere. The school YCL Committee cannot make a single step without the principal's and the teachers' approval, nor can the district and city YCL committees do anything without the approval of the district or city CPSU committees. Is this what the party's leadership of the Young Communist League should be like?

Let us try to rectify the situation together. The CPSU Central Committee will draw the proper conclusions from the current 20th Congress of the Young Communist League. We shall act with regard to the YCL, the political vanguard of Soviet youth, in the spirit of the Leninist traditions. Let's agree that the Young Communist League should have an interest in everything going on in the country.

A section of the young people have shut themselves off, trying to avoid the hustle and bustle of life. It is wrong for young people to act that way. That is why the social need for the Young Communist League to be an active political youth organisation is stronger today than ever.

The concerned and bold voice of the Young Communist League should be heard everywhere – at factories, farms, schools, colleges and universities, design bureaux or on theatre stages – urging people to action, creativity and innovation. I am convinced that the Young Communist League will find the strength and determination to overcome the old, and that a full life for young people and the interests of the country will become the content of its work everywhere. And I must say that here you surely can count on us, Communists.

Comrades, we are living in a complicated, contradictory but inter-connected world, as was said at the 27th Congress of the CPSU. Our society is changing, our ideas of socialism are being enriched, and spiritual values and ideological stands in the world arena are being collated. The Young Communist League is called upon to help young people evolve definite and clear-cut views of the world and life, via studies and discussions.

Incidentally, there seem to be too few discussions in the Young Communist League – there were some only when you were preparing for your Congress. But discussions within the Young Communist League are the main method of moulding its members' political and civic positions.

Even our students are not given a chance to discuss things at seminars in the social sciences. We have been preaching too much to our young people. Only by taking part in the political process, in all spheres of life and society, can one become a real champion of Lenin's cause, of socialism, and grow up truly human and political. I do not deny that lectures and an education are a necessary stage in life, especially in the life of a young person. But they are not what ultimately moulds the personality.

Linking studies with practical deeds in the Leninist way, the Young Communist League must give the young correct social guidelines, teach them to display a critical approach to the standards and morals of the bourgeois way of life, to perceive and assess social phenomena from a scientific, Marxist-Leninist point of view.

Ours is a complicated world, where certain forces are trying to promote false values, lead young people astray (and not only in the socialist countries, but in the West as well), away from active politics and community involvement, push them into the bog of philistinism and make them politically sterile. However, the Communists and our socialist system want to see young people active and politically mature, contributing to the resolution of all our issues.

In order to get our bearings in this world, we must see it well with all its interdependencies, complexities, contradictions and basic trends. Young people are particularly attracted by philosophical issues. Who has not pondered over moral values, the meaning of life, happiness and justice and humankind's future in their youth?

It is very important for our young people to draw on the life-giving source of Marxism-Leninism now that they are particularly receptive and their interest in life is great. This teaching emerged in response to the most pressing issues of mankind's life with all its concerns, worries and hopes.

In short, we must blend the revolutionary renovation of the country with the ideological and moral education of its citizens. Civic attitudes are generously fed by developments around us and this should also be done by our history.

Lenin thought it very important to help people learn history. He attached great political importance to preparing a book on the country's history that would be scholarly, easy to read and vivid.

Do we lack energy, scholars and literary skill to write a history of the nation and the Party? This must be an honest, courageous and fascinating book throwing light on the great and heroic road traversed by the country and the Party, the road of trail-blazers. This book must not be shy of the drama of certain events and some individuals' destinies. It must be free from blank pages, subjectivist pros and cons and opportunism.

We sometimes blame objective factors for all the defects in education. However, is man no more than a passive product of circumstances and are circumstances not created by people? I am sure that people of firm political views and moral principles will remain true to themselves in any circumstances. They will not seek 'worldly opportunism' or compromise with their conscience or look for ways to withdraw from community activities.

Millions of Communists and non-Party people did not forgo their principles and convictions even in the time of the greatest trials. This has made the major and fruitful changes now occurring in the country possible. This confirms our people's dedication to the nation and socialism and their profound patriotism. The patriot is not he who finds fine words to allege his love of the country. The patriot is he who energetically works against all odds, brushing aside pessimism, panic and egoism. This is how we see patriots. A genuine patriot is always an internationalist.

Our socialist record confirms the inseparable connection between patriotism and internationalism. It is through suffering that we came to see patriotism as the resolute negation of nationalism, chauvinism and racism.

Man is not genetically predisposed to be internationalist or nationalist. What kind of citizen he will become depends on himself, his education and community attitudes. Every new generation of Soviet people will have to develop internationalist attitudes through contacts, study and work with various ethnic groups. Ours is a multi-ethnic country and the friendship between nationalities is one of our major assets.

It moves me to speak about the thousands of young Soviet lads who went through the baptism by fire in Afghanistan. They proved to be genuine internationalists, helping the fraternal country to defend its revolution. They also showed themselves to be genuine patriots in upholding the security of our southern border.

On behalf of the Central Committee of the Party and on your behalf I want to tell the young people back from Afghanistan that the nation admires their courage, gallantry and bravery. The qualities you displayed in the most stressful circumstances are precious in peacetime too. We do not doubt that you will retain these qualities for the rest of your life. I take this opportunity to address myself to the members of the Young Communist League in the army, to those who have completed service with the armed forces or fought for the righteous cause in Afghanistan: tell teenagers about yourselves, your comrades, officers and advisers, about bravery, heroism and comradeship-in-arms.

Comrades, the Party clearly sees the difficult tasks and issues on the agenda of the Young Communist League. We understand guidance of the Young Communist League as constant comradely assistance, which is our prime duty.

Dear comrades, the younger generation always has the most immediate bearing on the future. This is all the more so today. The advance of civilisation is eroding away the line between the possible and the impossible. You are going to command tremendous research, technological and intellectual potentialities that have never been controlled by any generation anywhere. All that has been conceived can now be translated into hardware with the aid of technology, the good and the evil, the salutary and the disastrous. Assuming control over this power, you must remember that you are working for the future.

Every person wants to be happy. However, happiness comes only to those who ignore the small things and are motivated by noble humane considerations.

The Communists, all old-timers believe that young people will justify the expectations of the Party and the nation.

On behalf of the Communists the Central Committee of the Communist Party of the Soviet Union extends warm greetings to Congress delegates and guests, the multimillion-strong Leninist Young Communist League, all young Soviet men and women.

We wish you a bright future and good health.

12

Speech On the Occasion of
Mrs Thatcher's Visit

Esteemed Mrs Prime Minister,
  Ladies and Gentlemen,
  Comrades,
  Greeting you today, Mrs Thatcher, we are greeting the country with which
the Soviet Union, Russia, has had a long-standing relationship and common
interests. The two nations have gained much of what is useful from the four
centuries of communication since Moscow and London exchanged their first
embassies in the mid-sixteenth century.

There were other things, too, to the point of armed conflicts. But the two
countries joined forces to fight Nazism. That glorious page will forever remain
in history. It will never be obliterated from the memory of the Soviet people.

The times have changed. There are new problems, new concerns and hopes
today. Soviet-British dialogue is an inseparable and important part of today's
European and world politics. This is explained by the circumstance that the
Soviet Union and Britain are two great powers and that each has made a major
and irreplaceable contribution to world history. Both were among the founders
of the United Nations and are permanent members of the UN Security
Council. All this determines their international role and responsibility.

It is from these positions and in the spirit of realism and a desire better to
understand each other's way of thinking that we approach the current talks.

Your visit to Moscow, Mrs Thatcher, is taking place at a very interesting and
very responsible time, at a time which is crucial in many respects. And this is
making an imprint on our dialogue.

Speech given at a Dinner in the Kremlin in Honour of Mrs Thatcher, British Prime Minister,
30 March 1987

We have talked a good deal about the process of reorganisation in our country. I want to repeat in this context: our foreign policy today stems directly from our domestic policy to a larger extent than ever before.

We say honestly for all to hear: we need a lasting peace to concentrate on the development of our society and to tackle the tasks of improving the life of the Soviet people.

The West is scrutinising this open position for signs of the Soviet Union's weakness. It claims that the Russians have fallen hopelessly behind, that their system is not working and that the goal of socialism has proved altogether flawed. That is why, supposedly, any concession can now be wrenched from them if proper pressure is applied. It is a bad delusion.

The Soviet Union today is a result of immense socioeconomic changes and transformations, which her peoples have carried out in the seven decades since the revolution.

True, there have been difficulties, sometimes dramatic, and quite a few external obstacles. But one thing is clear: the efforts of the people have turned the country into a world power, whose role in international affairs is well known and commonly recognised.

The economic potential of the Soviet state, its political prestige and the ability of our society for more energetic advance are being turned by us to the good of world peace and progress.

The socialist system has demonstrated repeatedly and in many ways its advantages over capitalism. This is not boasting but a hard fact. Far from all its potentialities have been identified and put to use. The full development of the potential of socialism, the comprehensive perfection of the Soviet system, its new quality and a new level of the material wellbeing and the cultural and intellectual standards of the people are what reorganisation will give us.

At the same time it is socialism's invitation to peaceful competition with any other social system, and not merely an invitation but the manifestation of readiness to participate as equals in the development of an appropriate mechanism of this competition, cooperation and, if you wish, rivalry – but peaceful rivalry. This mechanism should promote and strengthen an atmosphere for the peaceful competition of states.

It is one of the fundamental aspects of new political thinking. Today's world needs it. Otherwise the age which gave rise to nuclear weapons wil be short and end in a tragedy for humankind.

It is alarming that the West continues to claim today that nuclear deterrence is the only way of averting war.

We do not understand how nuclear weapons can be lauded when there are four tons of explosives for everyone in the world including children, and when the explosion of even a small part of the existing nuclear arms arsenals will jeopardise life on earth. We cannot agree to this from the point of view of either politics or morality.

I would like to say, too, that the Soviet Union has pledged not to be the first to use nuclear weapons and will never turn them against those countries which have no such weapons in their territories. This is our immutable principle.

I have already had a chance to point out the evil of the ideology and policy of nuclear deterrence. I want to explain our position anew.

First, this tool is not failproof and as time goes on the risk of the accidental outbreak of a nuclear conflict keeps growing. It is the fuse of the charge which is capable of destroying civilisation. Second, deterrence is a policy of blackmail and threats and therefore a constant source of the arms race and the escalation of tension.

Third, the logic of deterrence, that is the buildup and upgrading of weaponry, means the subordination of politics to the interests of militarism with most grievous consequences for the wellbeing of the people and for democracy itself.

Old thinking, involving armed force as a means of achieving political goals and the presentation of other nations in the 'image of an enemy', led to two world slaughters. It bred the cold war and today's extremely dangerous situation, and has brought the world to a point beyond which unpredictable consequences begin.

Our unilateral moratorium, a programme for a nuclear-free world, announced on 15 January 1986, the Reykjavik initiative, the Moscow Forum, 'For a Nuclear-Free World, for the Survival of Humanity', and now the proposal to detach the question of medium-range missiles in Europe constitute manifestations of new thinking.

The basic outlines of an accord on medium-range missiles in Europe were agreed in Reykjavik. It would seem that there are no serious obstacles to rapid progress.

An accord would have major military and political importance and, moreover, change the situation psychologically: we have been arming ourselves till now but then would for the first time start dismantling nuclear weapons.

But what is happening in response to our initiative?

We see the problem of medium-range missiles being weighed down with a package of conditions upon and demands to the Soviet Union. We see the NATO countries retreating from the positions of their own 'zero option'. Things have gone so far that, instead of reductions in the nuclear arms arsenals, Europe is being offered a buildup of those arsenals, the deployment of US shorter-range theatre missiles.

We also hear statements that the West will trust the Soviet arms reductions proposals if the USSR modifies its political system, taking Western society as a model.

It is just not serious. To hope that we surrender our ideals at any time means to flee from reality.

The next few weeks will show if NATO really wants to remove a whole range of nuclear weapons from Europe, in accordance with the wish of the peoples, or if it is again trying to find a decent way of disguising its desire to retain Pershing and cruise missiles in Europe and even increase their number, or replace them with something more novel.

To the roar of nuclear explosions in Nevada, we had to cancel our 18-month unilateral moratorium on nuclear testing. But this does not mean that we have dropped our idea of achieving a solution to this key problem of nuclear disarmament.

The Soviet Union is prepared to return to the moratorium on any day and any month the US declares an end to its testing. Let me take advantage of this opportunity to remind Britain that it is a participant in tripartite talks on this issue.

We hope that the in-depth dialogue we are conducting with Western countries and our positions and intentions, which we have been talking about frankly and backing up with practical action, as well as this visit of yours, esteemed Mrs Prime Minister, and our forthright talks, will fnally form a subject for serious deliberation and invite reciprocal moves.

At this critical moment for Europe, it is its nuclear powers – Britain and France – that we are addressing in the first place.

The world today is one in which a struggle is under way between reason and madness, morality and savagery, life and death. We have determined our place in this struggle definitely and irreversibly. We are on the side of reason, morality and life. This is why we are for disarmament, and for creating a system for general security. This is the only possible way in which mankind can regain immortality.

Strength must give way to universally shared values and equal relations presupposing respect for the interests of every nation and for its right to an independent choice, the right to be unlike others.

It ought to be said that in the West there are still quite a few people with a penchant for talking about the freedom of choice. But they really mean the choice of the capitalist system.

However, when this or that people – in Nicaragua, Africa, the Middle East or Asia – actually reveals a desire to look for a different road of its own, which will suit it better, it finds its way immediately barred with dollars, missiles or mercenaries. They start with hypocrisy and end with bloodshed.

As a result, the 'volcanoes' of regional conflict are fuming.

The 'lava of strife' they are pouring forth has been burning the whole organism of the world community and filling it with smoke. We propose looking at this problem too in the light of new thinking and demonstrating an ability to reckon with the realities of specific situations and see the real causes of any conflict rather than zealously search for a 'hand of Moscow' everywhere.

Approaches to a settlement can be different. An international conference on the Middle East, activities by the Contadora Group, the UN Secretary-General's efforts for an end to the Iran-Iraq war, effective economic and political measures against the apartheid regime in southern Africa, coope-ration between the countries of ASEAN and Indochina as a factor for a settlement regarding Kampuchea – these and possibly other methods and forms could help to quench the fires.

So far as Afghanistan is concerned, we are for resolving the problem by political means through an end to outside interference.

The Afghan government's programme for national reconciliation has evoked broad response both in that country and elsewhere in the world. It is the only right way to take. Soviet troops have come to Afghanistan at the request of its government, and they will be returned home as part of a political settlement. The process of achieving national reconciliation and a settlement concerning Afghaistan has already got under way.

It is making progress. The main thing is not to hamper it and to put an end to any interference in the affairs of that sovereign country which wants to be and will be neutral and non-aligned. We are, however, only witnessing a step-up in efforts to scuttle the normalisation process on the part of certain Western forces.

The goal of 'humanising' international relations is served by continuing the CSCE (Conference on Security and Cooperation in Europe) process started in Helsinki. The CSCE process is a kind of university of political dialogue.

It has taught us more than one lesson in the difficult science of mutual understanding; it has been teaching us to see the opposite side not as an enemy but as a partner. The document adopted in Stockholm is proof that these lessons have been learnt well.

But further progress has to be made. We are waiting patiently for a reply to the Warsaw Treaty countries' initiative on conventional arms and armed forces and are prepared for a decisive scaling down of the military confrontation of the two blocs in a zone stretching from the Atlantic to the Urals.

Arms must be reduced to a level of reasonable sufficiency, that is a level needed only to cope with the tasks of defence. In the European building every flat is entitled to protect itself against burglars but only in such a way as not to demolish the next door apartment.

We are prepared to come to terms on a dependable and irreversible destruction of all chemical weapons.

So we count on the West, especially West European countries, being aware of its responsibility and taking reciprocal steps also in what concerns non-nuclear arms.

The CSCE process could be effectively assisted by a representative humanitarian forum we have suggested holding in Moscow.

But its interesting that as soon as we made the invitation to talk about human rights in a serious and businesslike manner and compare, in an atmosphere of mutual candour, how many people really live here and in capitalist countries, they have apparently grown nervous there and are again trying to reduce the whole subject to two or three individual cases, while evading a discussion of all the rest.

We are also prepared to discuss the particular cases in a humane spirit, but are strongly intent on talking about the whole range of related problems openly and loudly so that we shall be heard in the West by the millions of the unemployed, the homeless and the destitute, by those beaten by police and victimised in court, and by those whose civil rights and human dignity are subjected to glaring discrimination simply because of the colour of their skin, and so that we shall be heard also by the trade unions being deprived of the right to protect their members and thus of their inherent mission and by blue-collar and other workers denied the possibility to take part in running the factories they have been bound with by their whole lives.

If we are to talk about human rights, let's talk about all those rights and especially about those concerning millions of people.

Ladies and Gentlemen,

Comrades,

Face-to-face meetings are the best way of finding common ground and bringing positions closer together on specific matters. What is essential here is an ability not only to talk but also to listen, and not only to listen but also to understand each other and to look jointly for solutions to the most formidable problems of the modern world. It is in this vein that we would like to pursue our political dialogue with Britain.

The Soviet Union cherishes its economic, scientific and technological contacts with Britain. Our departments have prepared well for talks on these matters. You will have an opportunity to see this for yourselves tomorrow.

But things will not start to hum if the British side remains unwilling to remove the obstacles which keep everything that is most interesting for us out of the exchanges, prevent Soviet goods' access to your market or make offers by your firms non-competitive. In short we need reciprocity and understanding for each other's interests in this field.

We in the Soviet Union respect the British people's allegiance to traditions. We know the role your country has played in developing world trade and industry and appreciate the skills of its workers and the great contribution by its scientists, artists and writers to the cultural treasure house of civilisation.

We understand a feeling for one's historical 'roots' and share it. A nation disregarding its history puts a question mark over its future. But it is likewise true that he who does not think of his future devalues also the best in his past.

So let us address the problems of the times so that the people of the twenty-first century can appreciate the political thinking demonstrated by the leadership of the USSR and Britain in this complex, watershed period.

I wish happiness and well-being to you, Mrs Thatcher, and to all British guests, and peace and success in tackling their problems to the people of Britain.